UPHOLSTERY TECHNIQUES ILLUSTRATED

W. LLOYD GHEEN

TAB BOOKS

TAB BOOKS

Blue Ridge Summit, PA

FIRST EDITION
NINTH PRINTING

© 1986 by **TAB Books**.
TAB Books is a division of McGraw-Hill, Inc.

Library of Congress Cataloging-in-Publication Data

Gheen, W. Lloyd.
    Upholstery techniques illustrated.

    Includes index.
    1. Upholstery—Amateurs' manuals.   I. Title.
TT198.G48   1986   684.1′2   85-27612
    ISBN 0-8306-0302-6
    ISBN 0-8306-0402-2 (pbk.)

Cover photographs courtesy of HI-WAY FURNITURE, Route 5, Box 8
Leitersburg Pike, Hagerstown, MD 21740   HT3

Contents

Acknowledgments

I acknowledge with deep appreciation the following people for their special assistance and encouragement in developing and completing this work.

First of all, my beloved wife, Helen, for her extended patience and encouragement during the research, organization, and writing phases of this book.

A special thanks is extended to John C. Paulson, Robert B. Jensen, and Gordon Brian Hartley, manager and supervisors respectively of the physical plant upholstery shop, Brigham Young University, for their encouragement and cooperation in permitting the majority of the photos to be taken at that facility. Appreciation is extended to Dale Butterfield, owner and manager of Acme Upholstering; Robert W. Kirkham, owner and manager of Kirkham Upholstering & Carpet; Mike Anderson, sales representative of American Excelsior Company; Richard Williams, sales representative and Bruce George, warehouseman, both of United Foam Corporation; Kay A. Zirker, manager of Ramco Industries; No-Sag Spring Corporation; General Plastics, Division of General Tire and Rubber; Uniroyal Corporation; and to Joe Sargetakis of Silver State Suppliers for his kind and valuable assistance in providing information so vital to this project.

Last, but certainly not least, appreciation is extended to Drs. Jerry D. Grover and Garth A. Hill, past and present department chairmen respectively of the Industrial Education Department, Brigham Young University, for their active encouragement, cooperation, and assistance.

Introduction

Upholsery Techniques Illustrated has been written to make the reupholstering process more self-explanatory for the newcomer to the trade, for the apprentice, for the student, and for the do-it-yourselfer. Basic procedures have been photographed in a step-by-step sequence, with directional indicators included where tricks-of-the-trade might not be obvious. Discussion of tools and materials and procedures that are either phasing out or that have ceased to be a part of modern practices have been omitted. Technical information on the newer materials and tools has been expanded to help you make informed decisions rather than rely exclusively on my bias.

Upholstery is so diverse that one reading of a book or doing one piece of furniture will never allow you to develop expertise. Each different piece brings new challenges and problems to be solved. It is an ever-changing trade, an exciting trade. New and different tools, materials, and procedures are constant realities. For that reason this book cannot be the "last word," but is intended to be an improved word. I welcome constructive criticism and suggestions for additions and improvements.

Chapter 1

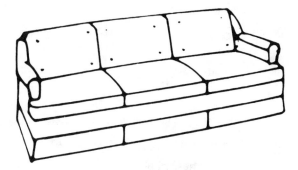

Overview

Within this book two "generic" terms will appear, upholstering and reupholstering. *Upholstery,* when strictly used, refers to the application of all new materials to a new frame, which may include any or all of the following: *foundation, base, padding, stuffing,* and *cover.* Used in a more loose sense, as is most often done in the business, it means "reupholstery." *Reupholstery* is the application of new cover material to a used piece of *upholstered* furniture. This may or may not include new foundation, base, padding, or stuffing materials. Whenever upholstery is used in this and subsequent chapters, it will really mean reupholstery (which is the scope of this book) unless specifically noted otherwise.

Upholstering new furniture or reupholstering old furniture remains a bit more of an art than it does a technology. Although there are technical aspects which will lead to a finished unit that is pleasing as well as correctly done, very few (if any) upholsterers will do the job exactly the same way. For example, variations in the way the same stuffing and padding materials are applied give not only

different "feels" to the furniture, but also result in differences in the appearance of the finished product. Some like the tight, rather squared look, while another may prefer the more subtle, soft, "puffy" look. Both effects can be achieved using identically the same materials. Small changes in how and to what extent the cover is fitted and pulled down can transform a piece from the tight to the softer look, and visa versa.

Based on my experience, there is no such thing as the one and only way of upholstering. To say, however, that there are no procedures which are better than others would have about the same validity as saying that because a stork often stands on one leg rather than both, he, therefore, has no need of the other. Now, to the observer of a picture in *National Geographic,* the consequence of whether the stork needs one or two legs may seem rather inconsequential, but to a living stork it would be a matter of quite serious merit.

Many beginning upholsterers (and a number of those having considerable experience as well) have encountered some degree of frustration at trying

Table 1-1. Symbols for Cover Fabric Identification.

Component Symbols		Location Symbols	
A	= Arm	Bot	= Bottom
B	= Back	C	= Center
Bx	= Boxing	F	= Front
C	= Cushion	I	= Inside
D	= Deck	L	= Left
K	= Cambric	O	= Outside
P	= Panel	R	= Right
S	= Seat	T	= Top
SK	= SKirt		
W	= Welt		

Complete the following mentally or on scratch paper.

IA	= Inside Arm	OA	= (?)
IB	= (?)	OB	= (?)
CBC	= Center Back Cushion		
RSC	= (?)		
LCSC	= (?)		
RBC	= (?)		

Note: Location symbols precede part or component symbols.

to understand exactly how to do a particular part of the job when they have been told one way of doing it, and then another person steps up and corrects their procedure saying, "That's not the way to do that. Here, let me show you how." The question naturally arises then, which is the right way? The answer?

Hold onto your hats because this is profound! Common sense and good judgment are often the most valuable guides. Strange thing about those two characters though, common sense does not seem to be so common and good judgment is often debatable. Just remember, whatever the boss says, that is the best way. What seems to work the best and be the easiest to perform by each person is probably the most sound guide to follow, coupled with a background of the "basics," of course. This text is designed to provide those basics and some of the tricks-of-the-trade at the same time.

For the novice, upholstering possesses many challenges and problems not previously confronted. "Where does this go? How should this be done? What now?" All these, and more, are very common queries. So, accept a bit of counsel at this point and don't get all hung up in finite details. Upholstering is a problem-solving activity! Do some thinking, try to envision what would happen if that task were to be done as you imagine it could. If thought over and it seems logical and that nothing would be seriously wrong if done your way, try it! But, don't fail to think.

Upholstery is fun! If for no other reason, I say so! There have been some who have tried it, however, who have said, "I'll never, ever do this again! Now I can see why they charge so much to reupholster a chair." But there have also been those who have started their own businesses, have hired into existing shops, or who have continued doing every piece of upholstered furniture they could find in their own homes. One vivid and true example of the joy possible through upholstery can be seen from this illustration: A slight of frame, energetic, sweet (always pleasant), elderly lady beyond her sixties not only did her own work, lifting and moving her chair around, making and correcting mistakes; she also made a rather lengthy trip to buy an antique loveseat, stripped it down, refinished the wood, and reupholstered it with diamond tufting and deep, piped channels in a striking deep red, heavily napped velvet (not an easy undertaking for the novice), and all because she enjoyed it so much.

Taking a class in upholstery, or just doing a piece of furniture on your own is guaranteed to accomplish four things:

(1) Tax your patience.

(2) Increase your tolerance to frustration (if the job is completed properly).

(3) Reveal some muscles that have long since been forgotten (overlooked?).

(4) Develop a confidence (that may have been concealed or lacking before) that you can tackle another piece and do it well, if you should so desire.

Note: It is not acclaimed to make you a competent upholsterer with one experience. Every piece of furniture seems to have its own personality which requires a slightly different approach and which possesses a few unique problems that were not previously experienced, or even conceived, for that matter. To illustrate: one experienced upholsterer (27 years in commercial upholstery) whom I esteem as a top-quality journeyman, commented that he still learns with each new piece of furniture that comes into his shop. This man, to give an idea of his expertise, has done work with fabric costing

Don't get all wrapped up in <u>finite</u> details.........

Oh boy! Think it through *before* doing it!

over $200 per yard (It had gold thread in it!); has done production and custom work; redesigned as well as designed furniture from the frame up; has worked draperies, sporting and personal equipment of all conceivable kinds that can be sewn or repaired on a commercial, straight stitch sewing machine (and some items that couldn't be done by most operators!); and has designed, with patents pending, athletic and gymnastic gloves and wrist supports that are in use at several universities and high schools already—and all this with no commercial advertising having been employed yet!

So, what does this all mean? Simply that the first, or second, or third time taking an upholstery class, or doing furniture on your own through using this text, or any other yet developed for that matter, will not give you ("experiencer" might be a more appropriate term, if we could find it in the

Table 1-2. The General Order of Stripping and Covering.

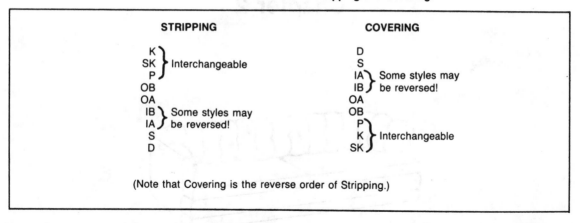

STRIPPING

K ⎫
SK ⎬ Interchangeable
P ⎭
OB
OA
IB ⎫ Some styles may
IA ⎭ be reversed!
S
D

COVERING

D
S
IA ⎫ Some styles may
IB ⎭ be reversed!
OA
OB
P ⎫
K ⎬ Interchangeable
SK ⎭

(Note that Covering is the reverse order of Stripping.)

dictionary, as reading alone cannot develop manual skill) all the skills and all the answers to the problems that will be encountered on the different types of furniture. Upholstering (reupholstering) is a problem-solving activity, not a science.

The first time a person strips a unit to the bare frame, either to make frame repairs or to replace badly worn or soiled materials, just looking at that skeleton of what used to be a piece of furniture is almost enough to instill panic and then despair. Take courage! All is not lost! If the stripping process is pursued as outlined in this book, a restoration of pleasing countenance can take place. Proceed, now, into the fascinating, challenging and rewarding world of upholstering. Remember, even when your finger is dripping blood because you got caught on a staple stub you forgot to get out during the stripping process, it can be fun! Even if your patience is taxed, muscles grumble at you because they haven't been used in quite this way for a long time, hair thins (from pulling), and blood is shed on those "gotchas"—even after all this—it can be fun. *Buena aventura!*

Chapter 2

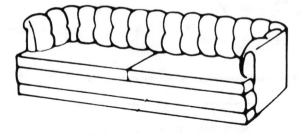

Upholstery Tools

The tools shown and discussed in this chapter are organized into three basic categories: essentials for the "do-it-yourselfer," the minimum for the small or part-time shop, and tools for the professional shop. An attempt has been made to list the tools to each category in a priority order, with the most essential first. This ordering, being basic, might be altered by individual circumstances. One might find that every tool is essential. Another, that some tools are not even mentioned should be. Yet another might determine that some of those tools mentioned are not at all necessary. The categories are intended as a guide only, and not as the last word!

Although tools are often used for many purposes, other than for what they were designed, the proper use of the appropriate tools will be illustrated in this and subsequent chapters. Use tools for the purposes for which they made. Take the time to find and use the right tool and the work will be a pleasure with a high chance for success. Taking short-cuts just because something else is handier at the moment was the stimulation for the Modern Upholsterer's Proverb: "He who takes short-cut with tools, finds longest and most rough way."

FOR THE DO-IT-YOURSELFER

Upholsterer's Shears. No one, after they have tried to cut some of the upholstery fabrics, would consider doing it (more than once) with a pair of common household scissors, Fig. 2-1, bottom. The heavy-duty upholsterer's shears (Fig. 2-1, top) really, are quite necessary. If a lot of cutting is to be done at one time, shears will be found much more "friendly"—they don't create blisters nearly so fast nor muscle cramps nearly so acute as do the common scissors.

Screwdriver. Disassembly, and subsequent reassembly, of some of the furniture pieces would be virtually impossible without the right screwdriver. There are several specialty screwdriver types that have come into use, but for most furniture assembly, the *straight-slot* and *Phillips* remain the most popular ones. A medium size would probably be the most practical for the

Use the right tool for the right job.

one-time upholsterer. However, the only way to preserve the driver blades and the screw heads is to use the right size driver for each screw size. What is the right size? If the driver fits snugly, it is the right size! If it doesn't quite enter the slot or cross, it is too large. If it only goes half way across the screw slot or wobbles without turning the screw, it is too small. Simple, eh?

Staple Remover or Ripping Tools. Only a glutton for punishment (or perhaps the inexperienced) would think of stripping a piece of furniture without the use of a *staple remover*, for stapled materials; or a *ripping tool* or *claw tool* for materials fastened with tacks (Fig. 2-2). Although the mallet is not yet mentioned, if a claw tool or ripping tool is to be used, some hammering device is certainly

7

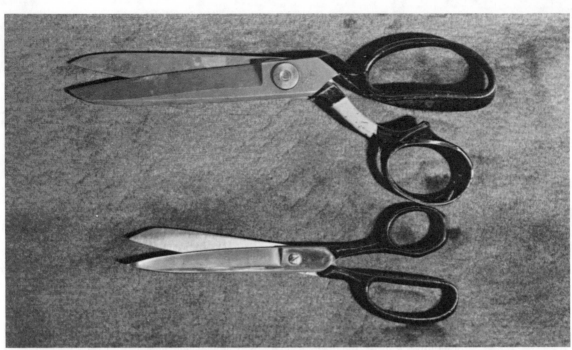

Fig. 2-1. Upholsterer's shears (top); heavy-duty household shears (bottom).

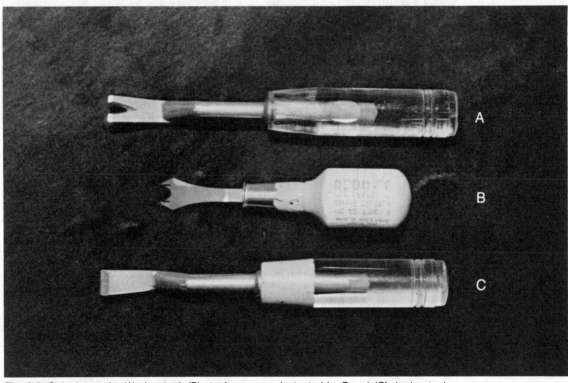

Fig. 2-2. Stripping tools: (A) claw tool. (B) staple remover (patented by Berry) (C) ripping tool.

8

Fig. 2-3. Flexible measuring tapes: top-steel rule, bottom-cloth tape.

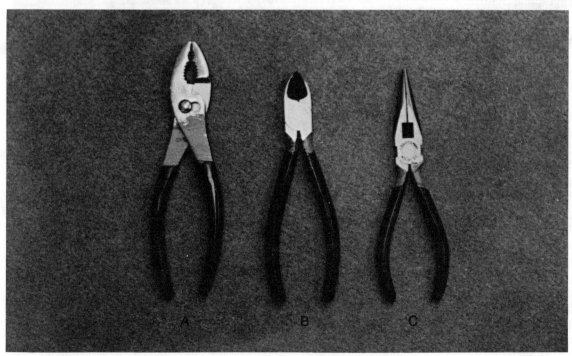

Fig. 2-4. Popular pliers: (A) slip-joint, (B) diagonal cutters ("dikes"), (C) needlenose.

necessary. *Note*: Only a karate expert would consider using the bare hand or forehead to drive these tools! The *straight slot screwdriver* could be used to remove both staples and tacks, but that is a torturous way to go.

Measuring Tape. Some flexible measuring device is necessary. It would be possible to use a piece of string and transfer measurements, but why go back to stone age procedures when we have measuring tapes available? Figure 2-3 shows two popular types of flexible tapes: (top) the *steel tape*, and (bottom) the *cloth tape*. Flexibility is essential as many measurements must be taken around curved surfaces and corners. Have you ever tried to bend a yard stick around a corner? Both of those pictured work well. However, there is one word of caution: don't try to communicate to another a measurement using the cloth tape pictured unless it is remembered that the actual measurement begins at the point of the arrow marked "start" and not at the darkened end of the tape. The added length is provided so the operator can have something to hold on to when measuring to corners, edges, and the like.

Pliers. A great aid in removing staple remnants, those sharp little critters that draw blood and inflict instant pain when least expected and never desired, is any one of various types of *pliers*. Handy pliers to have are the *slip-joint, diagonal cutters* (dikes), and *needle-nose*, shown in Fig. 2-4A, B, and C respectively. Each of these pliers has a specialty use in addition to being able to perform basically the same functions of pulling, cutting, and bending. *Slip-joint* pliers are especially useful for general grasping and bending, such as edge wires and other light spring wires. The *dikes*? They are the stripper's helper! One of the handiest tools to have as they can grasp very close to the frame surface, cut staples easily when they can't (or won't) be pulled out, and are flat enough to be used quite successfully as a "gotcha" (staple stub or broken or cut tack remnant) finder. The *needle-nose* find their specialty in being able to make small diameter bends in light wires and to get into some places too tight for fingers and other types of pliers to reach.

Tack Hammers. Although most of modern

upholstering is done with staples and staple guns, all of the *tacking* can also be accomplished with *upholstery tacks*. The *tack hammer* is an indispensable, yet inexpensive, tool for that job. Without it, bruised and sore fingers are the guaranteed and painful norm. Of course a good pair of tweezers could be used to hold tacks while driving them with a claw hammer, if one wanted to "putter away the time" doing the job. Four styles of *tack hammer* are shown in Fig. 2-5. All *tack hammers* have one end which is magnetized to hold a tack for starting with the opposite end being nonmagnetic for subsequent

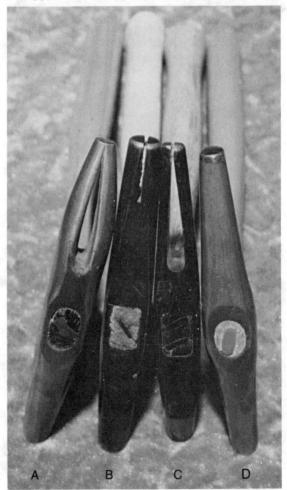

Fig. 2-5. Tack hammers: (A) split-end magnet (greatest curvature of both heads), (B) split-end magnet (least curvature of both heads), (C) split-end magnet (straight-end for magnet, curved head), (D) solid-end magnet (moderate curvature, both heads).

Fig. 2-6. Popular adhesives: (A) aliphatic wood glue (yellowish in color), (B) adhesive for foam, (C) adhesive for foam to substrate, (D) polyvinyl wood glue (white in color).

driving of the tacks once they have been started. Hammers A, B, and C all have the magnetized ends split. Model D has both ends solid. The magnetic end of all hammers is always the smaller diameter. All hammers shown work very well. Model B has less of a curve to the head, less taper, and is less expensive than the other models. Models A and D are the preference of most professionals. Models A, B, and C have relative flat sides which are used by many upholsterers to set and level *tack strip*.

Adhesives. Furniture frames occasionally need repairs or modifications. Good quality wood adhesives are frequently used. The most popular adhesives for woodworking are the yellowish aliphatics and the white, polyvinyl glues. Figure 2-6A and D respectively. Other adhesives quite necessary for the upholsterer are the foam adhesives. Those most popular are found in the

aerosol variety although they can be purchased in the bulk pack and applied via spray guns. Two varieties are helpful. An adhesive to attach foams to substrates such as wood, metal, cork or other fabrics is a general purpose contact adhesive. One such adhesive is the *Trim Adhesive* pictured in Fig. 2-6C. A less expensive variety works very well for glueing foam to foam, such as the *Foam and Fabric Adhesive* (Fig. 2-6B).

FOR THE SMALL SHOP

Although reupholstering can be performed successfully with the minimal assortment of tools above, doing more than one unit is made much more enjoyable and profitable with the addition of the tools listed in this category.

Staple Gun. An indispensable tool for today's professional is the *staple gun*. Figure 2-7 shows various types of guns. For the average home owner who doesn't have an air compressor handy, the manual model can be used. If the manual staple gun is desired, get the heavy-duty models that have two tension settings. Lighter, inexpensive models do not have the power to drive staples into furniture woods. *Tip*: Don't plan to use one of these for prolonged periods unless you have been hand-squeezing dozens of oranges lately! The *electric gun*, although quiet, is considerably more bulky (as can be seen in the photo) than its more popular counterpart, the *pneumatic*. Heavier staples are used in the electric guns than are used in pneumatics. The pneumatic gun, however, is the work-horse of the industry. It is used extensively in professional shops and educational programs. The *scissor stapler* is used primarily for stapling tucks and pleats in cover panels, dacron edges when lining cushions and other light duty and temporary work.

Clamps. The *C-clamp* (Fig. 2-8A) and the *spring clamp* (Fig. 2-8B) are each used in applications requiring pressure in small areas such as holding parts steady for drilling, holding parts together while glue is setting, or clipping fabric temporarily out of the way while working beneath it. The *C-clamp* is capable of exerting near crushing pressure, should it be necessary, while the *spring clamp* exerts a rather mild pressure.

Hand Drills. Making frame repairs frequently calls for the installation or removal of screws, drilling of pilot holes, or the drilling of dowel holes. A *brace* or a *hand drill* is used to accomplish these tasks. The *brace* (Fig. 2-9A) is used for holding and turning tools (drills and "bits") having tapered, square ends as does the *auger bit* in the photo. The square, tapered end fits into the notched, two-jaw chuck of the brace. The offset handle of the brace permits considerable rotational force to be applied for the turning operation.

Auger Bits. So named because they are formed like an "auger," *auger bits* are used exclusively for drilling wood. A lead screw draws the cutters into the wood during the drilling process, making the only real effort required that of turn-

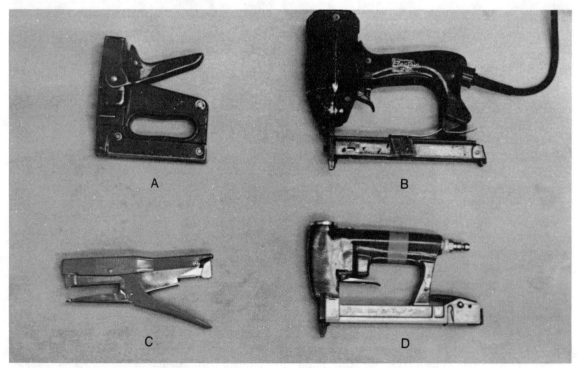

Fig. 2-7. Staple guns: (A) manual, (B) electric, (C) scissor (also manual), (D) pneumatic.

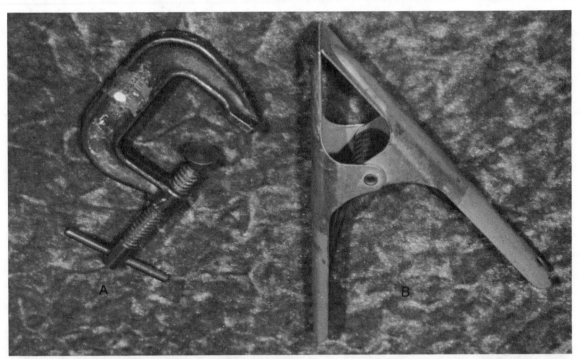

Fig. 2-8. Clamps: (A) C-clamp, (B) spring clamp.

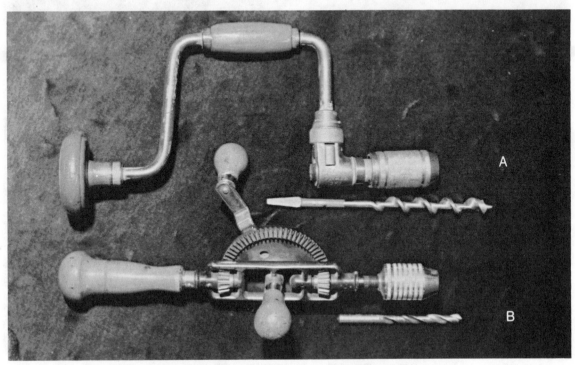

Fig. 2-9. Manual hand drills: (A) brace (and auger bit), (B) hand drill (and twist drill).

13

ing. Auger bits commonly range in size from 3/16″ to 1″ graduated in sixteenths. The number stamped on the shank of the bit means sixteenths. For example, a bit stamped with "9" would drill a hole 9/16″ in diameter. Twist drills, screwdriver bits, and other types of drivers, can be purchased with square drives to fit the brace. Some multi-blade screwdrivers, the kind that fit into one common handle, are excellent for use with the brace because they have small "ears" formed on the shank which prevent them from turning in the chuck.

The *hand drill* (Fig. 2-9B) has a three-jawed *chuck*, commonly called a *"Jacob's chuck"* (named after the inventor), for holding and turning drills and bits having round or hexagonal shanks. This tool has been nicknamed "egg beater" because of its similar appearance to some styles of the household appliance of the same name. Although considerably slower than the electric or pneumatic models (Fig. 2-15), it can do anything either of the power models can do—if one has enough stamina, that is. *Twist drills* (named such because they look like they have been mercilously twisted, Fig. 2-9B) can be used to drill metal, plastic, or wood. They have no lead screw so all cutting force must be applied by the operator. Screwdriver bits can be purchased for the hand drill or brace in either round or hexagonal shanks, or they can be readily made from an extra screwdriver merely by cutting off the handle.

Webbing Stretcher. If a unit has webbing that needs repairing or replacing, some kind of *webbing stretcher* is a must. A tool that has the capability of pulling the full width of the webbing evenly is really all that is necessary. Several types of webbing stretchers are shown in Fig. 2-10. Each type will be discussed for its particular advantages and disadvantages.

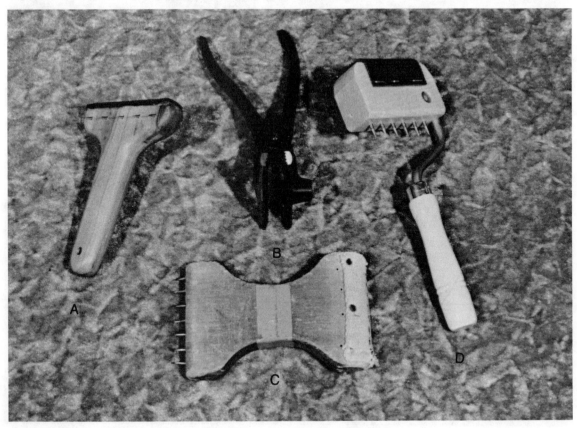

Fig. 2-10. Webbing stretchers: (A) lever, (B) webbing plier, (C) In-line, (D) offset.

Lever. This type was first designed for use with fabric webbing by the author in 1982 (Fig. 2-10A). It is currently undergoing improvement for marketing. The main advantages are: (1) it can be used on webbing as little as one inch longer than the frame it is to span, (2) it has direct lever action, permitting great leverage and stretching with minimal force required, and (3) because of the unique head design, is capable of providing ample travel to tighten even long strands with no slippage and no marring of the wood surfaces against which it is placed. Numerous users have indicated that this stretcher is the easiest and most comfortable to use of the four varieties pictured.

Webbing Plier. The plier (Fig. 2-10B) is one of the most versatile. It can handle fabric, plastic, rubber, and some metal webbing. This tool can grasp any of these and provide plenty of leverage to tighten them. The major disadvantage is that the pliers, being all metal, can scratch and mar a frame very easily. Good padding is needed between the pliers and show wood against which they might be placed.

Offset. A comfortable stretcher to use (Fig. 2-10D), once the webbing is attached to the tool, for fabric webbing. It has excellent leverage and a non-slip, non-mar head which can be used against show wood frames with no danger (unless the finish is relatively fresh, of course). Two minor drawbacks of this type are (1) it requires the operator to almost "thread" the webbing between the offset handle and the prongs while holding the handle in a rather awkward position, and (2) a slightly longer strip is needed for grasping than with the Lever stretcher.

Blade. This is perhaps the grandaddy of the industry (Fig. 2-10C). It has been around longer than any of the other types. It is used for fabric webbing and does an adequate job of stretching (obviously I am biased?). It seems rather awkward to use as it requires the operator to either have the hand(s) between the webbing and the stretcher, or working from the sides to achieve leverage. It does require at least six inches more webbing to reach the prongs than the outside dimension of the frame.

Any of these stretchers can be used on roll material, virtually of infinite length, except the pliers.

If webbing is being used directly from the roll then, the extra lengths needed for the offset and the blade units would be of no consequence. There is one other type of stretcher which exists, the *Band Stretcher.* That unit is used for installing metal webbing.

Sinuous Spring Puller. This tool (Fig. 2-11) is extremely handy when it comes to installing *sinuous springs.* The springs can be installed without the use of a puller, but when many pieces have to be installed, or when time means dollars, as it does in any business, the time and strain saved through the use of the puller is worth many times the nominal cost. It is constructed simply enough that a do-it-yourselfer could make one with a piece of wood and heavy sheet metal or light band iron and a 1/2″ steel rod.

Mallets. A *mallet,* to the experienced upholsterer, is an essential tool. Of the variety shown, two are more preferred: the *rawhide* (Fig. 2-12F) and the white, hard *rubber* (Fig. 2-12E). The rawhide is preferred for its endurance, light weight, nonmarring characteristic, solid face, and lack of splintering. The white rubber mallet is used quite extensively for installing tack strips; smoothing and contouring some slightly irregular padded edges, corners and shoulders (It is effective on some heads as well!); and for fitting seat units into their metal pans (such as theater seats). The black rubber mallet, although practically identical to the white, does leave occasional black marks. Note that all mallets used in upholstering feature nonmetalic faces.

Hand Screw. For applications where

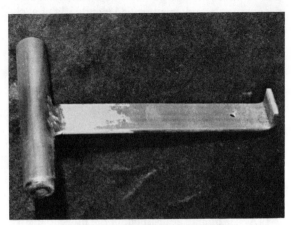
Fig. 2-11. Sinuous spring puller (homemade).

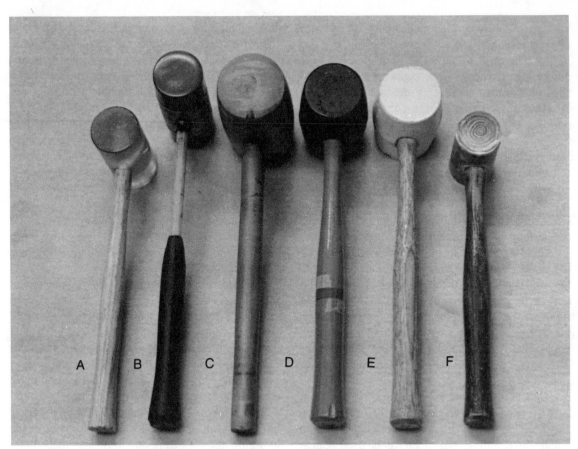

Fig. 2-12. Mallets: (A) plastic head; (B) lead head, plastic insert; (C) wood; (D) black, hard rubber; (E) white, hard rubber; (F) rawhide.

pressure is needed for parallel or slightly angled surfaces, the *hand screw* (Fig. 2-13) is a very handy tool to have. Each handle has right and left hand threads on the rod, can turn independently of each other, and when worked singly or in unison can exert tremendous pressure between the jaws. This tool is frequently used to clamp broken rails, uprights, slats or other frame members while a good quality wood glue is drying.

Bar Clamps. When frame repairs require application of "the squeeze" on spans exceeding 10 inches, *bar clamps* (Fig. 2-14) are about as handy for the upholsterer as skis are for the ski jumper. Since not all frames require this type of repair, the bar clamp has not been identified as necessary for the do-it-yourselfer. The pipe base bar clamp (Fig. 2-14A) has infinite adjustment of the moveable jaw,

shown at the extreme right of the photo, while the band base clamp (Fig. 2-14B) has fixed-stops (notice the notch on the bottom of the bar just to the right of the jaw).

Power Hand Drills. The two most popular types of power hand drills for upholstery are shown in Fig. 2-15. Figure 2-15A is a *pneumatic* drill shown with a 1/2″ chuck, chuck key, and a hex-drive *Phillips* screwdriver bit. Figure 2-15B is an electric drill with a 3/8″ chuck, chuck key and a *straight-slot* screwdriver bit. Both drills are variable-speed and reversible. Both reverse and variable-speed control is essential for inserting and extracting screws, probably the most popular use of the power drill in upholstery.

Stuffing Regulator. Occasionally (perhaps a little more frequently for the novice), some lumps,

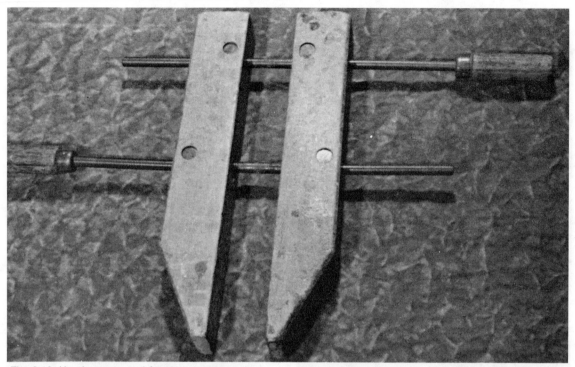

Fig. 2-13. Hand screw: used for clamping parallel and nonparallel surfaces.

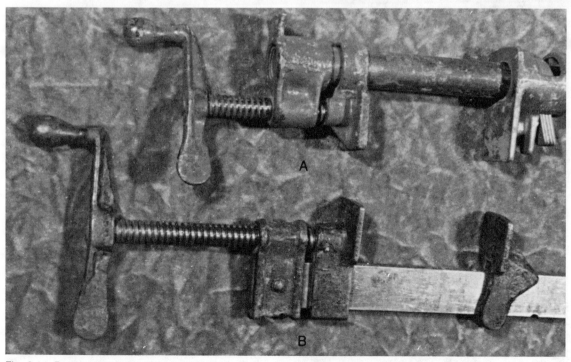

Fig. 2-14. Bar clamps: (adjustable from 0″ to the length of the bar); (A) pipe bar clamp, (B) band bar clamp.

Fig. 2-15. Power hand drills: (A) pneumatic (with chuck key and hexagonal shank Phillips screwdriver bit), (B) electric (with chuck key attached to power cord) and round shank, straight slot screwdriver bit).

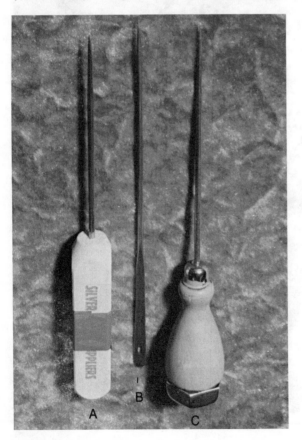

Fig. 2-16. Stuffing regulators: (A) standard ice pick, (B) upholsterer's stuffing regulator, (C) household ice pick (with scolloped flange filed off.

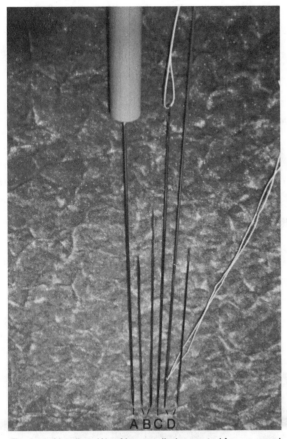

ripples, dips or blobs are observed after the cover has been tacked in place. The stuffing regulator is used to insert carefully through the cover and move small portions of padding to smooth the contour and at times fill some corner voids. Figure 2-16 shows the more common regulators: A—*Common Ice Pick*, B—*Stuffing Regulator*, C—*"Fancy" Ice Pick*. It should be noted that two of the three regulators are ice picks. Such is not at all uncommon in upholstery shops. In fact, many upholsterers prefer the positive control afforded with the wooden handle. The ice picks also have very sharp points, are very inexpensive (except for the fancy or "commercial" model shown, Fig. 2-16C), and the smooth, slim taper of the shank is precisely what is needed to give minimal disturbance of the cover fabric.

Needles. If any deep sewing (through a few inches of padding), tufting or buttoning is to be done, long, straight needles (Fig. 2-17) are essential. For taking long running stitches, the *single-point needle* (Fig. 2-17C) is generally used. For sewing where stitches are taken repeatedly through cover and padding, such as when sewing down the cushion retaining groove, the *double-point needle* (Fig. 2-17B and D) is used. Use of two points saves time by eliminating the need to completely reverse the needle direction each time it is inserted through the sewing materials. For installing buttons or for tufting, a *button tufting needle*, with a handle on one

A B C D

Fig. 2-17. Needles: (A) tufting needle (converted from a round double-point, (B) a diamond, double-pointed (eyes at bottom), (C) round, single-pointed (eye at top), (D) round, double-pointed (eye at bottom).

Fig. 2-18. Welt board: made from Adler wood 3/4″ × 1 1/2″ × 80″ (length and thickness are optional).

end (Fig. 2-17A), is the preference. Many operators (especially those tired of having their spleens punctured) have put a "handle" on the second point of the double-pointed needle, creating a personalized tufting needle safe and comfortable to use. The tufting needle shown in Fig. 2-17A was made that way.

Welt Board. More often than not the welt board (Fig. 2-18) is "homemade." All that is really necessary is a smooth, straight piece of close-grained wood (hard wood is preferred: alder, poplar, maple, birch, cherry) that is 1 1/2″ wide and of a length convenient and sufficient, usually ranging from 60 to 80 inches. It is extremely useful for marking welt strips preparatory to cutting them from the cover fabric.

Trestle. To ask an upholsterer to work without a *trestle* (Fig. 2-19) is like asking a cowboy to ride the range without a saddle. It is a tool of the trade. Many beginners, home owners and hob-byists, however, have done a lot of reupholstery working on the floor, on benches or tables. As one gains experience working on furniture, and on trestles, it soon becomes apparent that the furniture is much more accessible with much less contortioning required of the operator using the trestle than with any of the other alternatives mentioned.

FOR THE PROFESSIONAL

Professional shops, being concerned with doing a wide variety of jobs as easily and rapidly as possible, will have, in addition to the previously mentioned tools, most of those listed in this section.

Hog Ring Pliers. *Hog Ring Pliers*, as the name might suggest, are used to install *hog rings*. These fasteners are used extensively for fastening (1) two or more wires, such as edge wires and springs, together; (2) edge rolls to edge wires; and (3) cover materials to the metal and wire frame

Fig. 2-19. Trestle: features recessed, carpeted top (a must!); center shelf with raised sides and ends (very helpful!).

20

Fig. 2-20. Foam saw: electric with 8″ blade—sufficient for most needs (5″ cushion foam shown on right).

elements in auto upholstering. The most popular models are those that are spring loaded. The spring creates sufficient closing pressure to the plier so it can retain the hog ring within the slotted jaws with no additional pressure necessary from the operator. This feature is especially useful when the plier must be inserted into tight places to attach the ring. Without the spring tension, the ring often falls out of the jaws before it can be located and the clamping pressure applied. Both the *spring loaded* and *standard models* come with *angled* or *straight* heads.

Foam Saw. This tool (Fig. 2-20) is so time saving and does such smooth work that no commercial shop doing any extent of foam cutting will be without one. They are too expensive for most hobbyists to purchase for just a few pieces of furniture. In that case, it would be more economical to pay a commercial shop to do the cutting. These saws

can cut through foam rubber the full depth of the dual, counter-reciprocating blades which range from 6 to 18″ in cutting length, with great ease and a very smoothly (as smooth as the operator can move the saw anyway!). An occasional coating of silicone "dry" lubricant along the length of the blades and on the base plate greatly increases the life of the blades and increases the ease of passing the saw through the foam.

Sinuous Spring Cutter. *Sinuous Springs* are rather heavy gauge spring steel wire, and are real "tooth chippers" if one tries to cut them with dikes, slip-joint or needle-nose pliers. The safe and easy way to cut sinuous springs is to use the no-sag cutter, Fig. 2-21. This cutter is either wall mounted (as shown) or mounted on a table or bench. It not only cuts but also has a built-in end crimper for turning the outward-curving, cut end inward. Figure 2-22 shows the crimper readied to make the reverse

Fig. 2-21. Sinuous spring cutter with spring ready for cut.

bend. The completed bend is shown in Fig. 2-23. This reverse bending is necessary to prevent the spring end from (1) gouging into the frame, (2) tearing burlap and stuffing materials, and (3) squeeking as it rubs against the frame.

Sinuous Spring Benders. These are used in pairs to adjust bends and arcs in *standard* sinuous spring material. The benders are placed over adjacent loops of the spring and with counter-rotating pressure the spring is bent as desired in either direction. Used in this manner, straight bends can be made neatly and easily. Without the benders, twisting and nicking of the spring wires is common. *V - arcs* and *Z - arcs* are easy to make. Figure 2-24 illustrates, on a short piece, how the bend for a V-arc would be completed.

Button Machine. Most commercial shops and upholstery schools will have a *button making machine*. The unit shown in Fig. 2-25 is probably the most popular and lowest priced of the button machines. It is a small hand operated, portable unit capable of making professional quality buttons with ease. There are other models which are faster (and more expensive), even some which are semi- and fully-automatic, but none will do a much better job than these well designed hand models. Shown at the base of the machine is a strip of fabric, the cutting die, button dies, wooden plunger (home made), button cap and base. These components comprise everything necessary (except for a bit of elbow grease!) to make a fabric covered button. One other accessory which is very helpful is a piece of wood or fiber material to reduce the space between the upper and lower "plates." Several thicknesses of

Fig. 2-22. Sinuous spring crimper—ready to crimp (reverse) bend of cut end.

Fig. 2-23. Sinuous spring crimper—after crimp has been made.

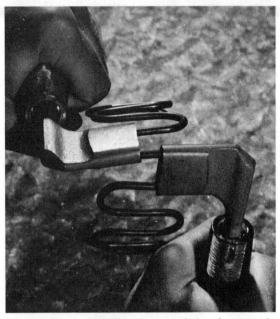

Fig. 2-24. Sinuous spring bender at conclusion of acute angle bend.

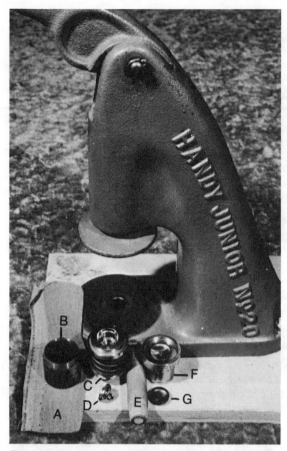

Fig. 2-25. Button making machine: (A) cover fabric, (B) cutting die, (C) button base retaining die, (D) button eye base, (E) wooden plunger, (F) cap retaining die, (G) button cap.

button cover so the convex face of the cap matches the concave center of the die.

5. Hold the cap retaining die (Fig. 2-25F) in one hand and with the wooden plunger force the button cap, cover and center of the die down until it stops. This takes considerable pressure if the fabric is heavy.

6. Place filled cap retaining die on top of the button base retaining die and pull the handle down until it stops solidly.

7. Remove the covered button and repeat for each button desired.

Another hand model is shown in Fig. 2-26. This model has a pivoting base which speeds up the but-

fabric can be placed on this spacer, the cutting die (Fig. 2-25B) placed on top, and the handle activated forcing the die down through the stacked fabric, cutting multiple "button covers" at one time. To make a covered button:

1. Cut the "button covers" as indicated above or by driving the cutting die through single layers of fabric with a mallet, refer to Fig. 2-12.

2. Insert button base (prong or eye, Fig. 2-25D) into the button base retaining die (Fig. 2-25C) with the prong or eye down, then insert the die into the bottom plate, button base up.

3. Place one button cover, outside down, into the cap retaining die (Fig. 2-25F).

4. Place a button cap (Fig. 2-25G) over the

Fig. 2-26. Two-headed button machine: (Increases production by as much as 50 percent).

Fig. 2-27. Klinch-it tool and staples.

Fig. 2-28. Klinch-it tool and staples: close-up; (A) bottom view of staple strip—showing partially curved teeth, (B) Klinch-It tool with bottom staple activated—showing how it is spread to "clinch" into cloth webbing, (C) top view of staple strip—showing crowned top that forms over spring wires.

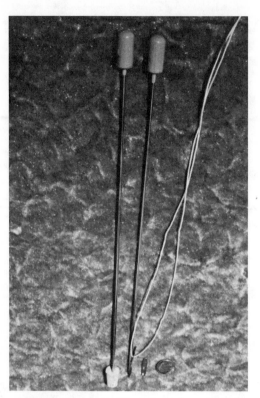

Fig. 2-29. Blind tufting needles and clips.

ton making process by as much as 50 percent.

Klinch-it Tool and Clips. Another of the indispensable tools for the professional is a *Klinch-It Tool* (Fig. 2-27). This tool is used to quickly and conveniently anchor coil springs to a fabric webbing base. Its use eliminates the need to fasten the springs by the old hand-sewn method. The tool is shown with strips of the clips on either side. A close-up of the business end of the tool (Fig. 2-28) shows the bottom view of the clip strip (A), the top

Fig. 2-30. Blind tufting needles and clips: close-up; (A) needle in protective cork retainer, (B) needle loaded with clip and tufting twine, (C) clip showing twine hole (center) and hole for needle hook (bottom end).

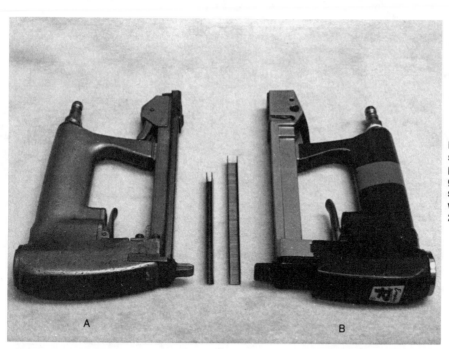

Fig. 2-31. Comparison of standard and gimp pneumatic staple guns: (A) gimp gun with strip of gimp staples, (B) standard gun with staples (Approximately 2× width of gimp).

view of the strip of clips (C), and the tool with a strip of clips loaded (B). The sharp points (four per clip) angle slightly outward. When the tool handle is compressed the clip is forced downward in the center while the outer edges are retained by the tool tracks. This action forces the points outward as shown with the bottom-most clip in Fig. 2-28 (B).

Were it to have been completely "clinched" the fabric clip carrier would have been torn from the remainder of the strip automatically, permitting the "clinched" clip to fall free.

Blind Tufting Needle and Clip. Use of this tool and its specially designed clip (Fig. 2-29) permits installation of eyed buttons to completely fin-

Fig. 2-32. Band clamps: (A) ratchet adjuster, (B) wrench, (C) nylon band, (D) corner protector brackets.

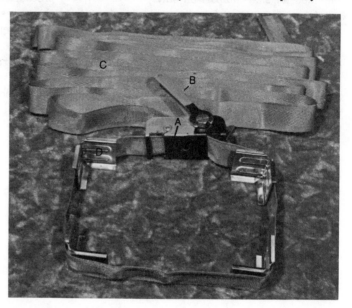

Fig. 2-33. Fabric saws: (A) rotary or disc saw, (B) reciprocating, double-blade saw, (equipment courtesy silver state suppliers).

ished furniture without the need of stripping any of the cover panels. The work is done entirely from the front side. The close-up (Fig. 2-30) shows the tufting needle in its protective cork retainer (A), fully "loaded" with the clip and tufting twine (B), and the clip showing the holes for the twine (center) and the needle hook (bottom) (C). The dime is included for size comparison only.

Gimp Gun. One of the "specialty" tools of the professional (Fig. 2-31, (A)), this gun is used for attaching ends and folded corners of *gimp* to furniture calling for the decorative trim. The staples are almost totally invisible when applied due to their narrower head. Figure 2-31 shows the difference in staple size between the pneumatic gimp gun and the standard pneumatic model.

Band Clamp. The *band clamp*, or strap clamp as it is sometimes called, (Fig. 2-32) is a rather unique tool. It is capable of exerting even pressure on all points of round objects, at all corners of square or rectangular items, and at almost any point along the convex curves or corners on irregular shaped pieces. As can be seen in the photo, the strap is of considerable length, commonly ranging from 12 to 20'. Obviously, it can girth rather large objects, even couches. The corner brackets are provided to protect sharp wooden corners from the abrading pressures of the tightening strap. The wrench, shown resting on the adjusting nut, provides sufficient leverage to hold most joints tight while glues cure.

Fabric Saws. The *fabric saw* (Fig. 2-33) is another of those specialty tools. It is used by shops and schools doing production work, cutting out multiple panels of fabric (up to 250 at a time) with relative ease and accuracy. Custom shops and most school settings have no use for such a tool, but, where multiple copies of the same panels are needed, the time saved over hand cutting each piece soon pays for these very expensive machines.

Chapter 3

Stripping

Anyone can tear apart a piece of furniture. But the trick is to tear it apart in such a way that it can be put back together in better condition than it was before the "tearing" began. And that is what *stripping* really is. Not the tearing apart, but the *systematic disassembly and removal of unwanted and damaged materials* in such a way that a marvelous restoration can take place.

PRINCIPLE OF STRIPPING

The principle of *stripping* is to remove only what is absolutely necessary, and no more! All too often, those having limited or a total absence of experience get carried away in their excitement of redoing a piece of furniture and end up tearing off, up, or apart items and pieces that really had no need to be disturbed.

Preparation

To properly strip and recover a unit accurate, rapid and simple communication (even to oneself) of (1) what is to be done, (2) what has been done,

and (3) what must yet be done will not only simplify but will also speed up the process and reduce frustration. To satisfy these three "what's," a checksheet is highly and almost urgently recommended. And to make the checksheet of most value the use of some standardized symbols (abbreviations) is recommended. While the expressions "thingy," "do-jigger," or "whachamacallit" might be acceptable terms to use when there are no options available, cutting and fitting a panel intended for the inside back to the outside arm area is not often considered a gratifying experience, especially when the fabric is costing well over $20.00 a yard and working time is limited—to say nothing about the frustration of trying to match the pattern and color of a discontinued fabric to replace the piece just destroyed. To avoid problems, learn well and consistently use the component identifications listed below.

Component Identification

Table 1-1 contains a listing of component and

Remove only what is *absolutely* necessary!

location abbreviations and their meanings. These symbols have been long accepted in the upholstery trade because of their simplicity and near self-descriptive character. It is advisable to commit them to memory until they become like trusted friends, unmistakable and constantly available when needed. A few are listed without their meanings. Try to define those just to convince yourself of just how logical they really are. If not absolutely sure of your accuracy, peek at the answers hidden a short distance beyond Table 1-1. It is important to be sure, and right, but it's a lot more fun to experience occasionally the thrill of discovery. So, try them first! Then, if you re not really sure, positive in fact, go to the answers.

Procedure

The most expedient stripping procedure is to take off first that panel or part that was put on last, and then remember accurately the whole sequence. Good mechanical problem-solving skills and a photographic memory would be great assets at this point, provided the latter would last long enough. But due to the rarity of both those gifts and the consistency for the need to solve the problems and to remember accurately over relatively long periods of time, a readily accessible and rather permanent aid has been devised: the Stripping Checksheet (Appendix A). Conscientious use of the checksheet will save many, many hours of trial and error work and frustrating puzzling over "impossible" tasks. Suggestions for using the checksheet are also found in Appendix A.

Answers to abbreviations in Table 1-1: OA = Outside Arm, IB = Inside Back, OB = Outside Back, RSC = Right Seat Cushion, LCSC = Left-

Center Seat Cushion (for units where there are four seat cushions), RBC = Right Back Cushion.

The general procedure is: start from the bottom and work upward, and from the outside and work inward. The basic sequence is listed in Table 1-2.

Although Table 1-2 indicates that the cambric (K), SKirt, and Panels may be removed in any order, be ye herewith informed that the cambric **MUST** be removed before the outside back or outside arms can be started. And, many times, legs and leg plates must be removed to get to the cambric. Also, from Table 1-2 it might seem that stripping begins at the bottom of the unit. Well, it does, generally! Sometimes, however, it might be helpful (if not absolutely necessary!) to remove a major portion of the unit before actual stripping begins. Figure 3-1 is a replica of an instruction card relating to a La-Z-Boy Recliner chair. Many manufacturers of furniture having removable elements will use similar instruction cards, most of which will be found attached to a frame member on the underside of the unit.

Stripping system: The "system" goes like this:

1. Look for special disassembly-assembly instructions, especially on recliners and units with very wide arms. **Danger**: Occasionally these tags may get torn or removed by accident, carelessness or ignorance. If such be the case, it could become extremely difficult to disassemble the unit unless you are lucky, gifted, or subject to divination, ESP, revelation, or pure inspiration. A good practice is to examine the unit very thoroughly, looking for levers, nuts (the kind used to attach bolts, not the edible variety), metal brackets, tracks and clips. Then try to figure out how it is intended to work before forcing something out of shape or into unintended pieces.

2. Prepare a checklist for disassembly and stripping. This alone will save untold agony when it comes time to recover and reassemble, and will be one of the best problem-solvers (or problem eliminators) available. For a sample of one style of checklist, refer to appendix A. Any type of checklist could be designed and used if the one featured is not quite what might be wanted. The important thing is to utilize some way to assure a knowledge

and memory of what, when and how it all comes apart. Failure to do so could be hazardous to furniture, composure and hairlines. Only a well-experienced upholsterer could hope to restore some pieces if careful notes and even some sketches are not recorded during the stripping process.

3. Remove hardware pieces (such as legs, plates or handles) and removable components (arms, backs or seat assemblies) that may be placed on top of and appear to prevent removal of fabric panels. It gets pretty tough to remove the cover if something has been attached on top of it. *Hint*: Replace or attach screws, bolts or special clips to the parts removed or the frame whence they came to avoid (1) an unnecessary puzzle of figuring out just which ones went where or (2) a prolonged search-and-rescue for the vanished items, which all too often defy rescue.

4. Remove and mark with chalk on the reverse side each piece of old cover material as it comes off, using the abbreviations of Table 1-1, which are now memorized, right? Use the general procedure outlined in Table 1-2 as a guide. Keep careful record of the exact order in which all components (fabric pieces and hardware) are removed—unless, of course, you find great enjoyment in doing things several times before it finally comes out right. A proverb for the beginner: failure to accurately note the sequence of actual disassembly may result in acute and perhaps chronic frustration! In this business, taking a short cut when you are not thoroughly ready for it is like making a 90 degree turn with a car where there is no corner. Something gets bent out of shape. In this case, the operator.

5. Put old cover panels aside for future reference. Do not plan to use these pieces for exact patterns! They are often stretched and distorted. Do use them as (1) reminders of fabric pattern and nap orientation, (2) aids to identify where and how the new cover panels are to be placed or sewn, and (3) silent sentinels, to assure that every old piece is replaced with a new one.

6. Save and protect padding and stuffing materials which are to be reused. These should be put aside where they will not be destroyed, scuffed or snagged. There is no need to replace old

TO PLACE BACK IN CHAIR—

Simply lift back to verticle position at rear of chair. Align track on back with mating link on body keeping both sides in line. With slight pressure push back down in tracks until it stops. Seen from rear of chair, on the back track there is a toggle lever – one each side. With a household screwdriver engage toggle lever. Using screwdriver tip apply firm downward pressure on toggle lever. Make sure lever is in down position for full lock.
To disassemble, reverse.

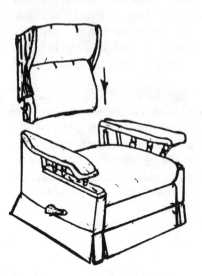

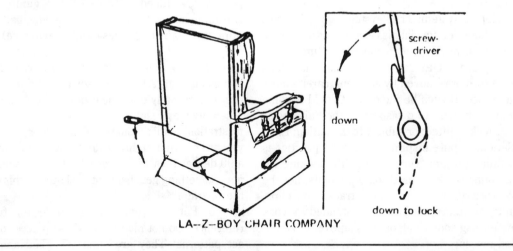

LA--Z--BOY CHAIR COMPANY

Fig. 3-1. Facsimile of assembly-disassembly instructions. Similar instructions should accompany all units having "special" fastening devices.

materials that are still in satisfactory condition. When to replace?

    a. If the stuffing and padding have become filled with dust, even though they still may seem resilient, they should be discarded. This is especially true for

those persons having any degree of allergy to household dust. Furniture is constantly bombarded with dust and even the most conscientious homemaker cannot keep all of the dust particles from being absorbed into the padding materials. Dust Check: Place padding on a flat surface (floor or table) and slap (just once will tell) with the flat palm of the hand. Sudden choking, itching, or blinding sensations indicate the presence of excess dust!

b. Even clean, matted stuffing should be replaced with new material if the unit is intended to have the supple, resilient feel. If a solid, more firm feel is desired, clean matted materials can be covered with a new layer of cotton felt or perhaps dacron mat.

7. Check and repair frame and foundation components as needed. Refer to Chapter 4.

STEP-BY-STEP SEQUENCE

Probably the most used tool in the stripping process is the patented, double-pronged *staple remover* (called by some, "Berry Picker." Why? Perhaps because it does such a nice job of "picking" out the staples? Or perhaps it has been nicknamed for the inventor, Mr. Berry?). This tool is designed so that it can be used on physically hard woods (oak, ash, maple, walnut, particle board), on structural foam (plastic) frame materials, and on softer frame woods (alder, soft maple, fir, poplar).

1. Visually examine the unit and note on the checksheet features to be remembered or altered such as location of seams and welts; sizes and shapes of panels, bands, welts, and skirts; and unusual depressions or lumps that should be changed. Figure 3-2 is a barrel-back chair ready for stripping. Are the seams where they will look the best on the new cover? Should there be more or less padding, and in what areas? Does the seat insert fit the contour properly and extend the proper distance to the front? These are some of the kinds of questions to answer and note before actually beginning the stripping process.

Fig. 3-2. Barrel-back style, ready for stripping. (Swivel base has been removed.)

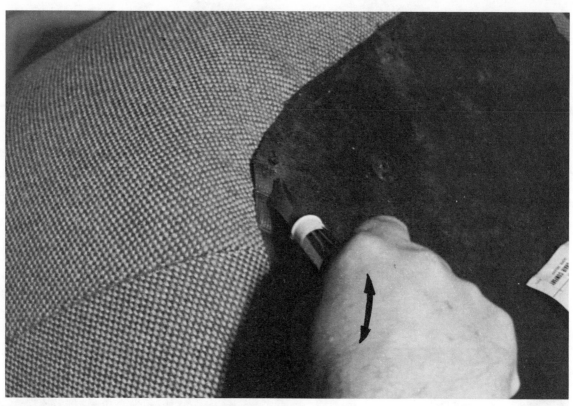

Fig. 3-3. Getting staple remover under staple in hard materials.

2. Remove hardware to get to the last panel of cover installed. The last panel is that one which is on top of any of the others.

3. Remove the cover panels in the reverse order to which they were installed. In this case it is the cambric (used on the barrel-back chair not as a dust barrier but as a finishing bottom panel).

Work staple remover under the staple. On harder woods, such as the base of the chair in Fig. 3-2, particle board, this is accomplished by holding the tool vertical, placing the point of one prong of the "Berry Picker" near one leg of the staple and applying downward pressure with an up and down motion as illustrated in Fig. 3-3. This forces the point far enough into the fabric and into the hardest of the furniture frame materials to get under the staple for extraction. Be careful! Watch the position of those hands. One slip of the tool with your hand in the wrong position (Fig. 3-4) and you come up with an "owie." It is presumed that upholsterers prefer to be engaged in the stripping process rather than that of blood letting, the ancient medical practice employed to rid the victi . . . patient of "bad blood." So, keep your hands from in front of the tool. Now, while holding the point of the tool under the staple, rotate it to either the right or left, depending on your position and that of the staple and your own personal preference (Fig. 3-5).

Also shown is the preferred use of this style of staple remover; one leg of the staple locked in the groove of the tool and the tool being rotated to the side away from the staple (Fig. 3-6). This procedure will tend to pull both legs of the staple out of the wood more frequently than any other process with this tool. This same approach also works well on the newer frame materials such as structural plastics (styrene, polyethylene, polypropylene and occasionally PPO (polyphenylene oxide)). On furniture with thick fabrics and softer woods (alder, soft maple, poplar, fir, pine (not a good choice for

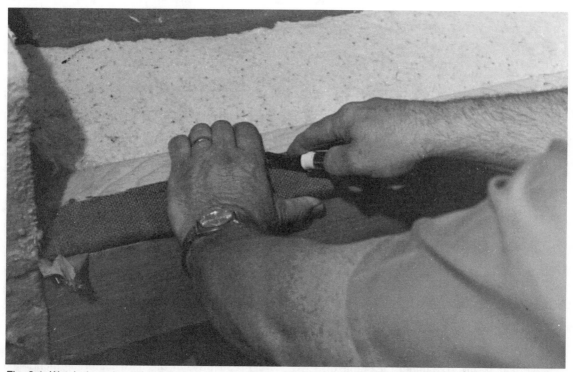

Fig. 3-4. Watch those hands! Left hand is in the wrong position!

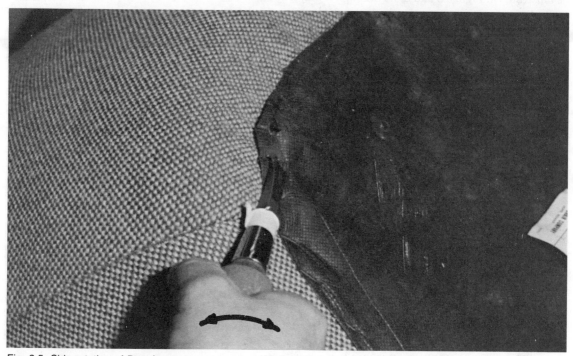

Fig. 3-5. Side rotation of Berry's staple remover to extract staple.

Fig. 3-6. Staple leg locked for removal. (Note that rotation is away from staple.)

furniture frames), gum, and bass) the staple remover can be inserted under the staple directly as illustrated in Figs. 3-5 and 3-6. Although it may take a little more time to get the staple thus locked, it will save time later by the full removal of the staple.

Frequently, in the hard materials mentioned above, and occasionally in softer ones too, the staple may break before one or both legs are extracted. The result is "gotchas" (Fig. 3-24), those sneaky,

Fig. 3-7. Cambric removed, staples extracted from bottom surface.

36

pointy little critters that delight in attacking the unsuspecting and unprotected finger, hand, arm or clothing.

4. Strip all fasteners on the bottom side of the unit. Figure 3-7 shows the barrel chair with the bottom cleared of staples.

5. Proceed to remove the "outermost" panel of material. Figure 3-8 has the operator lifting a folded seam, in this case the seat panel. Note that the under panel was stapled in place before the outer one was folded over and attached. Figure 3-9 shows the panel released and hanging with the pad seat raised to reveal the construction.

6. Remove the fabric from the unit. Notice that with the barrel chair all of the major panels (OA, OB, IB, IA) were sewn together before installing, (Fig. 3-10), and thus are removed as one piece. This chair style has only two places on the cover that are not sewn together before fitting to the chair. One is the seat panel shown hanging loose in Fig. 3-9, the other is the bottom rear joint between the outside arm panel and the outside back, shown in Fig. 3-8. Note also that all individual segments have been labeled. The straight lines beneath each symbol is the standard way to indicated the bottom of the fabric. Using this notation saves time when it comes to pattern and/or nap orientation.

Most furniture styles have each panel as separate pieces. These are removed one at a time and should be marked as they come off the unit, as illustrated in Fig. 3-11.

A *ripping tool* can be used for stripping stapled jobs as well those done with tacks (Fig. 3-12 and 3-13). Notice that in Fig. 3-12 the tool is placed so the back of the blade is basically flat with the frame surface and under the fabric. Used in this manner, it will tend to lift the fabric as well as either lift or

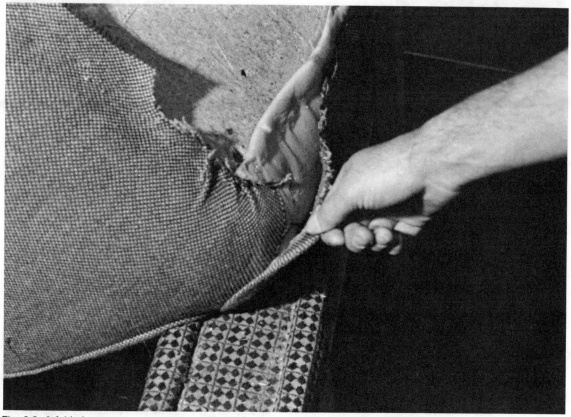

Fig. 3-8. A folded seam: sewn at top, stapled on bottom, stretched and folded in between.

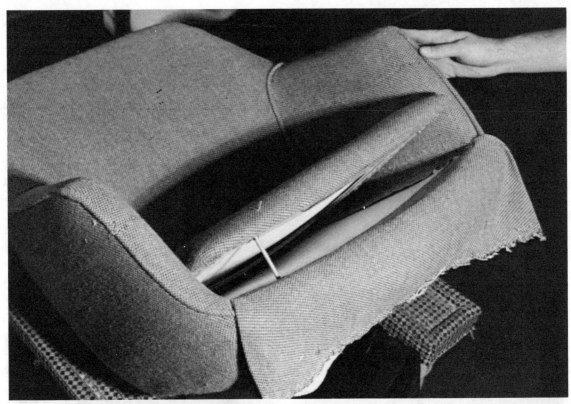

Fig. 3-9. Folded seat panel with bottom staples removed.

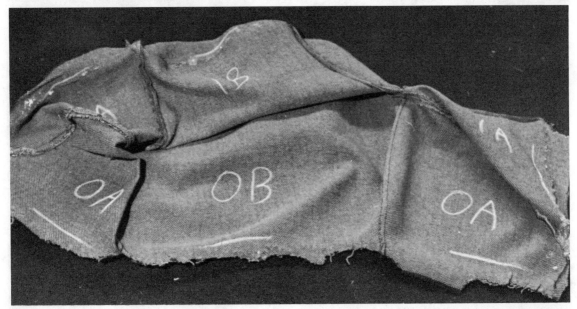

Fig. 3-10. One-piece, slip-over cover (IA, OA, IB, OB panels sewn together). On removal each component is marked for identification and orientation.

Fig. 3-11. Individual panels are marked after stripping.

Fig. 3-12. Using the ripping tool to strip stapled work.

sever the staple. Nice, huh? This can be a faster process, on occasion, if proper care is exercised. **Caution**: Great care must be taken when using the ripping tool to avoid gouging the wood excessively.

The *ripping tool* can also be used for staple clean-up (Fig. 3-13). The corner of the tool is used to wedge under the staple rather than trying to force it out with the flat face. Because most staples are put in so that the back is somewhat parallel to the edge and thus to the grain of the frame member, the tool blade will usually be directed against the grain and occasionally toward the edge. If the blade sinks into the wood near the edge of the frame and is tapped with the mallet, the result may well be a chunk torn from the edge. Gouges can also be ripped from the flat surface of the wood if care is not taken. Notice the marring of the surface at the bottom portion of Fig. 3-13? This is quite natural and not something to be concerned about. If your surface looks no worse than the one pictured, you're in good shape.

7. Remove the outermost panel. After the cambric is removed, usually the first major panel to be stripped is the outside back. This is accomplished by (1) removing the tacks or staples from the bottom (and side rails where necessary), (2) prying the tack strip from the sides by wedging the tool downward as shown by the arrow in Fig. 3-14, and (3) removing the tacking strip which is usually along the top back rail (Fig. 3-15). The staple remover is inserted between the OB panel and the frame and twisted, indicated by an arrow. At the same time, the other hand is pulling outward on the panel. These two actions together make it quite easy to remove the panel, except in the harder woods which know no easy way.

Once the tack strip has been released for a sufficient distance from one end, the faster method can often be employed, Fig. 3-16. **Caution**: the fast

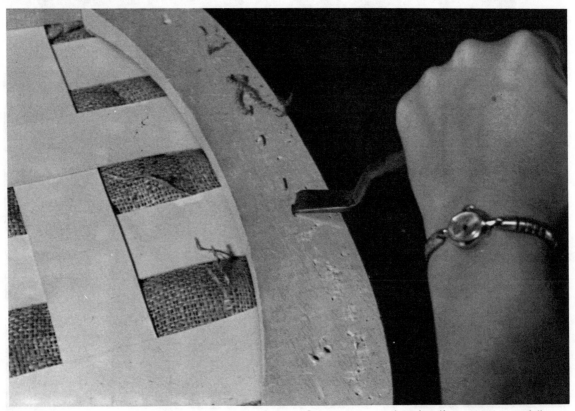

Fig. 3-13. The ripping tool to clean-up whole staples. Caution: Great gouges can be taken if you are not careful!

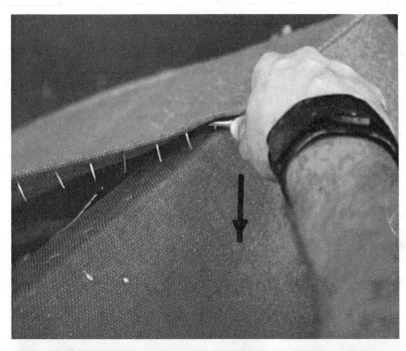

Fig. 3-14. Prying the tack strip free along sides of outside back.

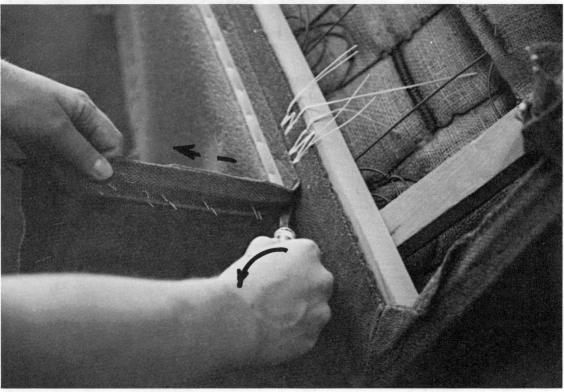

Fig. 3-15. Removing the tacking strip from top back rail.

41

method works well with strong fabrics and softer woods. The frame shown in this photo is made of alder and the fabric strong, therefore; the final part of stripping the outside back panel is fast and successful.

8. Check for frame and foundation damage. With the outside back removed, a quick visual check and good notes (mental for the expert, *written for the beginner*) will identify those internal repairs necessary before new padding or cover is applied. For the novice, don't trust the memory only, it will be regretted almost certainly. Notice the "sagging" webbing between the back uprights in Figs. 3-17 and 3-18. In this case, no back padding had to be removed, and the burlap covering the springs was also in good condition. But the webbing had to be reinforced or replaced. Reinforcement, in this case, was sufficient and less time consuming. To do this, only short sections of the burlap along the top back rail needed to be loosened, new vertical webbing strips installed, and the burlap stapled back into position. Chapter 4 shows how this was done. Reminder: Do not remove more than is really necessary! Continue with each panel, noting damage and needed repairs as the stripping progresses.

The last cover elements to be removed from most units will be the seat and deck panels. Occasionally the deck may not have to be removed, depending on its condition and style of unit. This determination can be made by visually examining the suspension system and burlap from beneath, and decking and padding from above. If the padding seems smooth and even and if the deck fabric is clean, tight and still strong, leave it alone.

Figures 3-19 and 3-20 show a chair and couch set that have a "hard edge" style seat. The hard edge is a strip of wood, ranging from 1/4" plywood to 1" thick hardwood depending upon the elevation desired at the front, that is attached directly to the

Fig. 3-16. Fast method to remove old fabric and tacking strip. (*Note*: Works well with strong fabric and softer frames.)

Fig. 3-17. Visually inspect frame and foundation for damages and record on checksheet after each panel is removed.

Fig. 3-18. Sagging webbing: reinforce, tighten, or replace.

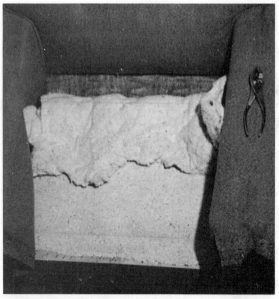

Fig. 3-19. Hard-edge seat construction with hard-edge strip, decking, and seat panels removed.

front seat rail. It is padded with one or more layers of cotton and provides a very solid support for the subsequent cushions.

In Fig. 3-19 the deck and seat panel as well as the hard-edge strip have been removed. Notice the crease in the cotton about two inches back from the front? That indicates where the rear of the hard-edge strip terminated. Figure 3-20 shows the operator removing nails from the 1/4″ plywood hard edge. Half of the padding has been left in the down position to show how it would appear immediately after the seat cover panel had been lifted.

In Fig. 3-21 the "hard edge" has been rolled toward the back to reveal how the cover is tacked to the bottom-back of the hard-edge strips. Notice that the panel is stapled a distance from the edge. This provides a space for the cotton padding to be tucked under that bottom edge and held in place as the cover is wrapped around (Fig. 3-23 shows more clearly how this was done). This also gives

Fig. 3-20. Removing hard-edge strip.

Fig. 3-21. Underside of hard-edge strip showing how seat panel is attached.

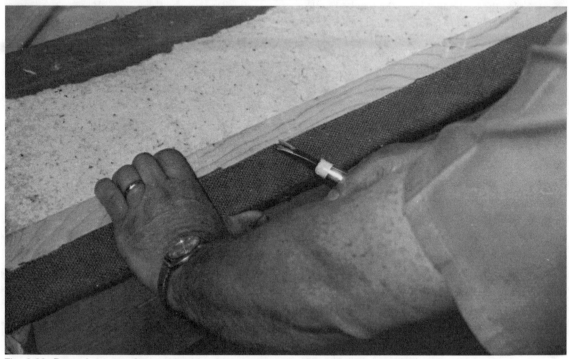

Fig. 3-22. Removing cover from underside of hard-edge strip. Note safe hand position!

Fig. 3-23. Padding is wrapped around hard-edge strip from back toward front.

the hard edge a nicely finished appearance.

The last step in stripping this style furniture is removing the seat panel from the hard-edge (Fig. 3-22). Note the hand position. If the staple remover should slip the operator would not encounter one of those stabbing pains. Nice, huh?

9. Remove the "gotchas." Back to the frame. To prevent injury, pain and staining the frame and

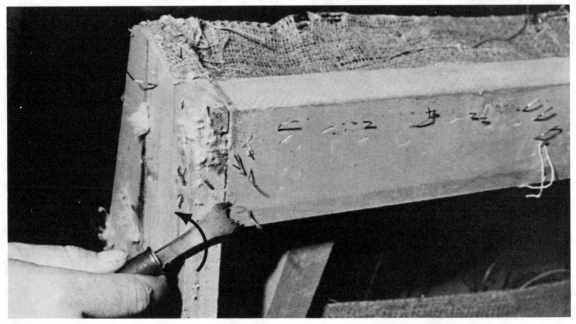

Fig. 3-24. "Gotchas," the themes of reupholstering. (Longer ones can be removed with staple remover.)

Fig. 3-25. Close-up of staple stubs. Warning: Get them all out or pounded in!

floor with blood, the gotchas (Fig. 3-24) should really be removed after each panel is stripped. A closer look (Fig. 3-25) reveals the merciless nature of those little critters. Get them out! All of them! Do not miss this step! More agony and irritation result from staple stubs than any other one factor in the upholstering business. There are plenty of other "gotchas" and "owies" lurking in

Fig. 3-26. Dikes, the stripper's friend—excellent for "gotcha" removal.

Fig. 3-27. The "planned" final check for staple remnants. Warning: move hands slowly and lightly!

the furniture without inviting the real demon into the picture. Take a few moments to assure their removal.

Among the tools best used for this work are the Berry Picker and the dikes. If the stub is long enough to permit locking in the groove, the staple remover works well (Fig. 3-24). However, the diagonal cutter has proven the best tool for this work (Fig. 3-26). A twisting motion provides a good leverage for removing metal remnants with minimal effort. The best cutter for this purpose is one that is slightly dull. Not so dull that the cutting edges no longer meet, but dull enough that it takes a little more than normal effort to cut the staples. It is better to remove the staples than to cut them off. The very short stubs left from cutting are real finger tearers! Even the shortest of them should be

hammered into the wood to prevent those painful snags (unless blood stained wood and sore fingers makes you feel better).

Slip-joint pliers can also be used, but they don't seem to grasp the staple pieces as well as the dikes. Don't use teeth! They chip easier than the staples pull!

As the final step, check the frame surfaces for any lurking stubs. If the fingers are used, as shown in Fig. 3-27, move them very lightly and slowly over the surface. The intent is to locate those sharp little protrusions so they can be pounded in or removed, not to take blood samples. An alternate method is to use the dikes as a detector and slide them lightly across the surface. Any protrusion will manifest itself as an obstruction to the smooth travel of the tool.

Chapter 4

Foundation, Stuffing, Padding and Muslin Cover

This chapter deals with all preparations for a reupholstered unit from and including the frame to the muslin cover. There will be a brief coverage of frame repairs and conditioning: spring installation, reinforcement and tying; the properties, installation (and in one case rejuvenation) of the currently more popular types of stuffing and padding; the advantages, disadvantages, and installation of the muslin cover.

FRAME CONDITIONING

Quality in upholstering is reflected from the frame through the padding to the final cover. There is no such thing as "covering up" a mistake or problem area. Those irregularities will be broadcast quite reliably to the outer appearance and feel. For example, uneven spring tension will be felt if not seen; a weak suspension section will be noticed by the "sitting IN" feeling rather than the expected "sitting ON;" lumps or depressions in the stuffing will be eventually both felt as well as seen as the unit "wears in." **COUNSEL:** Don't take short

cuts! Do top quality work from the frame outward.

One feature that is seldom found in furniture, except in those units which have been done by quality-minded craftsmen, is the rounding of sharp corners and edges of the frame. Production schedules seem to be more demanding than craftsmanship. Can the difference be noticed between units having sharp corners and those that have been rounded? Yes! In the reduction of wear of both padding and cover, in the ease of fitting, and in the final feel of most units. Is the extra time to round the corners and edges worth the bother? For the quality conscious do-it-yourselfer and for any true craftsman, definitely! For the production shop, hardly! For the custom shop, rounding of corners is often questionable. Yet, on units having especially rough frames in some areas it is not only worth the trouble but almost essential.

Figure 4-1 shows a new frame construction being rounded. Only the springs and burlap have been installed. Old frames, that are stripped to the frame, can likewise be rounded. If stripping would not normally be taken all the way to the frame,

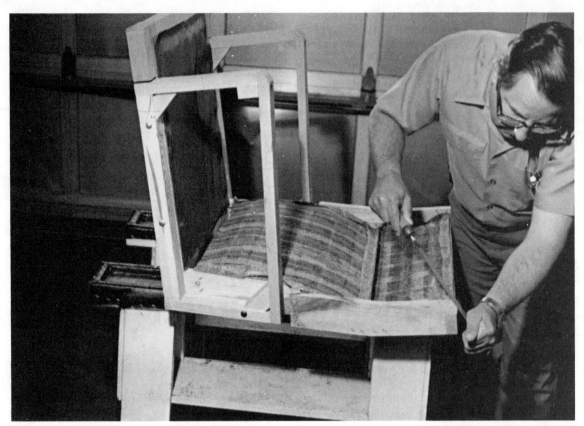

Fig. 4-1. Rounding edges on a new frame.

(Remember? Take off only what is necessary?) it would be unreasonable to go to that extra work just to round off the edges.

FRAME REPAIRS

Broken, badly gouged, and weak frame components should be either reinforced or replaced. The two center slats of the couch frame in Fig. 4-2 have been replaced and the two end rails reglued. Redoing the whole bottom on this unit was the best way to assure a solid frame. Notice the use of the four bar clamps to hold the joints tight while the glue sets. Failure to clamp glued areas will result in weak, brittle joints.

Reinforcing Sagging Webbing

Occasionally, the foundation may be in basically good condition with only the webbing sagging

(Refer to Figs. 3-17 and 3-18). One remedy is to tighten the old webbing. This can sometimes be done by drawing out the looseness and stapling the excess as illustrated in Fig. 4-3 (use 9/16″ staples). Another way to tighten the old webbing is to remove the top portion of the burlap, detach the top of the webbing, restretch (the webbing plier would probably be necessary), and restaple.

In some cases, existing, slightly sagging webbing is reinforced with the addition of new and tight webbing. Reinforcing webbing strips should be placed along the center line of the coil springs to provide the most solid support. The reinforcing webbing in Fig. 4-4 was not placed properly. Notice that it catches only the edges of the springs. For maximum benefit, it should have been directly in line with the centers of the springs. Old webbing can be reinforced by:

1. Place tack the new strand to one edge of

50

Fig. 4-2. Reinforcing a box-frame couch.

lustrated in Fig. 4-3.

Attaching the top, in this case, is simply a matter of pulling the webbing tightly across the inside of the top back rail and stapling. Figure 4-9 shows the place stapling. Notice also that the burlap has been detached only at the spots where the reinforcing webbing is to be pulled through. The webbing should be cut 1/2 to 3/4" beyond the back edge, the flap folded over and stapled on top of the main strand to minimize tear-out.

REATTACHING SPRING-EDGE WIRES

A unit with burlap wear as extensive as that shown in Fig. 4-10 may well mean additional problems beneath. Removal of the burlap from the bottom of this chair back reveals detached spring edge wires (Fig. 4-11). This repair can be achieved quickly and efficiently with the heavy-duty pneumatic stapler (Fig. 4-12). Merely relocate the edge wires, straddle the wire with the head of the staple gun and pull the trigger. Three-quarter inch, cement coated staples are recommended.

INSTALLING NEW SINUOUS SPRINGS

The first step to installing a new spring system

the frame, in line with the centers of the springs. (Fig. 4-5.)

2. Fold the flap down and staple securely in place. (Fig. 4-6.)

3. Stretch the webbing taut and place tack to the opposite rail, Fig. 4-7 (the stretcher is held in the right hand with the left hand doing the stapling).

4. Cut the webbing about 3/4" long, fold over the flap and finish staple as in step two above.

Another approach to reinforcing webbing is to attach additional strips to double the effect of those already installed. One such addition is shown in Fig. 4-8. Notice the tri-fold installation with the webbing coming from the bottom. This virtually eliminates any tear-out potential. The positioning shown (coming off the back edge of the rail) will give a "softer" back than the mid-point position il-

Fig. 4-3. Taking up slack in loose webbing when other foundation materials are in good condition.

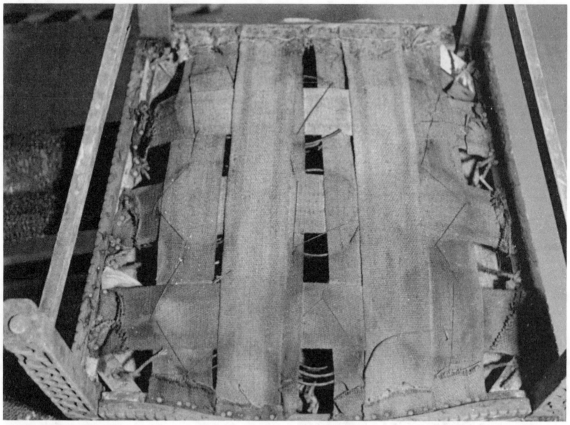

Fig. 4-4. Improperly placed reinforcing webbing.

Fig. 4-5. Webbing that has been spot stapled.

Fig. 4-6. Webbing that has been finish stapled in preparation for stretching.

Fig. 4-7. Stretching and spot stapling second end of webbing prior to cutting and finish stapling.

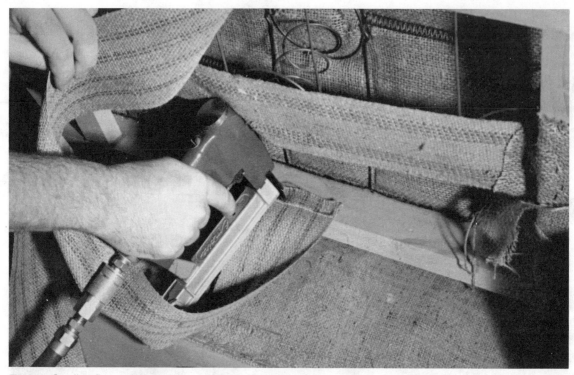

Fig. 4-8. Stapling first end of reinforcing webbing. Tri-fold stapled on top to minimize tear-out.

Fig. 4-9. Spot stapling of stretched webbing to top rail. (Notice that the burlap has been loosened only where webbing is to be placed.)

54

Fig. 4-10. This burlap should be replaced or covered with new material. (Caution: Worn burlap may be concealing other foundation problems!)

Fig. 4-11. Back spring modu-loop wires have broken loose.

Fig. 4-12. Reattaching modu-loop with heavy-duty pneumatic stapler.(Edge wires can be reattached in the same manner.)

Fig. 4-13. New couch frame redied for No-Sag springs. (Seat clips have been located and attached.)

is planning the layout. Figure 4-13 is a new-frame construction on which the sinuous spring clips have been located and attached (These were attached with the heavy-duty stapler pictured in Fig. 4-12.) awaiting installation of the spring sections. This sofa could just as well have been a used coil spring suspension that is being replaced with sinuous springs. The principle is the same. Determine the most desirable "hardness," then space and arc the springs according to Table 4-1.

Table 4-1. Sinuous Spring Calculations and Specifications

Distance Between Arms Along Front Seat Rail	Number of Strands	Center to Center Spacing of Clips	Spacing from Inside Arm Posts to Center of Two Outside Clips	Size of Connect Links
ORIGINAL NO-SAG XL				
20"	5	4"	2"	2 3/8"
22"	5	4 1/2"	2"	2 7/8"
24"	5	5"	2"	3 3/8"
48"	10	5"	1 1/2"	3 3/8"
52"	11	4 3/4"	2 1/4"	3 1/8"
72"	15	4 3/4"	2 3/4"	3 1/8"
78"	17	4 5/8"	2"	3"
86"	18	4 3/4"	2 5/8"	3 1/8"
SUPR-LOOP				
20"	4	4 3/4"	2 7/8"	2 1/4"
22"	5	4 1/4"	2 1/2"	1 3/4"
24"	5	4 3/4"	2 1/2"	2 1/4"
48"	10	4 3/4"	2 5/8"	2 1/4"
52"	11	4 3/4"	2 1/4"	2 1/4"
72"	15	4 3/4"	2 3/4"	2 1/4"
78"	16	4 7/8"	2 7/16"	2 3/8"
86"	18	4 3/4"	2 5/8"	2 1/4"

Space springs on frame by first positioning the two outside strands and then dividing the remaining area in equal parts. Spacing is calculated from center of clips. Courtesy No-Sag Spring Division, Lear Siegler, Inc.

Once the layout has been determined and the clips installed, attach the sinuous springs to the clips at the rear of the unit, then with the sinuous spring puller, pull them over and into the front clips (Fig. 4-14.) The operator's left hand is pressing down on the center portion of the spring to make attachment easier. The puller shown is a shop-made tool, and lighter duty, than the one pictured in Fig. 2-11. After all springs have been attached, the heavy-duty pneumatic stapler is a fast, sure way to secure the top of the clips. (Fig. 4-15.) (You just have to be a good shot to get the staple through both holes in the clip!) Clips can also be installed using barbed tacks or special nails that can be purchased from supply houses for this purpose. Figure 4-16 shows the completed seat suspension.

TYING SINUOUS SPRINGS

It is advisable to tie sinuous springs to provide a more consistent base for the burlap and padding.

The distance between sinuous ties is a matter of preference. Normally, two ties for seat and back springs will be sufficient. However, if more support is desired, additional ties may be used. A popular tie for this purpose is the "two-and-one tie." This tie is started by attaching one end of the tying twine to the frame at one side and securing it to the nearest loop of the first spring with a clove hitch knot. (Fig. 4-17.) From this beginning, go over TWO springs, around TWO loops; back ONE spring and around ONE loop as illustrated in Fig. 4-18. The tie name, "two-and-one," is derived from the over-and-around-two, back-and-around-one sequence. The object in this tying technique is to keep the twine snug without distorting the straight-line lay of the spring sections. To finish off, secure the twine at the other side, as illustrated in Fig. 4-19, first with a clove hitch on the last loop, and then stapled, tacked, or nailed to the frame. If a tack (number 12 or larger) or nail is used, secure the

Fig. 4-14. Using sinuous spring puller to attach springs.

Fig. 4-15. Locking spring clips with heavy duty pneumatic stapler.

Fig. 4-16. Couch seat with sinuous springs installed.

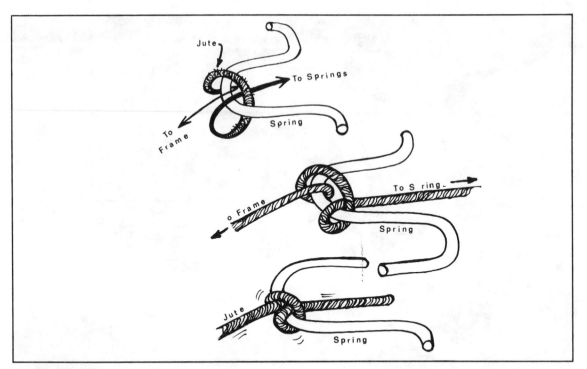

Fig. 4-17. Steps in tying the clove hitch knot to "lock" end spring unit.

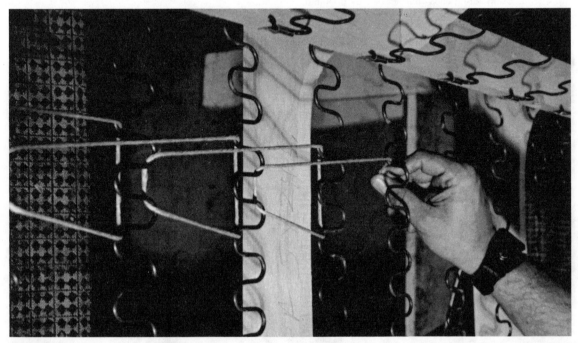

Fig. 4-18. The "two-and-one tie" for sinuous springs. (Provides added support for burlap and padding, and equalizes spring action.)

Fig. 4-19. Finishing off two-and-one tie with heavy-duty stapler. (Note clove hitch to prevent slippage (encircled.)

twine with a double-wrap as illustrated in Fig. 4-20. Notice that two wraps of twine have been made around the tack so that two layers of twine are between the head of the tack or nail and the standing part of the twine. This prevents cutting the standing part when the tack is driven tight against the twine and frame.

CALCULATING LENGTH OF TYING TWINE FOR SINUOUS SPRINGS

The length of tying twine, can be calculated by the following equation:

$L = (3n - 1) (S/(n + 1)) + 3n + 5$ where
L = total length of twine needed
n = number of spring sections
S = rail to rail span, taken over the top and at right angles to the run of the springs. (If spring sections are attached to the front and back rails, S = measurement over the springs from one side rail to the other side rail.)

Example: If a chair back had 6 rows of sinuous springs (an unusually wide chair) attached to the side posts and the top-to-bottom frame meas-

Fig. 4-20. The double-loop anchoring method for the double-strand tie.

61

urement (over the crest of the springs) were 35″, the twine length would be calculated like this:

$$n = 6, S = 35″$$
$$L = (3n - 1)(S/(n + 1)) + 3n + 5$$
$$L = (3 \times 6 - 1)(35/(6 + 1)) + 3 \times 6 + 5$$
$$= (18 - 1)(35/7) + 18 + 5$$
$$= 17 \times 5 + 23$$
$$= 85 + 23 = 108″$$

If the measurement (S) is taken in centimeters, the length (L) will be in centimeters. If (S) is taken in inches, (L) will be in inches.

ANCHORING COIL SPRINGS

Sewing coil springs to the webbing will work, but, attaching them with the klinch-it tool is much faster, Fig. 4-21. This is done by straddling the coil wire with the prongs of the clip, having the tool in-line with the direction of the wire as shown, and squeezing the handle while pressing down on the tool. The clip will penetrate the webbing, spread the prongs sideways, and release the clip in that one operation of the handle. Refer back to Fig. 2-27 and 2-28 to get a better idea of how this tool will work (It's tough to show much of this tool's action in a photo!). After coil springs are anchored to the base, they must then be tied across the top.

Calculating the Length of Tying Twine for Coil Springs

The formulas for calculating tying twine lengths for coil springs are significantly easier than that for sinuous springs. Both formulas include sufficient twine to tie all the clove hitches, binder and lock knots, anchoring loops, and wraps that will be used. This "quick and easy" formula is:

Double-strand tie: Quadruple the frame-to-frame* measurement.
Single-strand tie: Double the frame-to-frame* measurement.
*This measurement is straight-line, not arching over the springs.

TYING COIL SPRINGS

The tying of coil springs has a three-fold purpose: (1) to establish a given height (compression) of the springs, (2) to create a stable base for the burlap and subsequent padding, and (3) to hold the tops of the separate springs firmly in place. There are a number of different ways to tie these springs, but the two shown below seem to give the most reliable results.

The Double-Strand Tie

This is the first tie for coil springs. All height adjustment and front-to-back (or top-to-bottom for backs) location of the springs will be done with these ties. In its use, one strand of twine is doubled in half, anchored to the rear seat rail (or the bottom back rail) with a double loop (Fig. 4-20), and the springs tied in place, using one strand at a time. Normally, the ties are made from back-to-front for seats and bottom-to-top for backs, using both strands for each row. With the double loop anchored firmly to the frame, follow this procedure:

1. Take the first strand and tie a binder knot (see Fig. 4-28) around the rear of the third coil from

Fig. 4-21. Using the Klinch-it tool to anchor coil springs to jute webbing.

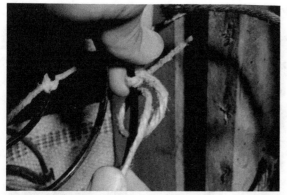

Fig. 4-22. The clove hitch being tied around a top coil.

the top of the rear spring, adjusting the spring so it is plumb (straight up and down). Figure 4-22 shows this knot already tied (beneath the clove hitch being tied). Notice that the twine is looped around the spring wire, tensioned as desired, and held from slipping with one finger while the over-and-around-and-under part of the knot is completed and snugged down firmly (Fig. 4-28). This knot is used most because it is fast and easy to tie and prevents any spring movement as long as tension is maintained. A lock knot (refer to Fig. 4-26) or a clove hitch (refer to Fig. 4-22) will be tied periodically to maintain a non-slipping tension on the binders.

2. Lock the first binder with a clove hitch at the inside of the top coil of the rear spring (Fig. 4-23, left).

3. Locate and secure the rear of the top coil of the center spring with another binder knot (Fig. 4-23, right).

4. Tie a binder knot at the front of the second coil from the top of that center spring (Fig. 2-24).

5. Go to the front spring and tie another binder knot at the rear of the third coil from the top.

6. Move to the front of the fourth coil down and secure it with a clove hitch. All six ties are shown in Fig. 4-24. *Tip:* Before securing the clove hitch, check to see that the springs are in line and at the same height.

7. Anchor this first strand to the front rail by making a double wrap around the first tack (Fig. 4-25) and drive it down tight.

8. Now, start the second strand by making a loop around the rear, top coil of the rear spring, pulling it down to the desired height and locking it in place with a clove hitch, as shown at the left of Fig. 4-26. If the spring foundation is to be flat, the level of this top coil will be the same as the rest of the springs. If the foundation is to be crowned, pull the rear of that spring down to the taper desired, and secure in place.

9. Move to the front of that spring and tie a double lock knot around the previous binder knot as illustrated in Fig. 4-26, right.

10. Follow the first twine to the middle spring and tie a double binder around the first binder knot, Fig. 4-27, and a single binder around the front of that top coil, Fig. 4-28.

11. At the rear of the third spring, tie a double lock knot around the first binder knot on the third coil from the top.

12. Go across the spring to the front of that same coil and lock that clove hitch with another double lock knot.

13. Secure the second twine to the frame with a double wrap around a tack or nail, the same as in Fig. 4-25.

14. Now, take the longest of the two ends to the top, front coil, loop over the coil, pull it down to the desired height (following the same procedure as in step 8 above) and secure that position with a clove hitch.

15. Move across to the opposite side of the top

Fig. 4-23. Finished clove hitch (left), binder knot (right).

Fig. 4-24. The first strand of the double tie in place. (Notice that the second strand is still laying on webbing.)

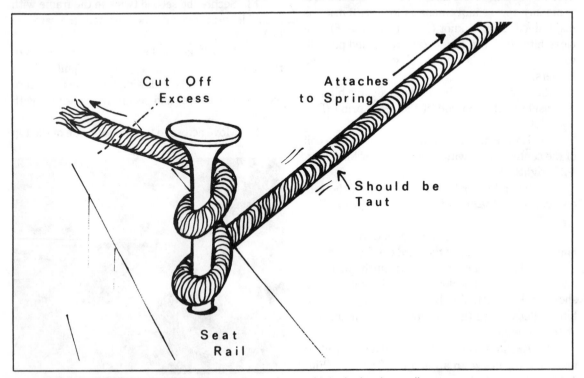

Fig. 4-25. Using a double-wrap to attach tying twine to frame with barbed tack or nail.

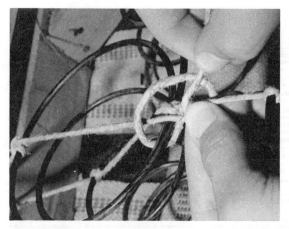

Fig. 4-26. Tying the double lock knot around the first clove hitch.

coil and secure it with another clove hitch.

16. Do the back-to-front ties on all rows, making each row straight and at the same height. Figure 4-29 shows the path and sequence for the double strand ties.

The Single-Strand Tie

The single strand ties are used to make all side and diagonal ties. See page 62 for the formula for calculating twine length. Figure 4-30 shows the sequence for the single tie. Proceed as follows:

1. Go to a side rail and anchor one end of the twine with a double loop, leaving a short end of about 10 inches extending from one of the tacks.

2. Begin with the long end and secure the outside, third from the top coil with a binder knot.

3. Lock the inside of the top coil of the first spring with a clove hitch.

4. Progress across the top of each spring to the inside of the last spring, tying binder knots, and secure the last one with another clove hitch.

5. Move down to the outside, third from the top coil, tie it with a binder knot and secure the twine to the opposite rail with a double wrap. (Many operators like to lock the side twines around the back-to-front ones with either a simple loop or a binder knot.)

6. Loop the remaining length of twine at both sides around the top, outside coil, pull it down to the desired height, and anchor it with a clove hitch. Make a binder around the center twine, and finish off at the inside top coil with a clove hitch that locks around the other twine.

Figure 4-31 shows a crowned seat with all the back-to-front and side-to-side ties in place. Tying the springs at four points each is commonly used for backs and where light use is expected, and is known as the "four-way tie."

Also shown are two diagonal ties, going from corner to corner. When all springs are tied at eight points, it would be known as . . .? You guessed it, the "eight-way tie." The eight-way is used mostly on seats and where maximum stability is desired.

The diagonals are started with a double wrap around a single tack, (Fig. 4-32). Notice that only

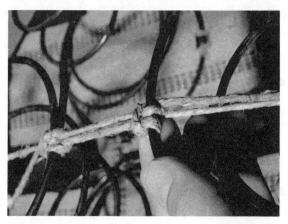

Fig. 4-27. A double binder knot tightened around a previous binder.

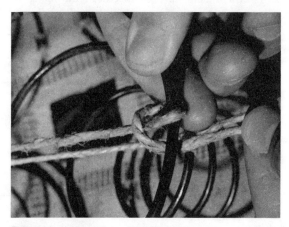

Fig. 4-28. A binder knot in the tying process.

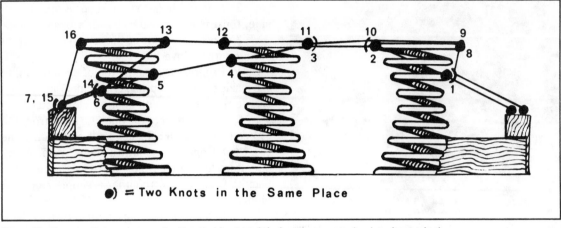

Fig. 4-29. The complete sequence for the double strand tie (used on seats, back-to-front tying).

one end of the twine will be used to make all ties. For the diagonals, all ties (which will probably be binder knots) will be made to the top coils only (and where it crosses the twine in the centers). Do not do any contouring with the diagonals! Figure 4-33 illustrates how to get the measurement to put into the single twine formula for each run—from tack to tack. *Note*: The tacks are placed so the twine will lie in a straight line when tying is completed. Figure 4-34 shows the seat with all but the final corner diagonals tied. For rounded seats (or backs), tie as illustrated in Fig. 4-35.

REINFORCING COIL SPRINGS

Seats of a coil spring construction utilizing an edge wire along the front which have insufficient spring for the persons using it can be strengthened by the addition of a home-made V-arc unit as illustrated in Fig. 4-36. The original coil spring is discernable by the black paint, while the new sinuous spring section appears almost white in the photo. For this application, the V-arc was attached with the same clip as an original reinforcing wire.

ATTACHING AND FITTING BURLAP

One of the popular methods of attaching the burlap is to snug it over the springs, sparingly staple in place (place tack), then fold the extra material over the top and finish stapling. This over-flap greatly reduces tear-out. The operator in Fig. 4-37 is finishing off the seat burlap (which in this case is a surplus piece of durable nylon fabric).

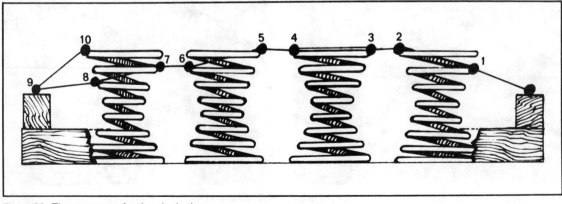

Fig. 4-30. The sequence for the single tie.

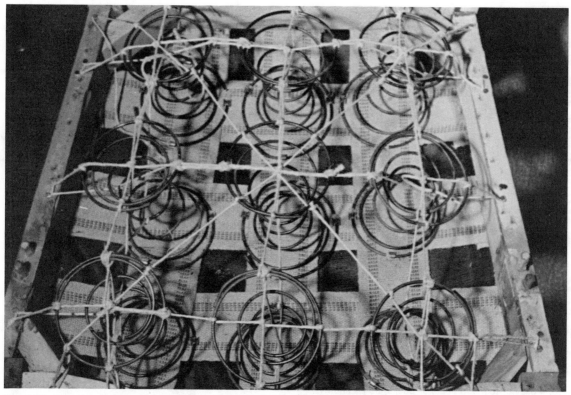

Fig. 4-31. A crowned seat with all the back-to-front and side-to-side ties in place.

The Y-Cut

With the spring foundation secured and tied, the burlap base is fitted and attached. Figure 4-38 shows another nylon fabric being used as burlap. Notice the bottom rail. The operator chose to apply the burlap cover with the flaps folded to the underside. Some prefer this method, expressing that it gives a more smooth base for the padding and final cover. The Y-cut shown in the center of the photo is strategic to the fitting process. This cut is used any time fabric meets a frame member straight-on, is to be finished against the face, and pulled around and finished against both sides— OR—when the fabric is to be stretched in two different directions, as is the case at the arm crest. The top portion will be pulled outward, around the front of the back upright, while the center portion will be pulled backwards between the back and the arm. Figure 4-39 shows a popular application of the Y-cut, fitting around a show wood arm post. Ac-

tually, the Y-cut is not really needed when fitting burlap, but by practicing it, fitting the cover will become easier. To properly make this cut (on a seat installation):

Fig. 4-32. Diagonals are started with a double wrap around a single tack.

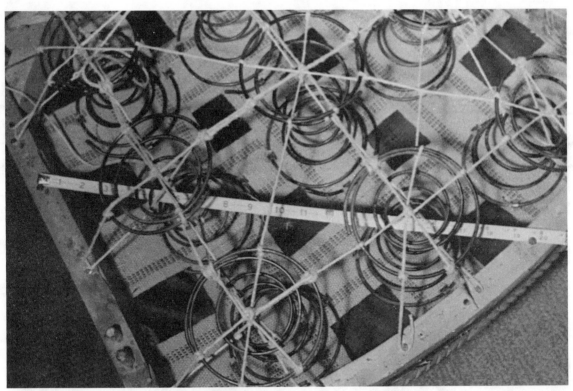

Fig. 4-33. For rounded seats or backs, tie as shown.

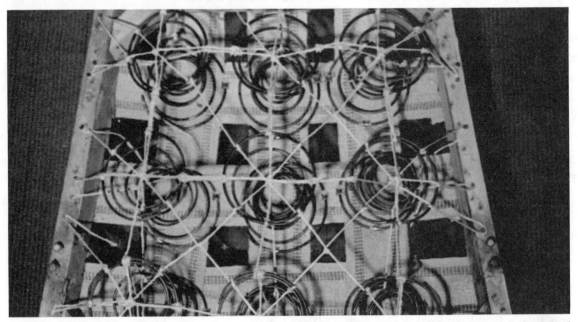

Fig. 4-34. Completely tied crowned seat. (*Note:* The corner diagonals were not tied on this job—a matter of personal preference.)

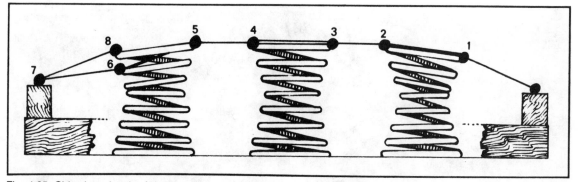

Fig. 4-35. Side-view sketch of the rounded (crowned) seat tying procedure.

1. Stretch and attach the fabric to the center portions of the front and back rails, leaving enough free to fold the fabric back from the sides to the face of the frame member that is to be fitted.

2. Mark and/or cut to fit. In Fig. 4-39, the burlap is folded back against the inside of an arm post and marked with chalk to show the location and direction of the cuts. The center cut is to be made straight toward the center of the upright or rail stopping 3/4" to 1" from where it is to be fit. The tab in the center is cut so that each leg of the cut will be approximately 1/32" short of spanning the width of the frame member around which it is to be fit and terminate just at the face of the frame member when the fabric is stretched tight. For the beginner, it might be a good idea to quickly sketch the chalk lines, as illustrated in Fig. 4-39, to assure one of where the cuts are to be made, and exactly where they should end. The experienced upholsterer will not bother with sketching lines, but just make the cuts. (Sharpening the chalk to a chisel point, as illustrated in Fig. 4-40, will reduce the width of markings and increase accuracy.)

3. Tuck the tab under so the folded edge meets the face of the frame member Fold the two flaps under and stretch tight along both sides of the frame member. Figure 4-41 shows the operator fitting the burlap around the front of the arm post. Notice how the tab finishes off against the face of the post (right side of the photo).

The Diagonal Cut

This cut is used when the fabric meets a frame member at a corner and is to be pulled around just two sides. To make this cut:

1. Attach the fabric, stretched to the desired tension, along the center portions of the adjacent frame sides, leaving enough free at the corners to make a diagonal fold across the edge of the frame member as shown in Fig. 4-42. For the novice, sketching the cutting line is recommended, as illustrated, straight from the fabric corner to the corner of the frame member.

2. Cut to the corner. For the stout-hearted, skip the sketch and cut diagonally to approximately 1/8" beyond where the fabric meets the frame edge. This gives space to stretch the fabric tight to the corner. If the burlap binds at the corner when stretched, make the cut a little deeper. Simple, eh?

3. Fold the flaps under and stretch, one at a

Fig. 4-36. Reinforcing spring edge along front of coil springs with a shop-made V-arc section.

69

Fig. 4-37. Finishing the burlap base. (Notice the over-lapping that reduces tear-out.)

time, along the side of the frame member to create the finished edges. In Fig. 4-43 the operator is fitting the front side of the diagonal cut to the back upright with the other flap still left on top of the burlap. The finished diagonal cut is pictured in Fig. 4-44, complete with the burlap over-flap to reduce side tear-out.

For the burlap base the "finished" edge is not

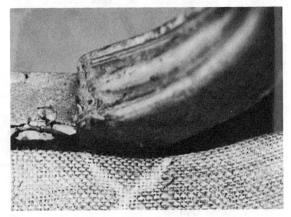

Fig. 4-38. The Y-cut used to fit fabrics (burlap, muslin, cover) around frame members and where the upper arm crowns.

Fig. 4-39. Sketching the cut lines prior to fitting to an arm post.

70

Fig. 4-40. Chalk sharpened to a wedge point to reduce width of marking lines.

nearly so important as it is for the cover, but by making even the burlap fit neatly, a good habit is being formed which will greatly enhance confidence and aid in fitting the final cover.

BASES FOR INSIDE ARMS AND OUTSIDE ARMS AND BACKS

There are several types of bases which are especially appropriate for the insides and outsides of covered arms, and at times the outsides of backs. For the sake of brevity this discussion will center on a base for an inside arm. However, the principle remains the same for both the other areas. This base will most frequently be made from a lightweight (0.020"-0.030") cardboard. Burlap or webbing are also used on occasion.

The Cardboard Base

The cardboard base shown in Fig. 4-45 provides a solid, rigid support for the padding. This is the quickest and most popular technique. It has the disadvantage of sounding like cardboard when tapped (but then, who goes around tapping upholstered furniture?). The cardboard piece is sized and cut so that it can be stapled easily to the framing

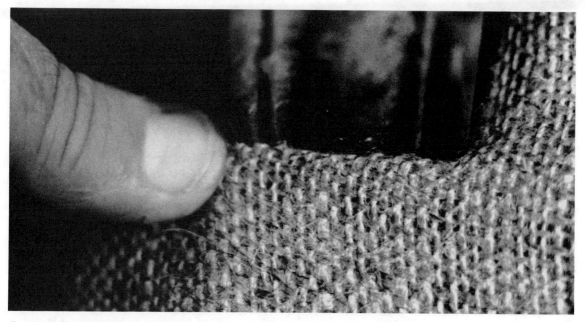

Fig. 4-41. Fitting the Y-cut. (Notice the finished edges at front and side of arm post.)

Fig. 4-42. Diagonal folding of the Burlap and marking for the diagonal cut.

Fig. 4-43. Folding first flap to finish diagonal cut.

Fig. 4-44. Completed diagonal cut. (Note finished edges along both sides of post.)

Fig. 4-45. Cardboard base for inside arm.

rails and uprights. It must be stapled to all sides to provide a solid base. On some styles, however, there may be a section that cannot be stapled, usually at the rear of the inside arm. In such a case heavier (0.040"-0.060") cardboard is used and only stapled to the top and bottom rails and the stump or post.

The Burlap Base

A burlap base provides a full and somewhat resilient support for padding. For those who do not want the possibility of a "cardboard sound" in the unit, this base is recommended. The burlap must be stretched tightly to be effective. It is recommended that the fabric be folded to the outside and stapled in place (Fig. 4-46). The outward folding minimizes tear-out. The most successful way to install this type of base is to:

1. Fold, stretch and staple the bottom edge in place.

2. Stretch fabric to top rail and staple in center.

3. Stretch diagonally up and sideways, stapling from the center along the arm rail. *Note:* staple sparingly at this point as final stapling will be done with the fabric folded over.

4. Fold burlap over and finish stapling.

5. Snug to center sides and staple in place. The finished inside arm foundation should look somewhat like the one in Fig. 4-46.

The Webbing Base

This is recommended where extra "forgiving" support and protection against impact is desired. It is especially suited for applications where knees and elbows may be factors with which to contend,

Fig. 4-46. Burlap base provides quiet support.

74

as in lounge or livingroom furnishings into, onto, and around which children are likely to be jumping, climbing or scuffling. For teenagers and apartments, place the webbing almost adjacent to each other to provide maximum support (and it still can't be guaranteed!). To install:

1. Determine where maximum support and contours occur. Locate the vertical webbing as desired.

2. Attach vertical strips, one at a time, at the bottom (Remember to fold a flap outward to minimize tear-out.). Stretch to arm rail and staple lightly.

3. Cut webbing 3/4″ to 1″ long, fold over and finish staple in place.

4. Locate horizontal webs as desired.

5. Attach, one at a time to the back upright, weave alternately through the vertical strips, stretch to the arm post or stump, and staple lightly.

6. Trim 3/4″ to 1″ long, fold over and finish staple. *Note*: Special consideration must be given to any contouring that is to be done. A close look at Fig. 4-47 will reveal (a) the strategic location of the leftmost vertical strip, and (b) the weaving of the topmost horizontal strip under the left vertical strip. Notice how that approach gives the inside of the arm a slight convex curvature to approach that of the arm stump.

CHARACTERISTICS OF STUFFING AND PADDING

The most popular stuffing and padding materials in modern upholstery practices are *cotton*, *dacron*, and *foam*. Within each of the three basic types are also various compositions which will alter the characteristics and properties, sometimes significantly. By blending or alloying materials, a stuffing or padding form can be tailored for almost

Fig. 4-47. Webbing base—quiet and extra strong.

any given application and will impart almost any desired firmness and resiliency. Yet with all the variations possible, all forms of padding, no matter what their composition, will have both a break-in and a break-down characteristic. Some persons, or even groups, may occasionally slip in an unintentional declaration that "X" material does not break down. The unintentional is stressed because it seems rather obvious to this writer that everyone would realize that such a thing as perpetual longivity of resilient materials has not yet been invented nor discovered. With this in mind, let us briefly identify what is meant by break-in and break-down.

The Break-In Period is a span of time during which new stuffing and padding materials will undergo changes in stiffness and cushioning characteristics. It is a period of stabilization. For example, resilient properties either seem to lose some of the springiness (as with cotton and dacron) or stiffness (as with the foams).

Cotton will have slightly more life during the first few months, then will settle down gradually and give years (5 to 8) of rather consistent support. Dacron and foam both possess a distinguishable "stiffness" when new. Each, therefore, will feel more firm when first installed than they will a few weeks later. Because of these break-in characteristics, no new or newly reupholstered furniture will possess quite the same "feel" as it will a short period after it has been put into use. So, if that newly redone unit doesn't feel quite like you expected, give it a month or two before counting to ten, or before stripping it down to redo it. Give it a chance to "break-in."

The Break-Down Period is the in-service life span of the padding material. When the "life" seems to be waning in the padding, it is going through the break-down period. All stuffing and padding materials will experience some form of break-down. Cotton will eventually mat down to a rather firm, solid layer showing little life or springback. That matting process is greatly accelerated by moisture, so don't spill very many glasses of fruit punch on the furniture! Cotton does not decompose to lifeless powders, nor does it just seem to evaporate, unless rodents, mildew or rot get into the act. Rather than a cell or fiber break-down, it just seems to compact. Dacron tends to mat much the same as cotton. However, during the life of its resiliency, after the break-in period, it has a much "softer feel" than does cotton.

On the other hand, all known foams undergo a cellular destruction as they break down. In this process, most foams will first mat, then decompose. Perhaps you have experience a foam rubber that has "hardened"? That is the matting stage. This usually occurs at the edges of cushions and points of major compression. This "hardening of the arteries," however, can be reversed, not indefinitely, but for a noticeable period of time (See "Foam Rejuvenation" below). Perhaps you have seen the situation where what once was foam rubber is now a pile of lifeless granules or powder? That is the advanced stage of decomposition—way beyond rigormortis. From this latter stage there is no known resurrection, yet! Although it has been suspected that all foams will experience that decomposition phenomenon, some sooner than others, there are newer formulations on the market that show promise in greatly increasing the time span between installation and "back to dust." Of especial note are the High Resiliency (HR) Foams. These are new enough that time has not afforded decomposition data to be established.

Cotton

The cotton used in upholstering is a composite material, made of a combination of several basic materials. The two major components of most cotton felts are known as first-cut cotton *linters* (which are the short fuzzy fibers on the seeds) and *binders* (longer, more coarse fibers of the cotton plant (pickers or gin flues) or polyester fibers). When purchasing upholstery cottons, the quality and content will be identified by two numbers, such as 70-30 or 85-15. The first number is the percent content of cotton linters, the second number, the percent content of binder. The higher the linter content, the softer and more lively the cotton felt. The higher the binder content, the heavier and stiffer will be the felt, and the quicker it will mat down.

Dacron

The word *Dacron* originates from the brand name DuPont gave to its line of polyester fibers. Thus, all dacron that is referenced in clothing or in upholstery is a polyester fiber. The material used for upholstering is much like the quilt batting familiar to many people. The most popular size for furniture upholsterers is 30 inches wide and 1 inch thick (in its relaxed form). A roll will weigh between 13 and 15 pounds and contain between 39 and 45 yards of material. It has a very low compressive resistance, which gives it the "soft" feel. To roll the fibers themselves between the fingers, however, will not give the impression of softness; they seem rather coarse and somewhat stiff. It is that stiffness that gives dacron the bounce or spring for which it is known.

Use. It is used primarily for the final surface padding of cushions, backs, and arms. It provides a very soft, almost "cushy" feel to the final product when the cover fabric is not pulled down too tightly. It is also used to provide a resilient "filler" in corners of cushions, inside back attached cushions and other areas where a filler may be desired that will not give the sensation of lumps.

Understanding Foams

Most, if not all, *foams* used in the upholstery industry today are polyurethane. Some people, even societies, will classify them as *foam rubbers*, while others will have them classified as *plastics*. Chemically, they are plastics. Behaviorally, they are rubbers. Take your pick and be content, this is one time when you can be right either way. Regardless of your stand, polyurethane chemistry is extremely diverse and complex. Thousands of formulations exist for making flexible urethane foam. That means that there exist thousands of differing foams. But we are fortunate, there are only a few formulations that are used extensively in furniture. Table 4-2 gives a condensation of the more popular foams; their major use areas, ILD's, densities, and manufacturers. To understand the terms, refer to the glossary.

To understand the basic characteristics of foams, the two properties, ILD and density, must be considered together. Basically it goes this way. The higher the density, the thicker the cell walls and the longer wearing (higher quality) the foam. The higher the ILD, the more firm the foam. Combined together, a high ILD with a low density indicates a stiff foam subject to short wear life. A low ILD and high density gives a soft foam that will endure a "longer" period of use. Due to the characteristics of the loads that are experienced in different applications, the same ILD will be rated differently as the application changes. Table 4-3 might help explain this. The ILD of 20-24 for backs is rated as "firm" while the same ILD for seats is rated as "soft." The ILD of 38-45 for seats is rated as "extra firm" while for church, bar and restaurant use it is rated as "medium."

The seeming confusion is really a matter of what is generally accepted as "proper cushioning." Consider, for instance, that the back of a chair or sofa receives relatively little weight or stress on it. For this reason, it requires little stiffness to give a proper cushioning effect. On the other hand, with church, bar and restaurant seating, usually the foam is over a solid wood or metal base. No "bottoming-out" is wanted, so, a stiffer foam is used as the norm. The best way to order and buy foam is to specify both the density and ILD desired. Anything short of that and there will be no assurance of accurate communication. The differences in ILD is readily apparent in Fig. 4-48. (Check Table 4-2 for the ILD and densities of the two United formula numbers.)

A relatively new foam that is rapidly becoming the essence of quality in upholstering is the *High Resiliency* (HR). As can be seen in Table 4-2, high resiliency foam has a significantly longer service life than any other foam currently on the market. It costs more, to be sure, but once a person has felt the difference between HR and "standard," the price differential almost becomes insignificant.

All foams are manufactured in much the same way. A liquid mixture is sprayed or poured on special conveyor belts. A chemical reaction causes

Table 4-2. Comparison of Upholstery Foams.

Use	Nominal* Density	ILD 25%	Formula No.	Company
Back Foams	.90	12-18	RA-15090-000	Crain
	1.00	12 max	2005	United
6 to 8 yrs	1.00	10-16	R10	Ramco
	1.00	18-24	R-21100-000	Crain
	1.10	12-18	2000	United
	1.15	18-24	2001	United
8 to 12 yrs	1.50	20-26	2049	United
12 yrs +	1.80	10	HR1810	Carpenter
Inexpensive Seat	1.05	30-36	RA-33105-880	Crain
	1.10	30-36	R22	Ramco
1 to 1/2 yrs	1.12	36-42	R34	Ramco
	1.15	30-36	2011	United
	1.20	24-30	2002	United
Mid-Range Seat	1.40	28-34	R250	Ramco
	1.45	32-39	R32	Carpenter
	1.45	27-33	RA-30145-000	Crain
3 to 4 yrs	1.45	33-39	RA-36145-000	Crain
	1.50	20-26	2049	United
	1.50	26-32	2009	United
	1.50	32-38	2010	United
	1.55	28-32	S28X	Carpenter
Top Quality	1.80	15-21	FA-18180-304	Crain
Seat	1.80	15-20	2080	United
6 to 8 yrs	1.80	26-32	2081	United
	1.80	32-38	2079	United
	1.80	48-54	2102	United
	1.80	28-34	R230	Ramco
	1.80	30-36	RA-33180.000	Crain
	2.10	45-50	S524	Ramco
	2.20	27-33	RA-30220-000	Crain
12 yrs +	1.80	28	HR1828	Carpenter
12 yrs +	1.80	35	HR1835	Carpenter
Church, Bar	1.30	40-48	2072	United
Restaurant	1.65	91-101	S91S	Carpenter
	1.70	70 min.	2145	United
6 to 8 yrs	1.80	41-47	FA-44180-304	Crain
	1.80	70-80	GA-75180-805	Crain
	1.90	80 min.	2108	United
	2.20	80 min.	2169	United
	2.50 min.	42-48	UL-45250-145	Carpenter

*Nominal Density = Average density

the liquid to expand rapidly up to 50 times the original volume, creating a flexible, rubbery slab which would be approximately 30 inches thick and of varying widths. This slab is then cut by automatic machinery to given lengths to permit handling, otherwise that "extruded" foam slab would be of infinite length and impossible to ship. The foams are then shipped to distributing warehouses where they are cut to customer sizes. Figure 4-49 shows a warehouseman (his arms may

**Table 4-3. Foam Firmness
Ratings for Differing Applications.**

Use	ILD	Rating
Backs	10 and below	Super Soft
	12-14	Soft
	16-18	Medium
	20-24	Firm
	26 +	Extra Firm
Seats	20-24	Soft
	26-30	Medium
	32-36	Firm
	38-45	Extra Firm
	46 +	Super Firm
Church	40-48	Medium
Bar and	50-70	Firm
Restaurant	80 +	Extra Firm

After the skins are trimmed off the bun, the remaining foam can be slabbed and trimmed to customer orders. Thickness ranging from 1/8″ to 29″ (or whatever the bun thickness will allow) can be cut as well as almost any conceivable size and shape. Most warehouses will utilize several horizontal and vertical foam saws similar to the ones pictured in Figs. 4-49 and 4-50. These saws are significantly larger and quite different from the upholsterer's foam saw shown in Fig. 2-20. Figure 4-50 shows an operator trimming a smaller piece to a "sample" size for customer reference, using a vertical band saw.

Rejuvenation of Foams

There may be times when a foam will seem to still have very good life, yet displays a matted or hardened section. If granularization has not started that section of the foam can be restored significantly. The extent of rejuvenation is totally dependent on the extent of decomposition. The process is a very simple one. Apply a jet of steam to the hardened area. This can be done with a commercial steamer, a steam iron, even a portable

be distinguished in the lower right corner) trimming off the top "skin" of a bun using a horizontal band saw. The two pieces of foam at the rear of the bun serve as a buffer to protect the saw blade from hitting the metal frame of the movable table. One of the rollers of the table can be seen just beneath and a short distance from the front of the bun.

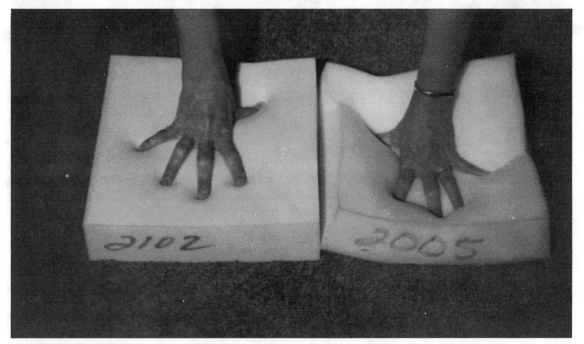

Fig. 4-48. The difference ILD makes. (Check table 4-2 for ILD ratings for the two foams.)

Fig. 4-49. Horizontal band saw used to cut foam buns to thickness. (The whole table moves on roller bearings.)

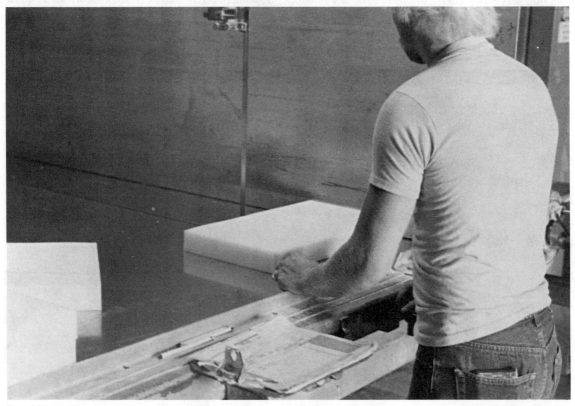

Fig. 4-50. Vertical band saw used to cut foam vertically and smaller pieces. (Table is also on roller bearings.)

clothes steamer. Do not touch a hot iron to the foam, just the steam! As the steam penetrates the foam it causes a relaxation of the compressed area, opening up the cells that have been compacted.

Stuffing and Padding

With the springs and burlap installed, the next step is applying the stuffing and padding. Almost any given "feel" can be imparted through a combination of modern materials. For our first example, we shall look at the arm rail.

Padding The Arm Rail

Many different "feelings" can be imparted to the arm. The fastest padding system is seldom the most desirable. For most furniture, built up layers of cotton has been the rule. For a brief time after installation, this padding gives resiliency and comfort. But with time, the cotton mats down and the result is a rather solid, lifeless armrest. Another "fast" way to pad an arm is to use a single layer of high quality, "standard" polyfoam. Both of these methods are frequently used in mass produced furniture. But, neither will give a resilient, comfortable arm rest that does not "bottom out". However, with the use of various combinations of foam; foam and cotton; or foam, cotton, and dacron; an infinite range of armrest properties can be created. For an armrest that has body, life and seems not to "bottom out," the following can be used:

Establish a firm, resilient base by using a layer of 1/4" to 1/2" high ILD foam. A very inexpensive yet satisfactory base can be achieved using good quality chopped foam carpet pad (New, not used!). Cut the foam to the size and shape of the arm and glue in place using a rubber based trim adhesive (Refer to Fig. 2-7).

    a. Spray both the arm rail and one side of the foam pad.

    b. Allow the glue to dry until it has lost the "wet" look and feel.

    c. Begin at one end of the arm and lay the foam down in a rolling motion. Try not to stretch or compress the foam in this

action. But to be sure,

    d. Check the length before pressing the entire pad down. Even with care, it seems that the foam gets either stretched or compressed a little. Figure 4-51 shows the operator "bridging" the foam to make sure that it will not extend beyond the point intended. By seating the second end in this manner, the remaining foam within the bridged portion will compress and adhere flat to the arm rail.

Stuffing And Padding The Arm

1. Establish the resiliency desired by covering the base foam and inside arm area with the desired foam (thickness, ILD, and density). The foam pictured in Fig. 4-52 is high resiliency, with an ILD of 30-35 at 25% deflection and a density of 1.80. For the photo, it was adhered to the outside of the arm rail, rolled over the top to locate where to make the cuts, then rolled back and cut partially through to show how the cuts are to be made. In normal installation the dangling rectangles would have been cut completely out. The rear cut is made so the foam fits against the back post. The second cut is made to leave enough material so that it presses beneath the projection that extends over the arm rail. This approach assures that no voids will be left in the padded arm.

2. Spray the underside of the foam, the surface of the arm rail, and the inside base, let dry past the wet stage, and secure foam to inside arm area.

3. Apply a layer of cotton padding over the foam. A layer of cotton on the outside of the foam gives a padding which feels cooler to the body than just the foam alone.

    a. Leave enough extra on the front to form a nicely rounded roll around the edges of the stump. The rolled edge will then form a "trough" for the panel that will later finish off the front of the arm.

    b. Leave about 1 1/2"-2" extra at the bottom of the inside arm and inside back areas. This is to be tucked under and between the arm, the back and the seat to close any gaps (Fig. 4-53).

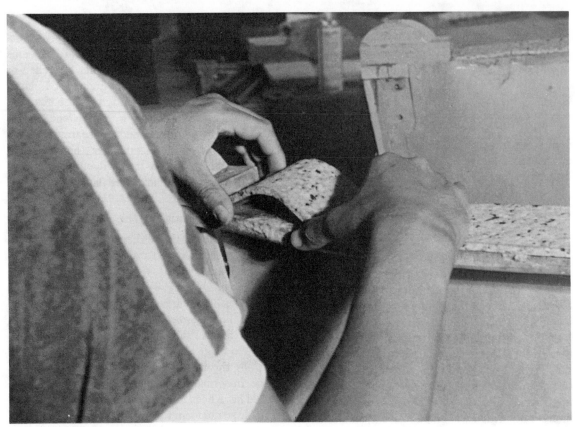

Fig. 4-51. Using 1/4″ bonded carpet pad to create a solid, "nonbottoming" armrest support.

Fig. 4-52. Contouring foam for inside arm.

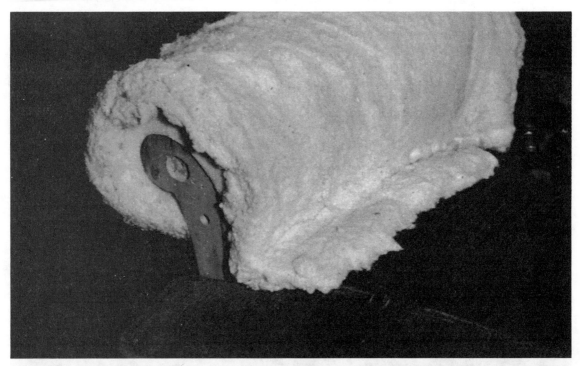

Fig. 4-53. Tear cotton padding oversize for inside arm and inside back. (Allow 1 1/2″ to 2″ extra at bottom for tucking under.)

Fig. 4-54. Stapling cotton to create a rounded or rolled edge.

c. Staple the cotton at the tucked-under, rounded edge in such a manner that no ripples or depressions are created. Notice how the operator is holding and stapling it in place in Fig. 4-54. The material around the top and right side will be formed and stapled in like manner.

MUSLIN COVER

Some of the higher quality furniture is finished with a *muslin cover*. This cover is fitted and stapled just as the final cover would be, with two exceptions—the bottoms of the inside arm and inside back panels must be stapled to the bottom arm and back rails respectively rather than the seat side and back rails. Installing a muslin cover can serve as an excellent teaching aid for the beginner! It provides experience in cutting and fitting with an inexpensive fabric. It also permits the novice upholsterer to see exactly what the covered unit will look like. Figure 4-55 shows the inside arm of a recliner-rocker covered with muslin. The ripples seen at the top, left-center indicate insufficient front-to-back stretching. There is no need to redo the muslin cover as the problem can be remedied when the final cover is installed.

Figure 4-56 shows the outside of the arm pictured in Fig. 4-55. A section of cotton has been placed over the muslin to fill a slight void which exists in the padding beneath the muslin cover—another of the benefits in using this interim cover. A light spraying of foam and fabric adhesive will hold the cotton in place. Figure 4-57 shows a properly padded arm, and how fully the contours of the padded portions are revealed by the muslin cover.

Advantages Of the Muslin Cover

1. Provides an inexpensive experience in cutting and fitting (the muslin fabric being much less expensive than all but donated cover fabrics).

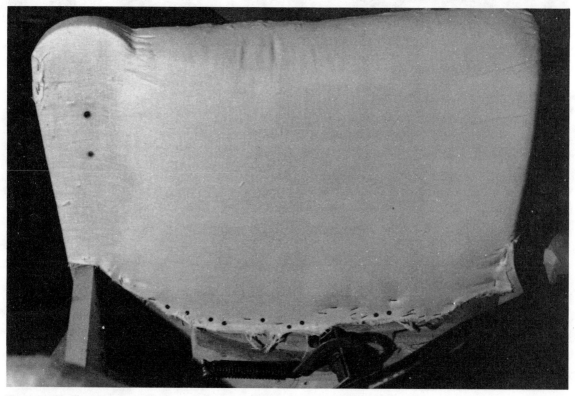

Fig. 4-55. Muslin cover on inside arm. (Ripples indicate insufficient stretch, front-to-back!)

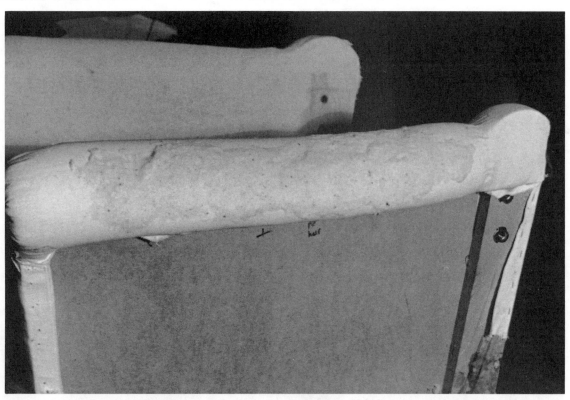

Fig. 4-56. Padding added to muslin cover to fill sight void. (A small amount of foam adhesive holds in place.)

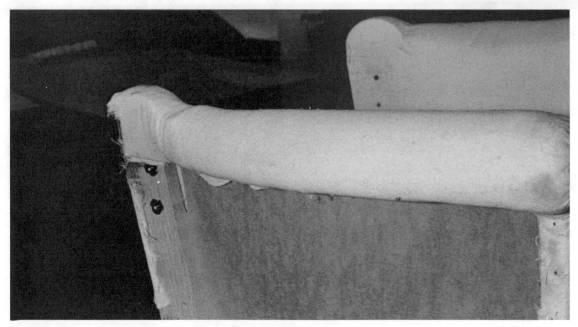

Fig. 4-57. Smooth contours reveal proper padding beneath muslin cover.

2 Holds stuffing and padding in place for application of cover.

3. Reveals the exact contour of the padded furniture and provides for last-minute adjustments, where necessary, without requiring removal of a cover panel.

Disadvantages of the Muslin Cover

1. Consumes significant extra time.
2. Adds to material and labor costs.

Chapter 5

Furniture Styles

The majority of American households in the late twentieth century are selecting upholstered furniture for function and personal preference involving a blending of contours and features rather than for a strict period motif such as Mediterranean, French Provincial, Victorian, Duncan Phyfe, Chippendale, Queen Ann, Louis XVI, Empire, Adam Brothers, Regency, etc. For that reason, the discussion on styles will focus on properties and shapes rather than historic or period features. (Besides, to adequately discuss the features of "period" furnishings is not the intent of this "how-to" upholstering book.) If one should wish a more specific exposure to historic styles the following two references are suggested: "Modern Upholstering Methods", Tierney (1965), and "Upholstery," Brumbaugh (1983).

An interesting experience awaits the visitor to almost any quality furniture store. The presentation by the experienced salesperson or interior decorator will center on "traditional" and "contemporary" styles. This is due to the "American eclec-

ticism" of furniture preferences. If a style carries a rather pronounced historic or period styling, it is called traditional. If the style is a combination of various period features (and most modern upholstered units fall into this category), then it will be classified as "contemporary", which simply means "that which the people want, now." The main discussion on styles will lead away from the "traditional" or period styles and will focus rather on styling as it relates to component features and contours.

BASIC SEATING DIMENSIONS

When it comes time to stuff and pad a piece of furniture, having a general reference for basic dimensions and what the resultant "feel" will be goes a long way to building self-confidence. For that reason the following "basics" are provided—basic because there is such a variation in upper body measurements (buttocks to shoulder) even between persons of the same height.

Backs

Four categories for back heights will be presented. The measurement ranges for each of these categories is the distance from the top of the cushion (with no one sitting on it) to the top of the back, along the face of the back (not the vertical distance!).

High Back-25″ +

High backs provide sufficient elevation from the seat to give a head rest for most adults. A back extending 25″ or more above an unoccupied cushion can be classified as a "recliner back" because it is high enough for adults to lean back and have support for the whole upper body without any slouching."

Medium-High Back—21-25″

Backs ranging from 21 to 25″ will provide back support for most adults to about the tops of the shoulders. For people 5′-5″ or shorter, the medium-high back will also provide a comfortable head rest.

Medium Back— 17-21″

If support to about the shoulder blade level is desired, the medium back will be sufficient for the "average" American adult.

Low Back— 14-17″

The low back is especially appropriate in conversation areas. A back extending between 14 and 17 inches above the cushion will generally allow an adult to turn partially sideways and rest an arm on the back of the unit with comfort. For that reason the low back could also be called the "conversation back."

Seat Depth

The "average" distance from the front edge of the cushion to the front of the back ranges from 19 1/2 to 21″. Within this range most adults can sit with comfort. However, if a unit is being tailored for occupants having long legs and it is primarily for their comfort (waving concern for guests of shorter stature), then longer dimensions (22-24″) will provide greater comfort. For those who may be built closer to the ground, a shorter seat depth (17″-19″) would probably provide the most comfort, so much so that their feet might even be able to touch the floor while sitting "normally" back in the seat. Now, wouldn't that be a pleasant experience, for those of you 5′-3″ and under?

Seat Height

The majority of upholstered furniture will have an unoccupied seat height, measuring from the floor to the top edge of the cushion, of between 15 and 17″. Balloon cushions and bench seats (not bench cushions) are two notable exceptions; balloon cushions because they are so much softer and compress much more and bench seats because they don't compress near as much and are designed more for short sitting periods rather than lounging. Now, moving away from the unoccupied status, it is really the occupied or compressed height that has the real meaning.

Soft Lounge Height

For the "sitting into" feeling, a unit which has an occupied (compressed) seat height of 11″ or less will do the trick. A seating height in this range is one from which senior citizens appreciate a helping hand to arise. However, this is the very height that it is quite comfortable to "roll" out of. This range (levity aside) provides that nice soft lounge comfort.

Comfort Lounge Height

The majority of upholstered furniture will fall into this category. A compressed height between 11″ and 14″ is what most American furniture is designed to provide. This range provides that "expected" lounge comfort. Livingroom furniture normally falls into this range.

Temporary Lounge Height

A seat having a compressed height between

14" and 18" is one that will be comfortable only for relatively short sitting periods. Dinette chairs and office furniture generally fall into this category.

Bench Height

Seats that have a compessed height of 18" or more fall into this category. For most of us, this seating height is meant for serious application and not for lounging comfort. Such things are piano and organ benches (upholstered ones of course!) and other chairs or benches that will require one to keep the back straight fit into this group very well.

Arm Height

The popular range for arm heights (the distance from the top of a compressed cushion and the top of a compressed arm rest) is between 8" and 10". Distances greater than 10" make the occupants feel like they are sitting on the down-slope of a hill, if they use the arm rest that is. Arm heights less than 8" seem to increase tension by dropping the shoulder abnormally low, or else cause the occupants to feel like they are sitting on the up-slope of a hill.

STYLING FEATURES

We will now turn our attention to the styling of upholstered furniture. In the discussion that follows, terms that are more descriptive of shape and function will be used rather than historical or designer names.

Bench Seat

The *bench seat* is simply an extra wide cushion that has no distinct divisions—divisions which are normally created by physically separate entities (two or more cushions for example), welts, or seams that are intended to be obvious. Figure 5-1 is an example of a bordered pattern bench seat and a pillow back. The arrows point to inconspicuous seams that are outside the striped borders of the basic fabric. This approach permits adding suffi-

Fig. 5-1. Couch with bench cushion and bordered pattern.

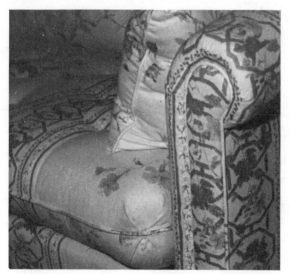

Fig. 5-2. Knife-edge cushion with rounded, double-tuck corners.

cient material to both ends to permit the very wide pattern to be centered on the unit, an especially good approach for fabrics having extra large or bordered patterns. A close-up of this unit (Fig. 5-2)

shows the details of a cushion with rounded, double-tuck corners (discussed later).

Jointed Seat Panel

One method used to break up long spans of solid fabric is to join panels at planned locations such as a centerline (Fig. 5-3) or where cushions meet. This unit also displays a camel back (a back with a center "hump" that flows out in compound curves) and a plain skirt with corner kick pleats.

SEAT BANDS AND SKIRTS

Narrow Band Accent. Several approaches are commonly used to give variety in seat styling. Figure 5-4 features a full width couch with extra thick cushions, the balloon cushion; a rather wide seat panel and a narrow band along the bottom front. The narrow bottom band is used to break up and add an air of lightness to the front proportion lines. This unit is accentuated with two extra-wide L- and J-cushions instead of having a third rectangular cushion in the center. This is especially appropriate because of the extra thickness of the

Fig. 5-3. Jointed (seamed) seat panel at center of couch.

Fig. 5-4. Balloon seat cushions and arms, narrow seat band.

cushions. The arms are also formed with the "balloon" effect, sporting an almost oval frontal panel sewn in as part of the IA panel. Use of the extra thick, soft seat cushions permits use of the shorter legs. The back is also padded extra-thick, made in two sections, and buttoned to add character and break up what would otherwise appear as a very puffy unit.

Matching Band And Seat Panel. Figure 5-5 shows a unit having extra-thick (5″) box cushion on the seat; contrasting, reversible, soft-stuffed, knife-edge cushions on the back; with a matching (same width) band and seat panel along the front. The arms are padded and rounded with a pronounced "plumpness." The inside arm panel is made of one piece of fabric which covers around the front of the stump, is rounded over the top with tapering outside tucks, and finishes off along the top to retain the parallel effect of the striped pattern.

Contrasting Fabric In Skirt. A contrasting skirt is used to accent the "hide-a-bed" featured in Fig. 5-6, providing another finishing approach to a "contemporary" design. Double-buttoned, full knife-edge cushions are finished off with double-tuck corners on the front and a sewn-in square corner on the rear. The roll arms are wrapped completely around, replacing the arm panel with the one-piece inside arm panel featuring the outside-tapering tucks at the top, front of the arm.

Broad-faced Seat Panel. Another method to finish off a seat section is the use of the broad-faced seat panel shown in Fig. 5-7 which blends in the balloon affect. The balloon motif is continued in the balloon arms (that again feature the outside tapering tucks to round the front, top) and crowned

Fig. 5-5. Wrapped arm, matching seat band, and box cushion.

Fig. 5-6. Contrasting skirt, double-buttoned, double-tuck corners on full knife-edge cushions.

Fig. 5-7. Wrapped arm; balloon, waterfall cushions; and channel crowned back with broad-faced seat panel.

back accented with channels formed in two inch soft (12 ILD) foam. Attention is called to the rounding edges of the cushions. This can be created through the use of a dacron wrap, extra-thick foam, and tucking around the corners. If the corners of the cushion panel are not tucked the edges will be basically perpendicular with minimal rounding. Figures 5-8 and 5-9 show other applications of the broad-face seat panel, giving a feeling of mass and strength to the units. Balloon waterfall cushions are a common complement to the broad-faced seat. Figure 5-9 breaks the balloon affect by lightly padding a level arm and adding an unaccented (without welt) arm panel that covers the entire front. Still another style of the broad-faced seat panel is the full-box frame topped with a double-layered, ultra-large biscuit tufted cushion as featured in Fig. 5-10. The "box" styling is maintained throughout by (1) sew-

ing seams along all edges. Figure 5-11, a close-up of the corner element of this sectional unit, reveals the locations and arrangements of these edge seams. This styling can be easily constructed to provide either a more relaxing lounge comfort (by making the base of rubber webbing or a casual bench seating by topping the box frame with a solid wood (plywood) base.

ARM STYLES

Rolled Arm. There are many variations that have been given to the arms themselves. The rolled arm, sometimes called "*Lawson*," is often finished off with a welted panel covering the stump and edge welting around the front and top edges of the outside arm panels (Figs. 5-1 and 5-2, 5-12, 5-20, 5-21, 5-26, 5-28, 5-35a and 5-35b). The unit featured in

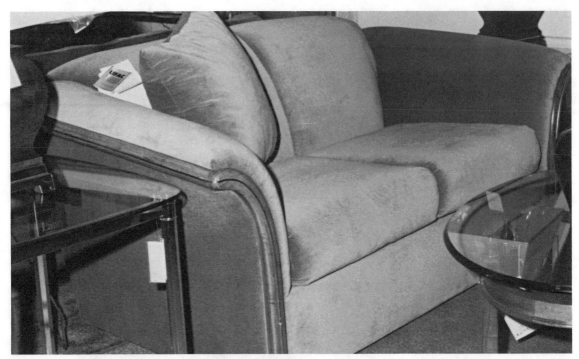

Fig. 5-8. Broad-faced seat panel and balloon waterfall cushions.

Fig. 5-9. Broad-faced seat panel with lightly padded arm and wide arm panel.

Fig. 5-10. Ultra-large biscuit-tufting on seat sections.

Fig. 5-11. Edge seams without welt to maintain squared motif.

Fig. 5-12. Rolled or Lawson arm, wingback chair.

Flap-Panels. The chair shown in Fig. 5-14 features a buttoned, flap-panel arm, a diamond tufted, knife-edged, pillow back; knife-edged seat cushion, and formed seat. This flap-panel is tacked along the top edge and at the side seat rail through the use of a stretcher. The buttons can either be of the double prong or eye style and can be attached prior to affixing the flap to the chair, or afterward. In the latter case, the prongs or ties would extend through and be fastened to the arm base, whether it be of cardboard, webbing, or burlap. Figure 5-15 shows another chair with the flap-panel arm, diamond tufted pillow back, and a box seat cushion.

Two modifications of the flap-panel are shown in Figs. 5-16, 5-17 and 5-18. Additional buttons are added along the top edges of the inside arm and inside back panels. The unit shown in Fig. 5-16 makes use of vertical channeling which is sewn

Fig. 5-12, however, is finished off with the welted panel and no welt around the outside arm panels. Also featured in Fig. 5-12 is the typical welted box cushion and a formed seat finished off with a welt around the bottom edge. The joint between the inside wing and inside arm is also accented with a welt (arrow, Fig. 5-12).

An alternative to the plain rolled arm is the lightly channeled version shown in Fig. 5-13. This style is pleasantly finished on the front through the use of a round-topped seat panel. A squared motif is accented with biscuit tufting on the knife-edged, square-cornered pillow back along with the formed-corner, smooth-topped seat panel, and finished off with the knife-edge seat cushion also with formed corners.

Fig. 5-13. Pulled biscuit tuft on back with lightly channeled arm and knife-edge seat cushion.

Fig. 5-14. Pulled diamond tufted back, buttoned flap-panel arms.

Wrapped Arm. A modern variation in arm styling is the wrapped arm, Figs. 5-5, 5-6, and 5-7. This is accomplished by wrapping a one-piece IA panel around both the top and front of the arm without sewing any seams or adding welting. This style eliminates squared edges and arm panels. Figure 5-5 displays the wrapped arm on a straight arm while Figs. 5-6 and 5-7 utilize the wrapping on a rolled style.

Button-Pillow Arm. Pillow arms are made in much the same way as the pillow back components—a complete assembly of multiple panels sewn together and then attached to the unit with one basic difference: the arm is usually more firmly padded than the back prior to attaching the "pillow." Figure 5-19 shows a buttoned-pillow arm accented with large, contrasting welt.

CONTRASTING WELT

The use of a contrasting color for welt trim is

Fig. 5-15. Pulled diamond tuft on back, buttoned flap-panel arm with welted box cushion.

along the lines of each set of buttons with the top buttons attached at the outside edges. The balloon seat cushion is also buttoned and the arm stumps are finished with panels. Notice the heavily padded seat panel which maintains the plump roundness of this style.

The top arm buttons in Fig. 5-17 are attached about three inches inside of the outer edge. This is shown a bit more clearly in Fig. 5-18. The top back buttons are attached as far forward as the frame will allow. An interesting contrast is created with the seat box cushion featuring a gathered boxing (Fig. 5-17) instead of the more traditional smoother sides (Fig. 5-15 or Fig. 5-20). The seat panel, however, retains the smooth, formed styling and is finished off with the plain skirt and kick pleats.

Fig. 5-16. Flap-panel, inside wrap-around, buttoned at top and center of channeling.

increasing in popularity Fig. 5-19. Figure 5-20 shows a wing back making use of this contrast on the arm panels as well as the seat box cushion. Panels of plain, contrasting colors also add a striking and pleasant accent to figured fabrics. The chair in Fig. 5-20 is finished with both the outside arm and back panels of a contrasting color.

BACKS

Tufting and channeling are among the most popular ways of accentuating a back. These techniques are used with virtually every kind of fabric. It should be pointed out, however, that not all fabrics lend themselves equally well to all types of tufting and channeling. Some of these differences will be identified below.

Folded Diamond Tuft. One of the more popular ways of finishing off a back made of real leather is by making diamond tufts by folding the fabric rather than sewing the seams, Fig. 5-21 (vinyl and cloth fabrics also are finished this way occa-

Fig. 5-17. Gathered boxing with loosely stuffed, flap-panel arms.

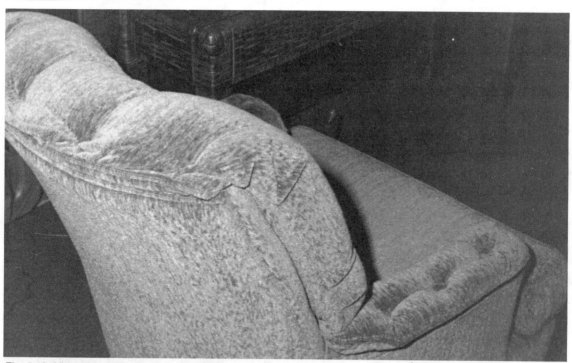

Fig. 5-18. View of top buttons on flap-panel arm and back components.

Fig. 5-19. Buttoned pillow arms and back, accented with contrasting welt.

99

Fig. 5-20. Wing back utilizing contrasting welt and outside arm and back panels.

Fig. 5-22. Sewn diamond tufting.

Fig. 5-21. Folded, diamond tufting on back and seat. (Done in leather).

sionally). One of the reasons why this style is more popular with leathers than other cover fabrics is that the folds stay in place better with the leather. The "softer" fabrics seem to let the folds relax (sag) out of their intended location with use.

Pulled Diamond Tuft. Often, when tufting is desired, the front fabric panel is cut oversize, which when installed, remains rather loose and almost floppy. Then, buttons are added, pulling the loose fabric into three dimensional contours of the design determined by the upholsterer, or customer. Figure 5-14 is one illustration of this pulled diamond tufting approach. This style of tufting works best with the softer fabrics—those not having stiff, extra tight weaves or backing.

Sewn Diamond Tuft.. Where tufting is desired that maintains an easily distinguishable tuft

Fig. 5-23. Pulled biscuit tufting on pillow back.

of channels. Figures 5-7, 5-16 and 5-24 are but a few of the variations possible. Figure 5-7 displays a crowned back with pronounced channeling made from 1 1/2" to 2" foam that is sliced to within 1/2" to 3/4" of the backing fabric (refer to Chapter 8 for instructions). Figure 5-16 exhibits a channeling sewn in a pillow-type cushion which extends completely around the insides of the chair. Figure 5-24 utilizes contoured channels to accentuate the curved lines of the chair. The seat cushion was removed and placed in front to show how it too was contoured to fit snugly into the irregular curves of the seat.

Camel Back

The camel back has either one or two smooth

Fig. 5-24. Contoured channeling on back with double-buttoned seat cushion.

line yet which gives a smooth contour, the sewn tufting is used. With this style, double-tapered tucks are sewn along each tuft line. The tucks taper into nothing at a distance slightly greater than the radius of the button from the point of intersection of the tuft lines. This permits the buttons to carry part of the fabric into the padding and still leave the remainder outward with less "wrinkling" than with the pulled tufting. Figure 5-22 is an example of the sewn diamond tuft.

Pulled Biscuit Tuft. Figure 5-23 is an illustration of the pulled biscuit tufting. Attention is called to the presence of wrinkles primarily around the sides of the tufting while the tuft lines are rather smoothly created.

Channeled Back

Numerous designs are created through the use

flowing "humps" along the top. The unit shown in Fig. 5-25 illustrates one of the popular contours for the single hump. The double-humped camel back is seen with fair frequency on loveseats (not shown).

Crowned Back

Crowned backs involve simply a single, smooth upward center arch along the back. Figures 5-7 and 5-26 are examples of this back style. Figure 5-7 retains the smooth crown contour while breaking the otherwise solid monotony with 9″ channels. Figure 5-26 features the crowned contour, accented with what one manufacturer calls the "nail-head, set trim" (described below) and lightly pulled tufting in extra wide channels (used to simulate separate back cushions) to match the buttoned, reversible knife-edge seat cushion lines.

Nail-head, Set Trim

This feature could be classified as either a finishing technique or a back style (as could several others herein listed), but because the sample presented (Fig. 5-26) deals more with the back than any other part of the unit it is included with back styles. With this styling the cushions are attached low on the front of the top, back rail, then a band is tacked on top of this, stuffed to the plumpness desired and either rolled over the top of the frame and attached to the rear of the rail or stapled to the top edge with another band or the OB panel finishing off the upper edge. Figure 5-27 gives a closer view of the decorative tack, band, and welt features.

CUSHION STYLES

Squared-crescent. This cushion style (upper cushion in Fig. 5-28) can be made either as a contoured toss pillow or a modified pillow cushion. The style shown is of the modified pillow cushion variety. The lower cushion is attached so its tapered

Fig. 5-25. Camel back sofa with rolled arms and center seamed seat panel.

Fig. 5-26. Crowned back with a nail-head, set trim and a pulled, deep channeled back. Double-buttoned, knife-edge seat cushions.

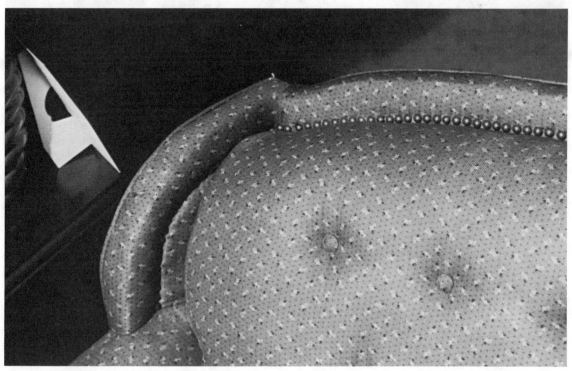

Fig. 5-27. Close-up of nail-head, set trim.

Fig. 5-28. Squared-crescent upper back cushions, gathered skirt and wings, accented with contrasting welt.

upper edge ends at about the point where the buttons are attached. One benefit of the modified pillow cushion styling is that the attached panels reduce the "dust and crumb trap" tendency by completely closing off the space between the cushion and the unit framework.

Flop Cushion. The idea behind the flop cushion is basically that of an enclosed pillow attached to a unit with an additional flap near the rear, upper edge. Figure 5-29 shows the concept with a double set of flop cushions propped up to show the underside (The white lines in the centers are zippers). Notice that the reverse side of the cushion makes use of a less expensive fabric than is used on the rest of the unit. Figure 5-30 shows buttoned, double-flop cushions. The buttons can be applied to the cushion only or they can button the cushion

to the foundation of the unit. Notice the multiple tucks at the rounded corner of the seat cushion. An interesting design is created with this approach which is shown in close-up in Fig. 5-31.

Ram-horn Cushion. This cushion design is created by forming a tapering padding over the top of a back or the front of a solid seat in such a manner that the side view will appear the shape of a ram's horn. Figure 5-32 shows this concept. To accomplish this style the cover is sewn to a backing panel so as to pull the cover around the edges to create the rounded appearance shown. At the seam of the two panels an additional piece of fabric is sewn which will serve to attach the ends to the back post (in this case). A panel is used to finish off the ends.

Clam-Shell Cushion. An interesting ap-

104

Fig. 5-29. Double-flop back cushions; single-flop arm; and eared, weltless knife-edge seat cushions.

Fig. 5-30. Double-flop back cushion; balloon, multiple-tuck seat cushion.

proach that breaks the traditional cushion design is shown in Figs. 5-33 and 5-34. In this style either a deep tapered seam is sewn in one panel or two separate panels are sewn together in the same man-

Fig. 5-31. Close-up showing detail of multiple-tucks on rounded knife-edge seat cushion.

Fig. 5-32. Ram-horn back cushion.

ner as sewn tufting. Gathers are taken in the center portions to create the clam-shell appearance shown in the above Figures. The center portion is drawn deeply into the stuffing by using a section of edge wire inserted into a sewn sleeve and pulling and attaching it in the same manner as buttons. Figure 5-34 is a close-up view to give a better idea of how this might be done.

Box Cushions with Welts. Figures 5-3, 5-5, 5-12, 5-15, 5-17 and 5-18, 5,20, and 5-35a are photos of units making use of box cushions having welts. All but Fig. 5-20 take the traditional approach and cover the welts with the same fabric as used on the rest of the unit. Figure 5-20 reveals that a contrasting color for the welt fabric can add an air of elegance and distinction. The contrasting welt is increasing in popularity.

Box Cushions without Welts. A streamlined appearance is given to the standard box cushion by leaving off the welt. Figures 5-10 and 5-11 and 5-36 are samples of the weltless box cushion.

Knife-edge Cushions. One might surmise from the long list of Figures (5-1, 5-2, 5-6, 5-13, 5-14, 5-16, 5-19, 5-23, 5-26, 5-28, 5-29, 5-30 and 5-31, and 5-35c) that the knife-edge cushion is quite a popular item. Not only is this style increasing in popularity, the inclusion of the contrasting welt is likewise on the upswing (Fig. 5-19, 5-20, 5-28).

Knife-edge with Double-tuck Corners. The double-tuck corner is used on knife-edge cushions when a rounded corner is desired rather than the square. Figure 5-1 features a box-frame couch with a squared (not rounding into the arm stump) seat rail, but a rounded, double-tuck bench seat cushion. A closer view (Fig. 5-2) shows more clearly the details of how the tucks are made. Figure 5-6 shows another use of the double-tuck, of a more narrow (distance between the tucks) styling.

Knife-edge With Multiple-tuck Corners. An alternative to the double-tuck corner is the multiple-tuck. Now, if you are thinking that the multiple-tuck would be especially appropriate where a greater radius bend is desired, score one point! That is exactly where they are used. The knife-edge seat cushion in Fig. 5-16 makes use of what might be classified as the "standard" multiple-tuck corner; the tucks are rather small and basically vertical. However, by increasing the width of each tuck a rather striking effect can be created, Figs. 5-30 and 5-31.

Knife-edge with Ears. Where a casual atmosphere is desired, the addition of "ears" to the outboard side of knife-edge cushions continues the motif. The overlapping concept of the flop cushion is continued by the overlapping ears of the end seat cushions on the couch shown in Fig. 5-29. Ears could be added to the center cushion, overlapping the end cushions, depending on the preference of the customer, do-it-yourselfer, or upholsterer.

Waterfall Cushions.. "Traditional" furnishings can be transformed into somewhat a more "contemporary" styling merely by replacing the standard box cushions with waterfall. One of the more contemporary features added to the waterfall cushion is the ballooning characteristic (making the cushions of an extra-thick, softer (lower ILD) foam. Figures 5-4, 5-7, 5-8 and 5-9) are classic

Fig. 5-33. Clam-shell back cushion.

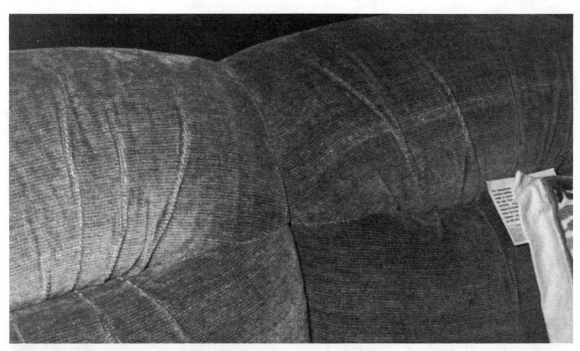

Fig. 5-34. Close-up clam-shell showing seams and gathers.

Fig. 5-35. Three popular seat cushion styles: (A) welted box, (B) Waterfall, (C) welted knife-edge.

Fig. 5-36. Single-flop, kidney roll cushion on back, weltless box cushion on seat.

examples of the "balloon" waterfall cushion. Although Fig. 5-9 is classified as a balloon cushion, it approaches the "standard" because of its lower profile. Figures 5-33 and 5-35b are standard thickness.

COMBINED STYLES

As was mentioned in the opening paragraphs of this chapter, the majority of American upholstered furniture is a blending or combination of various styling features. Figure 5-36 is just one example of this combination approach. Weltless box cushions are blended with a seamed balloon arm, the flop cushion back, and the broad-faced seat panel. By going back through this chapter now, one will be able to identify different styling features in

many of the units shown. The attempt has been to open the avenue to contour and function as styling features rather than the traditional "period" classifications. If period styles are desired, it is suggested that the upholsterer review some of the books written on historical furnishings.

FABRIC SELECTION

Fabric selection to portray any of the "styles" mentioned herein is strictly a matter of preference. Because of the modern attitudes to have furniture possess the looks and feel based on personal preference rather than portray a particular historical period or designer motif, the choice of fabrics has opened almost to infinity. What is desired by one person may almost cause another to shudder with a reaction to "poor taste." Some will go so far as to say that a tapestry or matelasse pattern just cannot be used on a contemporary piece of furniture. For the "purist," that would be very true, but to the customer, there may be no period restrictions involved. Professional interior decorators will probably specify styles as they have been taught, whether that teaching was by the experienced tradesman or from vocational or collegiate courses. And the raw reality of it all is that not every interior decorator and not every upholsterer will agree unanimously on fabrics and styles. The bottom line is, put on what you like and what seems to go well with the rest of the furniture in the room where it will be used. Now, if there is a lack of confidence on one's part to make that decision, by all means, consult with not one experienced professional, but several. Then, after getting several opinions, the choice becomes one of selection among ideas extended by the experts.

Chapter 6

Fabric Selection And Layout

One of the questions asked most frequently of an upholsterer is, "What is the best fabric to use?" While that is a very relevant question, it carries about the same vagueness as asking, "What is the best apple?" or "Which car is the best?" The answer to any question of this nature will either be a pronounced bias of a personal preference or additional information will be sought to determine "best for what?" No attempt will be made in this chapter to identify what is the best fabric in any general sense of the word. Rather, information will be presented from which the reader should then be able to determine which is best for the particular application. We will first look at the primary types of fibers that are used in "general" upholstering.

TYPES OF FIBERS

Fibers used in upholstery cover fabrics are classified as either natural or synthetic. Natural fibers are those which come direct from either plant or animal. Among those coming directly from plants are cotton and jute, each being taken from

plants bearing the same name. *Side Note*: It could be said that one form of natural fiber is also made from metals (gold, silver, brass, aluminum) but these are not to be found in the domain of general usage but rather among the high level "special" fabrics. Of the various natural animal fibers only two are used in upholstery: silk (seldom to be found in modern, commercial upholstery fabrics) and wool. *Synthetic*, another term for polymer, is chemically speaking, really a "plastic". Of the scores of different polymer bases, only five of them are commonly used in upholstery textile fibers: rayon, nylon, acrylic, polyester (Dacron) and polypropylene (Herculon or Olefin).

Blending. Each of the natural and synthetic fibers has a peculiar set of properties that makes it basically and distinctly different from any others. As a result of these distinct differences and the relatively few types of fibers found acceptable for upholstery fabrics, it has been found very beneficial to blend fiber types to obtain combinations of properties. There is really no limit to the combinations

111

that could be made. But one principle seems to hold some degree of reserve on the multiplication of fiber combinations that are being offered to the upholstery industry. That principle is volume sales. In manufacturing industries it is generally not in the best economical interest to produce quantities of "special" fibers that have limited demand. Such "specials" would cost too much for the general public. Therefore, most textile production is limited to a relatively small number of high volume "generals."

Textile technology has advanced to the point where a basic fiber composition can be modified to imitate others. For example, the popular natural upholstery fibers (cotton and wool) can now be treated and processed to look, feel and react very much like almost any of the synthetics. Neither of them can be processed to wear like several of them, however. Synthetics can be processed to exhibit many of the properties and characteristics of other synthetics as well as the natural fibers, even to the "itchy" feel of wool. Chemical changes in processing the fibers themselves, changes in surface treating chemistries, and even mechanical treatments such as polishing, crimping, twisting, buffing, or roughing can alter significantly the final appearance and feel of a fiber and hence the fabric. In reality, a good chemist can create textiles that will confound even the "experts." But the cost to do so would be prohibitive for general textile production and usage. For that reason, the majority of fabrics produced from the various mills are made to take advantage of the basic chemical properties of each fiber.

BASIC FIBER PROPERTIES

The properties that seem to be of most concern in fibers have been assembled and condensed into tabular form (Table 6-1). The information contained therein has been gleaned from two primary sources (1) and internationally recognized polymer chemist and fiber specialist, and (2) several upholsterers having a combined experience in the trade of over 100 years. *Note:* Although significant agreement exists between the two "expert" sources, complete consensus does not exist. Table 6-1 presents the

condensed properties of the fibers with a clarifying discussion following.

Acrylic Fibers. Wear resistance across the length of the fiber (as in flat and looped weaves (frieze is one example, Fig. 6-5)) is relatively low which makes it one of the least used fibers in twisted or braided weaves. End wear resistance, however, is exceptionally high making them especially suited for cutpile type fabrics (velvet and plush, Figs. 6-7, 6-8, 6-9). Acrylics have the highest resistance to ultra-violet light of all the fabrics. Processing is relatively high in cost, thus acrylics are on the average, higher in price than most of the other popular fibers. Another of the outstanding features of this fiber is its high degree of softness which imparts that "luxurious feel" to the velvets and plushes.

Cotton Fibers. Although rated quite low in wear resistance, the addition of surface treatments such as Scotch Gard or Dow Gard significantly increase wear and cleanability. Without these treatments, cotton stains easily and cleans with difficulty. Cotton is especially suited for thin, delicate fabrics, such as chintzes (Fig. 6-3). Cottons have long been recognized for their "breathability" which is superior to other fibers, imparting a cool feel. Cotton fibers have not been processed (to date) to be able to retain the "new" look but for a short time. Because of this latter characteristic, cottons will be found in blends more frequently than alone. Polyester is one of the most popular blending fibers for cotton.

Nylon Fibers. This fiber has come to be recognized as the "work horse" of the fiber industry. It has the highest cross-fiber wear life of those developed thus far. For this reason it is used extensively in woven patterns both for home and automotive applications. Nylon does not exhibit good end-wear characteristics, yet, which explains why few nylon "velvets" will be found. Recent modifications in formulating have developed fibers which can impart an extremely soft feel which permits a wide range of textures to be produced. This is the only fiber that has full elastic recovery. That gives nylon fabrics the "no sag" characteristic after prolonged or hard use.

Polyester Fibers. *Dacron*, by DuPont, is the

Table 6-1. Property Ratings on "Popular" Upholstery Fabric Fibers.

Fiber Type	Abrasion Resistance* (wear)	Flex Life (90° bend 1000 cycles)	Color Retention* (Fade Resist.)	Fiber Strength (Retention)	Feel (1 = smooth 10 = harsh)	Look (1 = shiny 10 = dull)
Acrylic	5-10a	4-5	10b	10b	4	1-10c
Cotton	3	.3-.5	7-8	6	6	8d
Dacron (poly-ester)	7-8	4-5	9	9	1-10	1-8e
Herculon Olefin (poly-propylene	9.5	17f	2	2-3	1	1f
Nylon**	10	20	3g	7g	1-10	3-10g
Rayon	1	.075	6	4-5	4	1-10h
Wool	4	20	1	1-2	10	10h

*Based on a scale of 1 to 10, 1 = low quality, 10 = high quality.

**This is the only fiber that has 100% elastic recovery.

a—End wear (as with cut pile (velvets), is exceptional, side wear (looped weaves) is somewhat less.

b—Has chemically built-in, ultra-violet screen, virtually unaffected by sun's rays.

c—Can be processed to have highest luster of all fibers.

d—Can be "polished" but loses "new look" rapidly-sheen can be somewhat restored with surface treatments such as Scotch Guard.

e—Has excellent "new look" retention.

f—Flexing causes fibrillation (breaking into smaller diameter fibers, which increases light refraction giving the appearance of color loss and "frosting."

g—Although ultra-violet light creates some frosting and yellowing of the polymer, nylon has been one of the most popular fibers for automotive upholstery.

h—Can be produced with high shine but dulls rapidly with use.

most well known brand name for polyester fibers. This fiber is recognized for that "new" look retention for significantly longer periods than most other fibers. Polyesters also have excellent color and fiber strength retention when exposed to sunlight. One recent formulation has imparted a superior softness to the fiber making it a top candidate in automotive "plush" upholsteries (Rolls Royce plush velvet for example). One draw back with polyester fibers is a rather low side flex resistance which means if the fabric will experience a lot of bending or waving it would not wear well.

Polypropylene Fibers. Two very popular brand names for this fiber are *Herculon* and *Olefin*. These fibers have exhibited very low ultra-violet resistance both in color and fiber strength retention. However, if the fabrics are kept from U-V light, they are extremely strong and wear resistant. The fiber takes dye very well and is one of the lowest cost fibers to process. High strength and low cost are the major factors in its "mass production popularity." This fabric will be found on most of the lower priced furnitures.

Rayon Fibers. This fiber family has the lowest flex life of all fibers in use. It does not wear well in either end or cross-fiber applications. It "fuzzes" easier than other fibers. However it does have some advantages: brilliant colorability, excellent dye fastness, and soft feel. It is used in blends where high color contrasts are desired making it suited for brocatelles (Fig. 6-2), demasks (Fig. 6-4), tapestries (Fig. 6-10) and matelasses (Fig. 6-6). It can be produced with high luster but will dull rapidly in use—a short-lived "new look."

Wool Fibers. Normally rated low in cross-fiber wear resistance, wool exhibits a very high end-wear resistance. It is second only to acrylic in cut pile wearability. Wool possesses a "natural look" that is difficult to match by other fibers. This is due to the scales along the fibers which not only impart a natural harshness, the "itchy" feel, but defy creation of a shiny or lusterous fiber. Because of the absence of shine in addition to the natural air pocket structure, wool has that built-in warmth that is also difficult to match. The major disadvantages of wool include a high allergenic property and relatively high price.

PATTERN ORIENTATION AND NAP

Most upholstery fabrics are woven on looms. Threads running the length of the loom are the *warp* threads, those going across the loom, the *woof* (some call these "filler" threads). Patterns and nap are *usually* oriented along the warp rather than the woof. If a pattern has a floral pattern, for example, the flowers will be oriented to appear upward when looking from on end of the roll. If the fabric has a nap, it will be oriented, likewise, along the length of the fabric. Notice that we have said usually. Some patterns will be oriented along the

woof. Some will have the flowers sideways to the nap of newer velvets. The actual orientation is very important to the upholsterer. Every panel that is to be placed on the unit must be oriented in the proper direction or the unit will appear to be covered with fabric of different hues or the patterns will be going different directions. Both of these conditions are avoided wherever possible. *Note*: The use of "wherever possible" is strategic, there *will* be exceptions which cannot be avoided. The attempt is to follow the general rule in the trade which is: **Rule**: Flowers up, nap down. This is easy to remember because FLOWERS usually grow UPward, and when a person takes a NAP, they usually lie DOWN. The arrows in Fig. 6-1 are showing the "down" direction for most of the common panels.

WEAVE TYPES

There are numerous types of weaves that are used in upholstery fabrics, but due to the large number of them and the relative similarity among many of them, only the more distinguishable of the different types will be discussed here.

Borcatelle

A fabric showing significant relief (third dimension contouring) in the majority of the pattern. Some use the terms Brocade and Brocatelle interchangeably-both have a distinct embossed property. Popular fibers are cotton, rayon, and nylon. The figure and background are usually tightly woven, as indicated in Fig. 6-2.

Chintz

A thin, light weight, printed fabric (Fig. 6-3), usually with small delicate designs. Cotton and rayon are the more popular fibers. This material comes polished or unpolished. The sample shown is polished (a slight sheen can be distinguished in the photo). *Side Note*: Because this material is so much thinner and lighter than the majority of upholstery fabrics, perhaps the term chintz ("chintzy") was coined to signify inferiority or "cheapness?" That is not the case, however.

Fig. 6-1. The "down" direction of various cover panels on a chair.

Fig. 6-2. Brocatelle weave (the "embossed one").

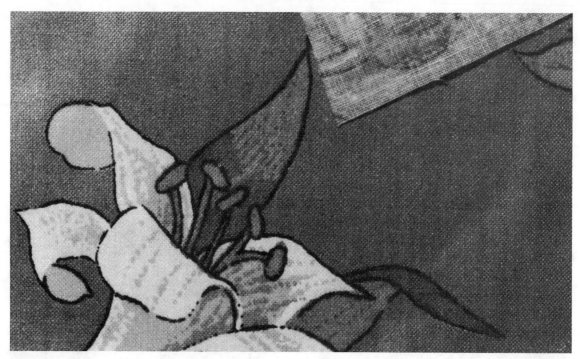

Fig. 6-3. A chintz print (the smooth, flat fabric).

Damask

A flat, tightly woven fabric that, unlike most others, is virtually reversible. The back of the fabric has the weave oriented exactly in reverse to the front, as can be seen at the fold line in Fig. 6-4. The popular fibers used include wool, cotton, rayon, and occasionally linen.

Frieze (Pronounced "frizay")

A woven, distinctly looped pile fabric wherein rather narrow loops extend upward creating a springiness to the surface. This weave can have all the loops of the same level, or can be figured with the background of a lower profile than the loops (Fig. 6-5). Fibers used include wool and rayon with nylon being by far the most popular.

Matelasse (Pronounced "Mat-la-zay")

A double or compound woven pattern which gives a double-relief characteristic wherein the pat-

tern raises and the background appears to be negatively embossed. This weave is basically two separately woven layers that are interwoven together at the pattern locations. A section has been cut out of the right side of Fig. 6-6 to show this characteristic. Cotton, nylon, and polyester are popular for this weave.

Plush

A deep, thick, cut pile that imparts a super-soft surface feel, Fig. 6-7. The nap has been brushed in different directions in an effort to illustrate the pile depth and the significant change of light reflection and absorption. The pile is deeper, and thus feels softer, than that of velvet. Wool has been used previously with acrylic now taking over the majority of this weave type. Polyester has recently entered as a "top-of-the-line" plush fiber.

Velvet

A short, thick cut-pile fabric (Figs. 6-8 and 6-9)

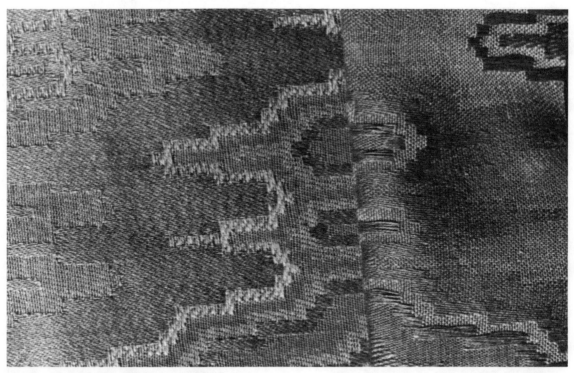

Fig. 6-4. Damask (the reversible weave).

Fig. 6-5. Frieze (the high-looped pile weave).

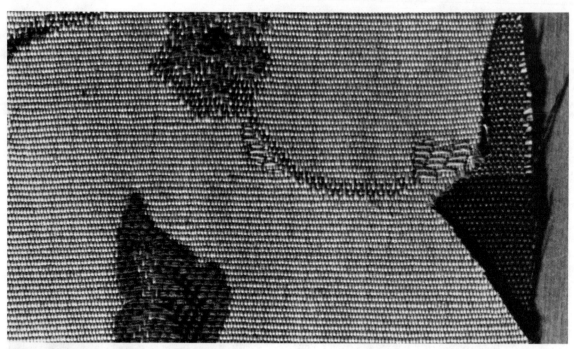

Fig. 6-6. Matelasse (a double fabric woven together).

made from thin fibers of cotton, acrylic, rayon, nylon, and viscose with polyester and polypropylene coming on line. The sample in Fig. 6-8 has had the nap brushed in opposite directions to indicate the shortness of the pile (in comparison with the plush sample in Fig. 6-7) and a similar change in light reflection. Figure 6-9 is a patterned nylon velvet possessing a very high shine to the fibers (this gives it the snowy appearance because of the white light reflections).

Tapestry

A low-profile, tight looped weave. The individual threads are usually tightly twisted, giving a rather hard feel to the weave and a corresponding absence of any **fuzz** (Fig. 6-10). Wool and cotton are the more prevalent fibers used in this weave.

ESTIMATING YARDAGE FOR COVER

There are three basic ways to identify the amount of fabric necessary to cover or recover any piece of upholstered furniture: *yardage charts, pattern layout,* and *educated guessing* (experience).

Yardage Charts

Yardage charts have been used for decades by upholstery shops and schools alike to help customers and beginning upholsterers gain a "feel" for the amount of fabric necessary to cover a unit. These charts, published by various fabric manufacturers, provide illustrations and yardage estimates for numerous of the more popular furniture styles. Figure 6-11 shows one of the charts, put out by General Plastics, a division of General Tire and Rubber. Figure 6-12, produced by Uniroyal Corporation, is one of the more popular charts in current use. Notice that no dimensions are provided with the illustrations, generally, so the user is left to interpret the illustration size similarity to the unit in question. Under most circumstances, even the novice can select from among the alternatives with reasonable reliability. One of the outstanding features of these charts is that the estimates are sufficiently generous to accommodate pattern repeats up to 15″ when a pattern layout is used with care.

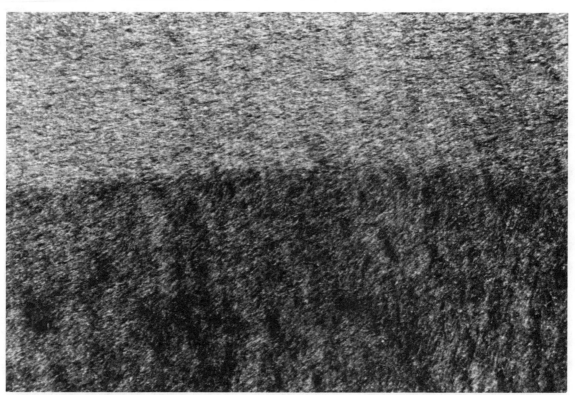

Fig. 6-7. Plush (a long, delicate cut pile).

Fig. 6-8. Velvet (a plain, short cut pile).

Fig. 6-9. Velvet (a very short cut pile with a pattern).

Fig. 6-10. Tapestry (tight, low loops with pronounced warp threads).

Note: These charts do not contain illustrations of all possible furniture styles, only some of the most popular. But, long field usage has indicated that from those styles that are shown, close estimates can be "guessed" for many other styles.

Pattern Layout

The pattern layout is the most accurate of the three estimating methods. This is the recommended method for the learner. Using the layout will build confidence to actually cut into that expensive fabric. It will also build confidence in the estimating charts by increasing an understanding of the layout principles. The layout is especially useful to assure that (1) every piece of cover is accounted for, (2) nap and pattern are oriented properly, and (3) there is, in fact, sufficient material to do the job. It can be a sickening, worrysome experience to approach the end of a job and find that there is not enough fabric to complete the project. The pattern layout is an excellent teaching tool. A significant additional benefit of using a layout is that the inexperienced can confidently cut out every panel of cover, mark it on the reverse side, and stack it in the order they will be installed on the

Avoid a heartache. Use a pattern layout.

Upholstery Yardage Estimator

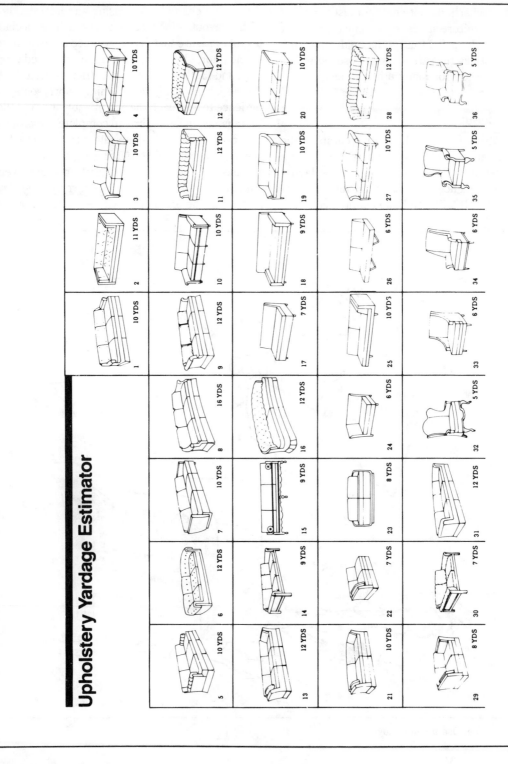

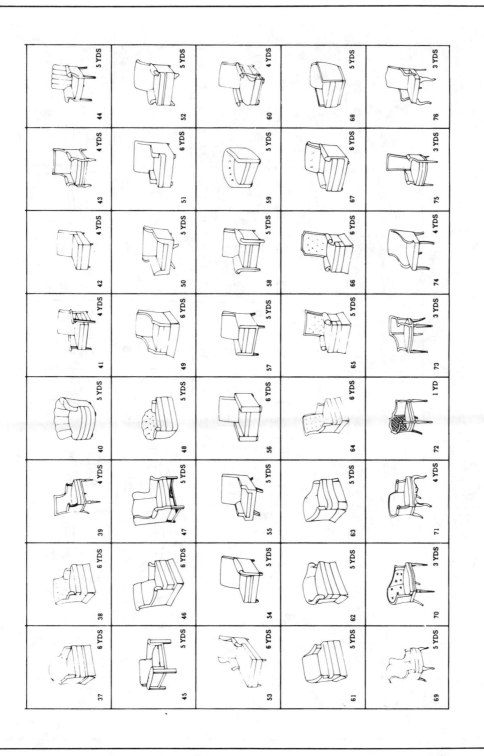

Fig. 6-11. Estimator chart from a U.S. vinyl manufacturer (General Plastics).

123

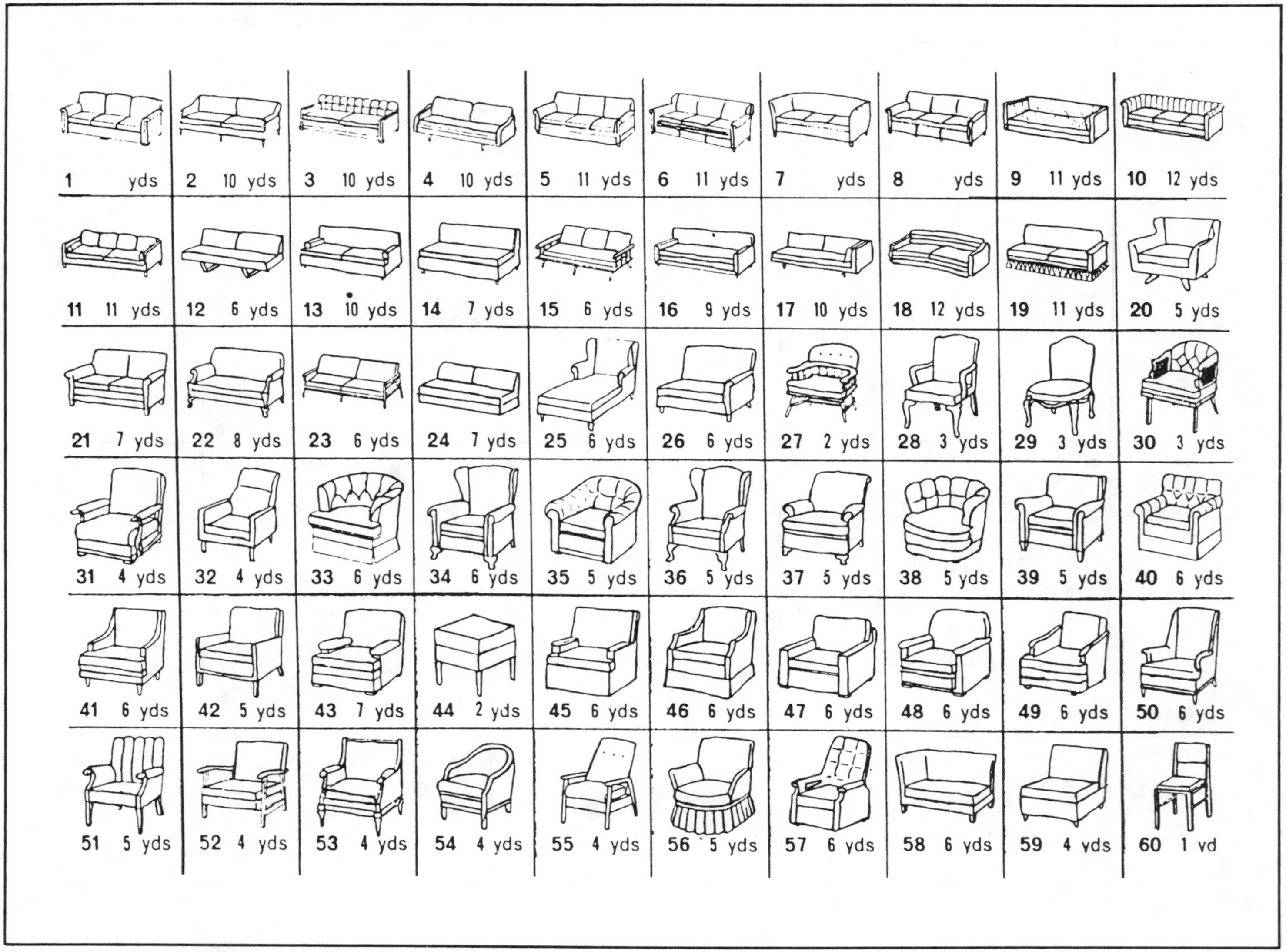

1 yds	11 11 yds	21 7 yds	31 4 yds	41 6 yds	51 5 yds
2 10 yds	12 6 yds	22 8 yds	32 4 yds	42 5 yds	52 4 yds
3 10 yds	13 10 yds	23 6 yds	33 6 yds	43 7 yds	53 4 yds
4 10 yds	14 7 yds	24 7 yds	34 2 yds	44 2 yds	54 4 yds
5 11 yds	15 6 yds	25 6 yds	35 5 yds	45 6 yds	55 4 yds
6 11 yds	16 9 yds	26 6 yds	36 5 yds	46 6 yds	56 5 yds
7 yds	17 10 yds	27 2 yds	37 5 yds	47 6 yds	57 6 yds
8 yds	18 12 yds	28 3 yds	38 5 yds	48 6 yds	58 6 yds
9 11 yds	19 11 yds	29 3 yds	39 5 yds	49 6 yds	59 4 yds
10 12 yds	20 5 yds	30 3 yds	40 6 yds	50 6 yds	60 1 yd

Fig. 6-12. Yardage chart (by Uniroyal).

124

unit. This can save a significant amount of time over cutting a panel and fitting it to the unit, then going back to cut another panel, fitting it, then repeating this process for each panel. Two samples of pattern layouts (Figs. 6-13 and 6-14) are included for reference. Figure 6-13 is for a padded, high back, open-armed rocking chair with no skirt. Figure 6-14 is for a couch measuring 67" between the arms with three reversible seat cushions and a plain, unpleated skirt all around.

Note 1: Neither of the layouts makes any allowance for pattern matching. If a fabric had a repeat of 27 inches, the yardage necessary might have to be increased by one third to one half.

Note 2: The couch layout (Fig. 6-14) calling for a minimum of 14 yards is unusually high. On this particular unit the back panels for the back pillow cushions and the decking were all made from the cover fabric. This is done only when the fabric is cheaper than sewing labor or the customer prefers the matching fabric on all areas. Some have suggested that the use of the cover fabric for all panels is a sign of higher quality. This is NOT necessarily an accurate assumption.

Note 3: Any deviations from a standard flat covering, such as gathers, pleated skirt, deep channels, etc. will increase the required yardage significantly.

Note 4: The single, short lines to the right of each panel in Fig. 6-13 and those at the bottom of each panel in Fig. 6-14 are orientation marks. These indicate the "bottom" or "down" direction of each panel. Putting these marks on the reverse side of the actual panels can save significant time when it comes time to orient and fit them to the unit.

Tip 1: Be sure to use the maximum dimensions for each panel and mark those dimensions on the layout, as shown. From these overall dimensions (1) a constant check is possible to verify that the width (generally 54") is not being exceeded, and (2) the total linear measurement can be quickly and accurately determined simply by adding up the dimensions along the edges.

Tip 2: Freehand sketch the layout with some attempt to represent proportion rather than taking the time to make straight lines and accurate, pro-

portional measurements. Figures 6-13 and 6-14 have been free-hand sketched and reproduced in that form to affirm that meticulous care is not necessary and is certainly not suggested. A representation is all that is necessary on the layout sketch. The important elements are that all panels are accounted for, oriented properly and that there is sufficient fabric.

Educated Guess

When it comes to getting things done, in any business, there is just no substitute for experience. Most experienced upholsterers can exercise the "educated guess" and estimate within one-third to one-half of a yard the amount of fabric needed to do almost any job. The main problems with this method are (1) it takes a considerable time to gain the extent of experience necessary to confidently estimate yardage for the different styles and sizes, and (2) it requires a good perception for differences and then a good memory to keep track of all the variations and their respective fabric requirements.

PATTERN MATCHING AND PATTERN REPEAT

A picture of a heavy plaid fabric, Fig. 6-15, reveals what is meant by pattern matching. Notice that the same plaid pattern is matched from the inside back cushion, onto the seat cushions, (even when interchanged or reversed), over the seat panel and continued onto the skirt. This is not really difficult to do, it just takes planning. Figure 6-16 shows the inside arm panel as it is mismatched to the decking. Although the decking on this unit was of the cover fabric, no attempt was made to match the pattern in either direction (and this is quite acceptable for the majority of work). *Side Note:* It would look nicer, when the seat cushions were removed, to have the decking match the back, seat, and IA panels, but then who uses a couch without seat cushions?

The view shown in Fig. 6-17 reveals a slight mismatch between the vertical pattern of the pillow back and the inside arm panel. Good quality workmanship would definitely match these two

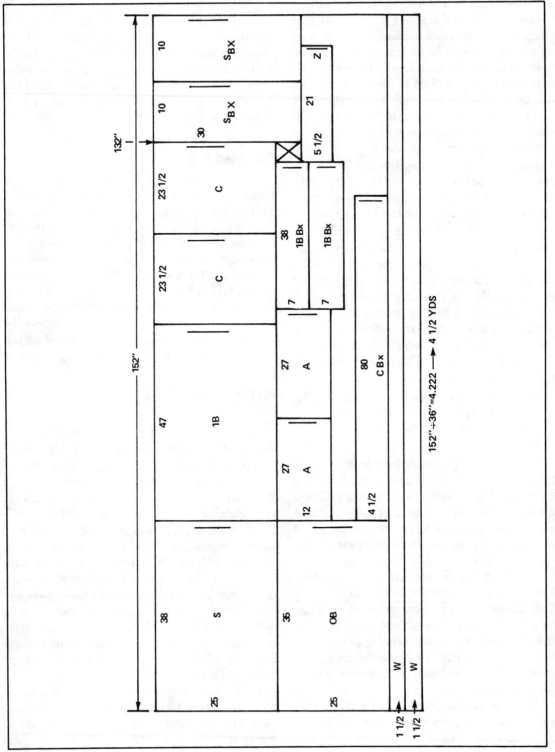

Fig. 6-13. Pattern layout (sketch!) for an open-arm chair.

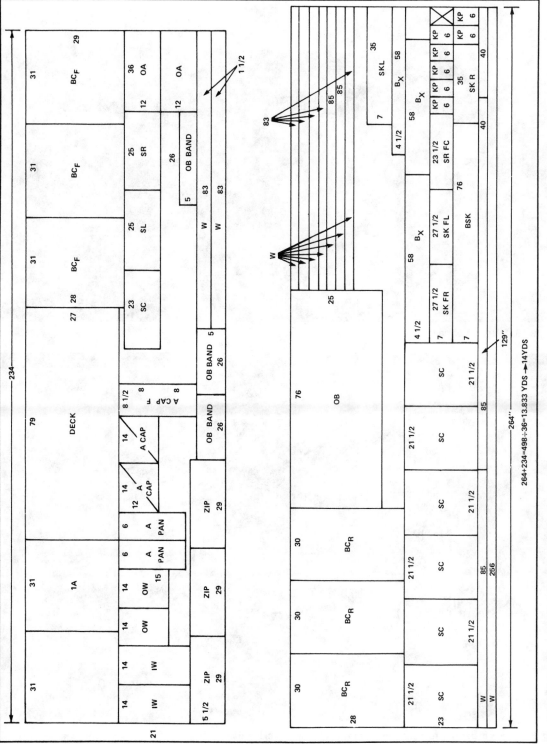

Fig. 6-14. Pattern layout (sketch for a 3-cushion couch).

127

Fig. 6-15. Matching of pattern from back to skirt.

Fig. 6-16. View of decking revealing mismatch of IA, IB and decking panels.

Fig. 6-17. View of IA and IB showing slight mismatch of horizontal plaid (not always intended).

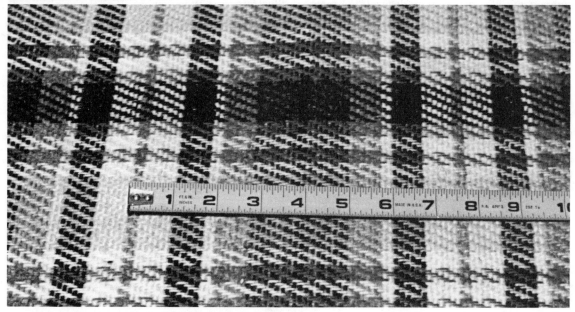

Fig. 6-18. Pattern repeat, vertical direction on unit.

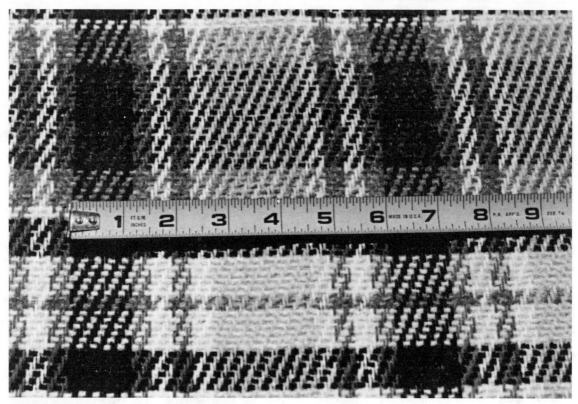

Fig. 6-19. Pattern repeat, horizontal direction on unit.

components. If a match were desired, the match could be simplified by installing the inside back before the inside arms. Following this procedure, the smaller inside arm panels could be moved to match the pillow back and also the decking with greater ease and less material loss than matching the back to the arms. To match the IA panels to the rest, they must be either cut sufficiently oversize, or laid out with that matching intent in the first place.

The illustrations shown in Figs. 6-18 and 6-19 illustrate the pattern repeat along the vertical and horizontal axes respectively. Notice that the vertical repeat is 7 1/2″ (Fig. 6-18) and that the horizontal repeat is 6″ (Fig. 6-19). All fabrics that have a distinct pattern to them will have a definite repeat in both directions, with one exception. Some fabrics having a very pronounced pattern will have only one such pattern across the entire width of the woof threads. These will usually be bordered patterns such as illustrated in Figs. 5-1, 5-2, and 5-25.

Chapter 7

Industrial Sewing Machine

Sewing is almost as much a part of an upholsterer's activities as is stripping or fitting. Few units exist that don't require at least some sewing of welt or cushions. Numerous styles require extensive sewing. One example is the barrel-back chair (Fig. 3-2) with virtually all panels being sewn together before being fitted to the unit. Another style requiring extensive sewing is the recliner-rocker which requires between nine and thirteen panels to be sewn together for the back attached cushion assembly alone. Such extensive use of the industrial sewing machine merits instruction on its use, maintenance and basic adjustments, thus the purpose of this chapter. Only the straight-stitch,walking-foot machine will be treated as this is the most popular machine for furniture upholstery. The photographs in this chapter apply exclusively to the Pfaff, Model 145-H3 or Model 145-P, because those are the machines that are being used at the time of this writing.

The principles of threading, tensioning and sewing on the Pfaff models relate almost directly to any straight-stitch, industrial sewing machine as well as being fundamentally the same for straight-stitch domestic models. Some of the primary differences that exist between the industrial and domestic machines, and which will be immediately noticeable to one who has used a domestic machine, are:

1. The industrial machines have noticeably more power, being driven by a much larger motor.

2. The machine for upholstering has a walking foot as opposed to the stationary or sliding foot on most domestics.

3. The foot treadle operates with three functional positions: (1) Neutral-achieved by depressing the toe (rear of the treadle) slightly but not enough to engage power drive. Neutral is especially useful to permit turning the handwheel for timing and other adjustments. (2) Variable-speed power drive-achieved by depressing the toe beyond the neutral position. The further the toe is depressed, the more power delivered to the motor, hence increasing sewing speed. (3) Brake-applied by depressing the heel of the foot (front portion of treadle). This applies an instant brake to the drive

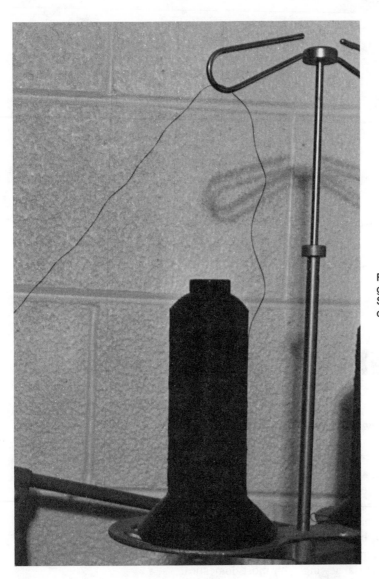

Fig. 7-1. Spool for needle thread. (First thread guide is used to discharge thread straight up. Spool must not be required to turn to discharge thread!)

system and an instant stop to the sewing motion.

4. The industrial machine will "coast" to a stop when the treadle is released, unless the instant brake is activated.

5. The very sound of power of the industrial machine almost unnerves some who have experienced only the domestic models, or who are naturally timorous around machinery.

Now, a look into the threading, adjustments, maintenance, and a few sewing tips on these machines.

THREADING THE NEEDLE

The primary concern in threading a machine is to assure a sustained, unobstructed path for thread travel. The first requirement for this, for most machines, is to have the thread that goes to the needle come off the spool with no friction. This is accomplished by having it pull directly upward from a stationary spool. In Fig. 7-1 is shown one of the two spools of thread on one type of standard thread stand. The thread *must* go from the spool upward through the guide. Please recognize that the purpose of any thread guide is to keep the thread "out of the way" and "moving freely." *Use Them*!

Figure 7-2 shows the basic threading path for the needle thread. Thread the machine in this order:

1. *Guide post on top of the machine.* It is there to keep the thread out of the working mechanisms to the right and top of the machine. In that post there are two holes drilled at 90 degrees to each other. It is intended that the thread pass through both of them. However, some operators will use only one. The only difference noticed by the author in using one or both holes is that with the two there seems to be just enough "drag" to give a more smooth thread travel.

2. *Needle-tension guide and roller.* Pass the thread through the hole in the plate on the right side (Fig. 7-3A); over and between the rollers (Fig. 7-3B); to the right, around, and snugged between the polished disks of the thread tension adjustment (Fig. 7-3C); and straight off the bottom of the tension assembly to the bottom of the thread take-up spring assembly (Fig. 7-3D).

3. *Thread take-up assembly.* Hook thread into lock at the top of thread take-up assembly. This action will require using the right hand to hold the thread from moving (between the top post and the needle tension guide is a good spot) while pulling upward with the left hand on the free end to move the spring and thread past the lock, Fig. 7-4. Moving the free end slightly toward yourself and relaxing the tension with the left hand will permit the

Fig. 7-2. Threading path from spool guide to needle: (A) thread guides, (B) needle thread tension assembly, (C) overarm take-up assembly, (D) overarm, (E) pressure foot height adjustment, (F) pressure foot spring, (G) pressure foot tension adjustment, (H) fulcrum for pressure foot spring, (K) attachment point of spring to pressure foot bar.

Fig. 7-3. Needle thread tension and take-up assemblies: (A) thread guide, (B) tension roller guide, (C) tension disks, (D) overarm take-up assembly.

Fig. 7-4. Locking thread into overarm take-up hook.

Fig. 7-5. Take-up hook loaded and spring in relaxed position. Notice thread looped over hook, goes down through spring loop, up through guide (A), through overarm (not shown), and back down through opposite side of guide (B).

spring to take the thread downward from the hook to its natural position, Fig. 7-5.

4. *Overarm guide, overarm, and overarm guide again!* Pass thread upward through the right side of the overarm guide, (Fig. 7-5A); through the hole in the overarm, and back down through the left side of the overarm guide (B). This can usually be done by holding the thread taut between the fingers and passing it beneath the overarm guide hook (C).

5. *Needle bar guide.* Hook thread into slot on the bottom, left side of the needle bar (Fig. 7-6).

6. *Needle.* The last step is threading the needle. Always thread from the outside toward the

inside of the machine! Figure 7-7 shows the needle in its upmost position and the pressure foot down to permit easy access to the eye of the needle. The completely threaded needle is shown in Fig. 7-8. Notice that the thread is going though the needle from the outside (left, in this case) to the inside.

THREADING THE BOBBIN

1. *Open the bobbin cover.* Depress the spring

Fig. 7-6. Needle bar thread guide. Loading is easiest by holding thread taut and sliding into groove.

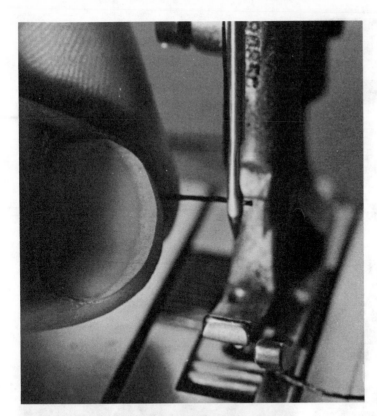

Fig. 7-7. Threading needle: always thread from outside to inside!

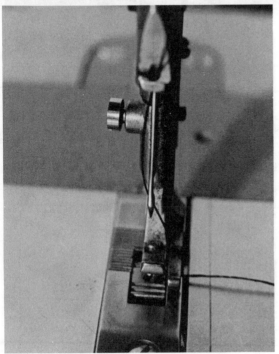

Fig. 7-8. Needle and bobbin threaded. Ready for sewing. Pressure foot is down with bobbin cover shown not fully closed.

bar to the right of the needle and on the base of the machine, and slide the bobbin cover plate to the right. This will reveal the bobbin case, bobbin cap, and needle pick assembly (Fig. 7-9).

2. *Lift the bobbin cap lock.* (Fig. 7-10).

3. *Remove the bobbin cap from the post.* (Fig. 7-11).

4. *Replace empty bobbin with a full one.* Be sure that the thread comes off the bobbin in such a way that when pulling on the thread it will hold itself into the slot and tension spring in the bobbin cap (Fig. 7-12). Holding tension on the bottom of the bobbin with the left hand, pull the thread into the slot and beneath the spring. The operator is beginning this step in Fig. 7-12.

5. *Lock bobbin thread in cap groove* (Fig. 7-13).

6. *Replace newly loaded bobbin cap into bobbin case and lock in place* (Fig. 7-14). Be sure that the thread will pass with relative ease through the small opening created by the grooves in the bobbin cap

and case, illustrated at point "A," Fig. 7-14.

ADJUSTMENTS

If the sewing threads (needle and bobbin) are not interlocking near the center of the fabric being sewn, something obviously is out of adjustment. Any change in thread size, either to the needle or to the bobbin, will upset the fine tension adjustments to either. It is necessary, therefore, for the operator to know how to make the two basic thread tension adjustments.

Needle Thread Tension.

The tension adjustment for the needle thread is found on the front of the machine head. Refer to Fig. 7-2B. Screwing the thumb wheel in increases tension on the thread, out reduces it. (*Note:* If the pressure foot is up, a cam at the rear of the machine activates a push-rod that releases the

Fig. 7-9. Top view of bobbin cap and case: bobbin cap lock is in locked position.

Fig. 7-10. Bobbin cap lock released: ready to remove cap and empty bobbin.

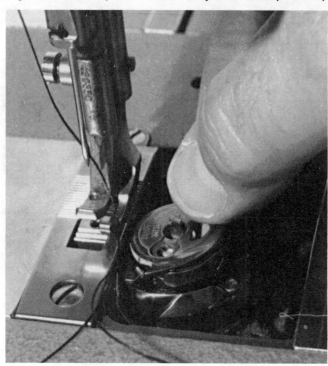

Fig. 7-11. Removing bobbin cap with bobbin (bobbin still has thread in it).

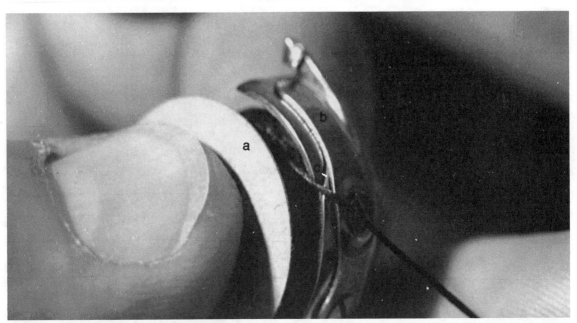

Fig. 7-12. Loading bobbin into cap: the thread must come off the top of the bobbin (A) from the left, to enter groove (C), and be pulled beneath tension spring (B).

thread tension. This is to permit easy pulling of the thread at the end of a stitch.) This is the preferred tension adjustment because it is much easier to make, and not nearly as sensitive as the bobbin ten-

sion adjustment, the latter of which is shown in Fig. 7-15.

If the two adjustments are set properly, the interlocking loops of the needle and bobbin threads

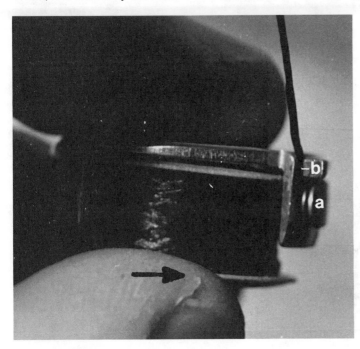

Fig. 7-13. Face of bobbin cap: Thread is beneath tension spring (A) and into cap notch (B). If properly loaded, bobbin will turn in direction of arrow as thread is pulled from cap notch.

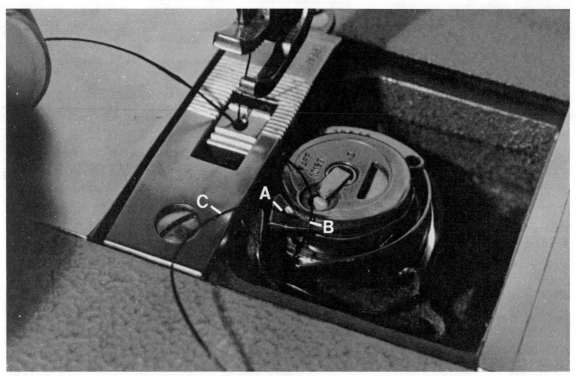

Fig. 7-14. Bobbin and cap loaded with thread properly exiting thread notch (A). Needle thread (B) is shown coming around to pick up bobbin thread (C).

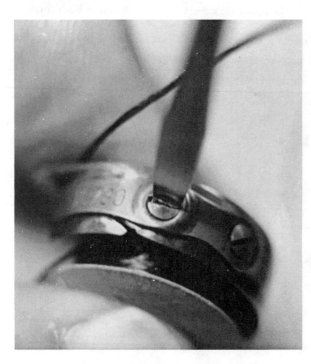

Fig. 7-15. Bobbin thread tension adjustment. (Caution: This adjustment is extremely sensitive!)

will meet somewhere within the materials being sewn. Figure 7-16 illustrates a stitch having proper thread tension adjustments, no loops can be seen on the top or on the bottom sides of the stitch. Figure 7-17 shows a stitch in which the needle thread tension is too tight. Notice that the interlocking loops of the needle and bobbin threads are visible on the top side. To correct this condition, normally, decrease tension on the needle thread. Figure 7-18 depicts a stitch with excessive bobbin tension. It can be seen that the interlock is now on the bottom side of the fabric. To correct, first try increasing needle thread tension. If the condition cannot be corrected before the tension gets so great that it breaks the needle thread, reduce the needle thread tension considerably, then reduce the bobbin tension by turning the screw, *slightly*, counterclockwise, Fig. 7-15. Caution: This adjustment is extremely sensitive if the bobbin spring is still in

good condition. A small fraction of a turn of the screw makes a significant difference in the tension. If it is still too great, loosen it. If it seems too loose, try reducing the needle thread tension first. Work back and forth until the optimum tension is achieved (Fig. 7-16). Important: The needle and the bobbin thread tensions are interactive. That means that if significant changes in either tension adjustment must be made, the two of them should be "balanced" by working alternately with each to achieve the proper adjustment. Changing one affects the action of the other.

Timing

The most frequently needed major adjustment for the upholstery sewing machine is the timing adjustment. If the bobbin pick just isn't picking up the needle thread, or in other words, if the machine isn't sewing, there are two major causes. Either the

A

B

Fig. 7-16. Stitch showing proper needle and bobbin tensions. (A) top side of stitch; (B) under side of stitch.

A

B

Fig. 7-17. Results of needle tension too tight: (A) top side of stitch, (B) under side of stitch.

A

B

Fig. 7-18. Stitch with bobbin tension too tight: (A) top side of stitch, (B) view of bottom of stitch.

142

needle pick drive dog has been "popped" or the timing is off. The drive dog will "pop" if the pick experiences an excessive drag in its rotation. Such drag is most often caused by the thread double-locking around the bobbin case or getting caught beneath it. The timing can be knocked out of adjustment by hitting something hard with the needle or the needle pick rotation being obstructed. Now, before revealing how to make the adjustments, let us see what it should be. To check the timing, the bobbin cover must be opened and the foot plate removed (Fig. 7-19).

Two extremely handy tools for working on the machine are two modified screwdrivers (Fig. 7-20). The first is a small offset screwdriver, straight-slot. This can be purchased or a standard, small screwdriver can be bent at 90 degrees (see bottom, Fig. 7-20). The second tool is a stubby straight-slot screwdriver. It, likewise can be purchased or the handle of a medium-sized driver can be cut off and filed smooth as the one shown at the top.

Timing Check

The correct timing can be identified by the relative position of the needle pick to the needle. To establish this check, turn the machine *in the forward direction* with the handwheel until the pick is just approaching the needle from the front side of the machine. If you should go beyond the desired point to make the check (Fig. 7-21), continue turning the machine in the forward direction to bring the pick up the needle from the front. Do not turn the machine backwards! Backward motion may result in an inaccurate timing check.

Fig. 7-19. Removing foot plate to check timing. (Notice that the second screw, at right, has already been removed.)

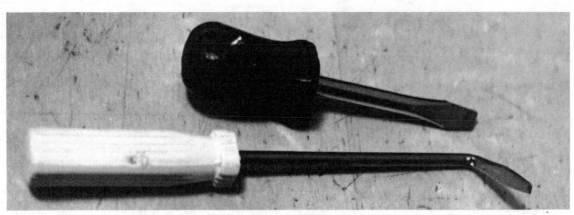

Fig. 7-20. Two handy screwdriver modifications for sewing machine repairs.

The pick should be reaching the front edge of the needle with the point of the pick about 1/16″ above the top of the needle's eye with the needle traveling upward. If the pick position is correct but the needle is traveling downward, the timing is way off!

Timing Adjustment-Needle-bar

Sometimes the timing can be adjusted by moving the needle bar either up or down as required. **Warning**: This is a limited adjustment! It requires coordination with the pressure foot, which will be specified later. To make this adjustment, first re-

Fig. 7-21. Proper timing setting: thread pick is approaching needle: A = eye of needle, B = point of pick. (Needle must be moving upward, indicated by arrow, as pick approaches!)

144

Fig. 7-22. Head cover plate. Arrows indicate two screws to loosen for plate removal.

needle bar to be moved with a little pressure. If it is loosened too much, the bar will slip downward, further upsetting the timing adjustment. Move the needle bar to establish the needle position indicated in Fig. 7-21, then tighten the set screw. Now to the second adjustment regarding the needle bar.

The needle bar cannot be lowered to the point where the bottom of the bar will contact the walking foot. Figure 7-25 shows the needle bar in about as close a proximity to the walking foot as can be tolerated. It should be noted that the pressure foot is in the raised position and the needle is full-down. Thus, if the needle would have to be lowered to a point beyond the position shown, the needle bar adjustment cannot be used. The gear adjustment is the other timing alternative.

Fig. 7-23. Removing head cover plate: Rotate bottom forward (1), lift upward (2) to locate enlarger groove beneath screw head, then pull plate straight out.

move the head cover plate, on the left side of the machine. The two screws, identified by arrows in Fig. 7-22, need only be loosened, not removed. Pivot the plate toward the front, then raise it upward as indicated by the arrow sequence in Fig. 7-23. This will permit the plate to pivot out of the bottom screw and be slid over the head of the top screw.

Loosen the needle bar set screw, identified by the tip of the screwdriver in Fig. 7-24. **Caution:** This screw must be tight, therefore care must be taken to not let the screwdriver slip and destroy the slot. Considerable torque may be required to loosen it, be prepared. Loosen it only enough to permit the

145

Fig. 7-24. Needle bar set screw (for timing adjustment). Loosen to raise or lower needle bar. Screw must be very tight when operating machine.

Timing Adjustment-Thread Picker Gear

The more sure timing adjustment is made by altering the position of the bevel gears located beneath the bobbin assembly. To get to these gears, tilt the machine backward on its hinges to reveal the underside, Fig. 7-26. One of the sources for sewing malfunction is also depicted in this photo. The drive dog is out of its track (points A). This particular problem is easy to remedy, and will be shown later in close-up detail. Point "B" is the cover to the thread picker bevel gears. To get to the gears, remove the housing screw (Fig. 7-27). The operator's hand is supporting the back side to avoid moving the machine (sometimes it takes a bit of pressure to loosen the screw!). Remove the cover to expose the gears (Fig. 7-28).

The gear to be moved is the smaller of the two. There are two set screws in this gear. One of them

is visible in Fig. 7-29. Loosen the first one, then tighten it again until the screw "snugs" lightly against the shaft. Rotate the handwheel forward to expose the second screw, loosen and "snug" this one also. Now, position the point of the thread picker to be just at the front portion of the needle, as indicated in Fig. 7-21. Holding the picker and bobbin assembly firmly with one hand, carefully and slowly rotate the handwheel until the needle is traveling in the upward direction and in the same position as indicated in Fig. 7-21. *Note*: This adjustment is rather touchy, a seemingly insignificant deviation up or down, will cause the machine to either skip stitches or not pick up the bobbin thread at all.

Tighten the set screws, semifirm, on the bevel gear and, without replacing the gear cover, try sewing a couple layers of upholstery fabric. If the adjustment is proper, the stitch will be even and complete. If skipping or nonsewing occurs, try again. *Hint*: If the needle bar even touches the raised pressure foot, raise the needle bar slightly, tighten the set screw firmly, and reset the timing

Fig. 7-25. Needle bar to pressure foot adjustment. Needle bar is in full-down position, pressure foot is in raised and full-up position.

Fig. 7-26. View of underside of machine: Drive dog and groove, points (A); thread picker bevel gear cover (B).

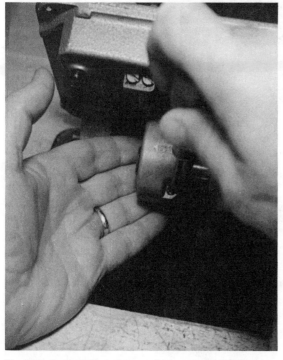

Fig. 7-27. Access to bevel gear adjustment screws. (Remove cover screw. Support unit with hand to avoid closing machine inadvertently.)

Fig. 7-28. Removing bevel gear cover.

Fig. 7-29. Bevel gear adjustment. Loosen then "snug" lightly both set screws, only one of which is visible.

with the gear adjustment. If the timing is right, tighten all screws firmly, replace covers, and go to work! Bon voyage!

Pressure-Foot Height Adjustment

For best results in sewing, the walking foot must raise high enough to "walk over" the fabric without dragging it. As sewing thicknesses change, so also must the height of the walking foot. Although this adjustment is relatively easy to make, it becomes very bothersome to change it for every function, thus, a "general" position is most often selected, and left there except for the exaggerated cases.

Figure 7-30 shows the rear of the machine. Near the center of the photo can be seen a wing nut just to the left of a darker bracket (point B). This is our adjustment. Loosening the wing nut, moving the bolt all the way to the top of the slide, and retightening it, as shown in Fig. 7-31, will raise the walking foot to its maximum walking height which is approximately 5/16 inches (Fig. 7-32). Moving the adjustment all the way down will give the minimal walking clearance of about 5/32 inches (Fig. 7-33). The latter is used for lighter fabrics. On this particular machine, the "general" position is indicated in Fig. 7-34 which works well for most furniture sewing needs.

Pressure-Foot Pressure Adjustment

That impressive assemblage of black steel run-

Fig. 7-30. Rear view of machine: (A) pressure foot hand release lever; (B) walking foot height adjustment assembly.

ning lengthwise along the top of the machine is the pressure foot tension assembly. The two long bands of steel are the adjustable spring units which apply the pressure to the foot to squeeze the fabric tightly together for each stitch. The best tension adjustment is the lightest that will squeeze the materials together tightly. The lighter the pressure, the lower the power requirements to drive the machine and the lower the wear on parts will be. But, like the pressure-foot height adjustment, rather than change the pressure adjustment for every deviation in sewing thicknesses and fabric "hardness," the adjustment is set to handle the "average" of the majority of the work being done. This adjustment is seldom changed.

If very light, soft fabrics are being sewn most of the time, reduce the pressure. For heavier, tougher materials, increase the pressure. How is this done? A little observation almost gives this answer. Notice that the spring bars are attached to a vertical shaft at the head of the machine, (point

"k", Fig. 7-2), pass beneath a fulcrum (point "h"), and end at the adjustment sight (point "g").

Figure 7-35 shows a close-up view of the adjusting assembly and the results of moving the adjusting and lock nuts, point "C." The fulcrum ("A") maintains a constant downward pressure on the spring bars ("B"). Due to the fulcrum action, an upward movement at point "C" will produce an increase in downward pressure at the pressure foot bar (point K Fig. 7-2). Downward movement at point "C" (Fig. 7-35) will reduce downward pressure at point "K" (Fig. 7-2). In Fig. 7-35, the operator is making an adjustment. Because of the heavy spring tension, it requires a little bit of effort to turn the adjusting and lock nuts.

TROUBLESHOOTING SEWING PROBLEMS

In this section, some of the most commonly occurring troubles will be highlighted. Immediately beneath each will be a listing of the probable causes

149

Fig. 7-31. Walking foot adjustment set for maximum height. Refer to Fig. 7-32.

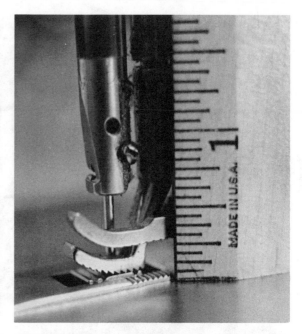

Fig. 7-32. Walking foot shown at maximum height. Adjustment shown in Fig. 7-31.

   c. Bobbin thread intact—Check drive dog. If it is engaged, as illustrated in Fig. 7-36, check for broken needle or timing

and the most likely solutions separated by a dash (—).

Stitches Suddenly Cease

  1. Bobbin thread no longer feeding:
    a. Bobbin out of thread—Put in new bobbin (That one was easy!).
    b. Bobbin thread broken—Check for entanglement, knots, and thread tensions.

Fig. 7-33. Walking foot shown adjusted for minimum height. Adjustment would be at bottom of groove, Fig. 7-31.

Fig. 7-34. "Universal" setting for walking foot height for a majority of furniture up-holstery materials.

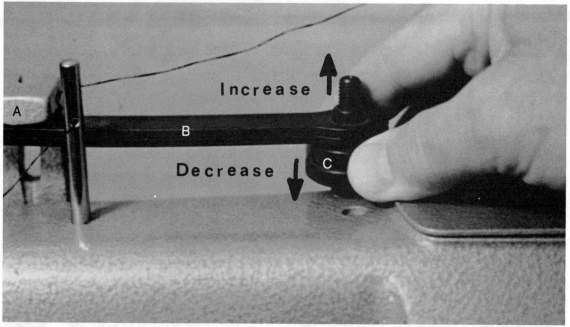

Increase

A

B

Decrease

C

Fig. 7-35. Pressure foot pressure adjustment: Rotating finger nuts (C) to force spring (B) upward increases foot pressure. Fulcrum (A) creases pivotal pressure on spring.

Fig. 7-36. Drive dog assembly (to thread picker) in engaged position.

Fig. 7-37. Drive dog "popped" (out of groove).

problem. If it is disengaged, as in Fig. 7-37, rotate handwheel, while holding the shaft with the other hand, to locate latch directly over the groove (Fig. 7-38). Depress the spring loaded retaining pin as illustrated in Fig. 7-39. This will permit the latch to snap back into the groove ready to drive the pick assembly again. If the pin will not depress, try putting the blade of a straight-slot screwdriver on top of the latch and sharply tapping the handle downward with the palm of the hand. This usually will snap the drive dog back into the groove.

d. Drive dog "pops" out too easily:

1. —Raise machine head and try rotating the handwheel. With tension off of the belt from the motor to the head, the handwheel should turn freely. If it does not, thread is probably caught in the bobbin or picker assemblies.

2. —Check bobbin and picker assemblies for entangled thread. If it looks like thread has been drawn beneath the bobbin case and it cannot be worked out from above, remove the bobbin cap and bobbin (Fig. 7-9 through 7-11). Remove the bobbin case by:

a. Extracting the three screw in the retaining ring, Fig. 7-40;

b. Removing the retaining ring, Fig. 7-41; and

c. Taking out the bobbin case by lifting straight up on the center post with the fingers (Fig. 7-42). *Needlenose pliers were used only for a clearer view of the action.* The entangled thread will immediately be exposed and removable with ease.

If the base of the thread picker seems to be dry of oil or there is an accumulation of lint, it should be cleaned and oiled (The lint pictured in Fig. 7-43 would be considered very minimal). To accomplish this:

1. Extract the center screw, Fig. 7-43 (it will be in tight!). A handy way to do this task is to release the motor drive belt from the handwheel, then while holding a screwdriver tightly in the slot of the

Fig. 7-38. To reset the drive dog, first position the latch over the groove, and then depress the spring or snap the dog down.

Fig. 7-39. To engage drive dog, depress spring loaded pin beneath latch, as illustrated.

Fig. 7-40. Removing screws (three in number) to bobbin case retaining ring. This is necessary when thread gets caught beneath bobbin case.

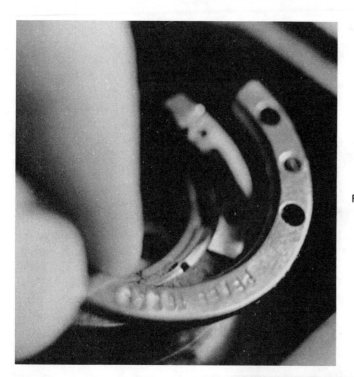

Fig. 7-41. Removing bobbin case retaining ring.

Fig. 7-42. Removing bobbin case. (Bobbin cap, bobbin and bobbin case retaining ring will have been removed before this step.)

155

Fig. 7-43. Removing mounting screw to thread picker assembly. (Necessary only to clean, oil, or replace assembly.)

screw, rotate the handwheel so the picker assembly will want to rotate clockwise and the pressure will tend to turn the screw. This is a lot easier than trying to get the hands in there and turn the screwdriver!

2. Position the thread pick as shown in Fig. 7-44 (arrow) by rotating the handwheel.

3. Lift the assembly out, with fingers, at an angle as indicated in Fig. 7-45. Wiggling the assembly slightly makes extraction easier. The drive disk, "B" in the photo, can be removed easily by lifting straight up. (When replacing this assembly, be sure that the drive nib on the disk engages in hole "C" in the picker assembly.)

3. —Increase compression on latch spring. Figure 7-46 shows the back side of the drive dog assembly with the adjustable tension pin at "A" and the access entrance to the adjusting screw at "B." Figure 7-47 illustrates making the adjustment.

2. Needle thread no longer feeding:

a. Spool out of thread—Replace with new

Fig. 7-44. Proper position of pick to remove assembly. (This is about the only position that will permit removal!)

spool (Another easy solution!).

b. Needle thread broken:

1. —Check for entanglements or improper thread path, Fig. 7-1 and 7-2.

2. —Pick may be burred, thus cutting needle thread. Refer to Fig. 7-44, arrow. Closely examine the point of the pick. Remove it and either replace it with a new one, remove the burr, or sharpen it. Burrs can be removed and the point can be sharpened by using a small, fine grit abrasive stone (slip stone). Do not use a file!.

3. —Timing slightly slow making pick enter and sever the thread. Reset timing a indicated in Fig. 7-21.

Chugging Sound When Sewing

This is simple one. Check the overarm take-up mechanism. The thread has probably slipped out of the proper path. Relocate thread in the proper path as illustrated in Fig. 7-4 and 7-5, making sure it does not loop around the adjusting screw outside of the take-up spring.

Sewing Tension Changes

1. Needle thread tension increases—

a. —Check thread path from spool. It may have slipped down around the base of the spool.

b. —Check thread path on machine. Reaching over the head, shifting of fabric or other body movements could have moved altered the normal threading path.

2. Bobbin thread tension decreases:

a. —Check bobbin placement in cap. It may have been put in backwards and the thread slipped out from under the spring.

b. —Check bobbin thread tension by pulling thread from bobbin cap. If tension on spring is insufficient.

1. —Try tightening tension adjusting screw. If tension does not increase noticeably.

2. —Remove old spring and replace with a new one, then adjust tension.

Fig. 7-45. Remove pick assembly by lifting up at point A to achieve angle as shown: (B) = drive plate; (C) = index hole for drive nip in upper side of drive plate.

Fig. 7-46. Rear view of drive dog assembly: (A) spring loaded latch pin; (B) access hole to latch pin adjustment screw.

MAINTENANCE

The very best maintenance on any piece of machinery is preventive maintenance. The first element in long and reliable service for a sewing machine is keep it clean!. Sewing produces significant quantities of "lint," which is fine particles of fabric created by the needle piercing the fabric, thread friction against fabric threads, and foot motion across the fabric. Figure 7-48 shows a very light distribution of lint beneath the cover plate. The most popular way to clean lint is to blow it out with compressed air, then lightly oil the moving parts. The oil will tend to wash migrating lint to the outsides. If an air gun is not available, there are commercial aerosol units of clean, dry air. They work well. A fine, soft bristle brush also works very well. Figure 7-49 shows a bobbin area recently cleaned with compressed air. The second element in preventive maintenance, one which can be but seldom is overdone, is lubrication. A lightweight machine oil should always be used. Every machine has most of the important lubrication spots identified in the operator's manual. In the event the manual is not available just remember that any location where a sliding or rotating interface is encountered, lubrication will be required. Best results, however, will most always be obtained by following the manufacturer's instructions from the manual, so keep it handy.

Figure 7-50 shows an operator applying oil from a polyethylene squeeze-bottle oiler to one of the oil "wells" located beneath the head cover plate. That same spot is identified as point "a" in Fig. 7-51 with five other locations identified by "o." In Fig. 7-52 ten additional oil spots are identified by white or black dashes while Fig. 7-53 shows two (marked "o") that are reached from the underside of the machine. The two spots marked "o" in Fig. 7-54 also require frequent oiling. To get to the upper spot requires the removal of both the the the bobbin cap and case retainer ring (Figs. 7-10, 7-11, 7-40, and 7-41) to get to the small felt pad (that has been removed in Fig. 7-54). All moving parts should be oiled. Frequent, light oiling is far superior to infrequent, heavy oiling. This is *not* a situation where, if a little is good, a lot is better. Frequent, light oiling will cause both the machine and the operator to sing along. "A lot" will just mess things up!

SEWING TIPS

Although this book makes no attempt to pro-

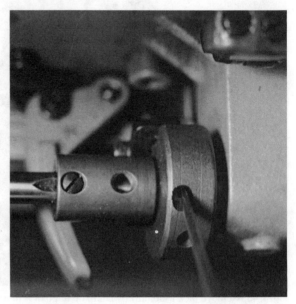

Fig. 7-47. Adjusting tension to drive dog latch.

Fig. 7-48. Bobbin well with small amount of lint. This would be considered only slightly dirty. Caution: It takes relatively little sewing, especially on napped materials, to build up lint deposits. Clean frequently!

Fig. 7-49. Bobbin well after cleaning with air gun.

Fig. 7-50. Polyethylene squeeze-bottle oiler gives positive control of oil at all times.

vide complete sewing instruction, a few tips are included in hopes that they will make this aspect of upholstering a bit more pleasurable, and successful (especially if this is the first experience on a commercial machine).

Needle Types

There are needles designed for specialty uses as well as for general purpose sewing. They vary in size (diameter), length (H3 or H4), and in point configuration. Figure 7-55 shows four different point configurations with their major use identified. Although some operators may say that any needle will work with every material, some will work "better" and smoother than others in given materials. Using the needle designed for a particular material will consistently produce superior quality stitching as well as reduce the "wear and tear" on the machine through the easier penetration the needle design is intended to give.

For most custom shops and for general purpose sewing which will involve cloth and vinyl fabrics primarily the round point will be the preference. The #17, H3, round point seems to be preferred by most upholsterers for this general purpose sewing. Many upholsterers will use this one style needle for all work that goes through their shop. Unless much work is to be done on a specific type of material, like leather, most operators feel it would be a waste of time to change needle styles.

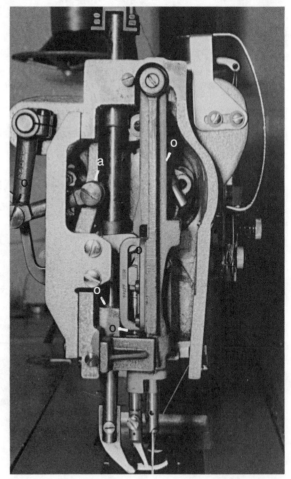

Fig. 7-51. Six oil locations (beneath head cover plate).

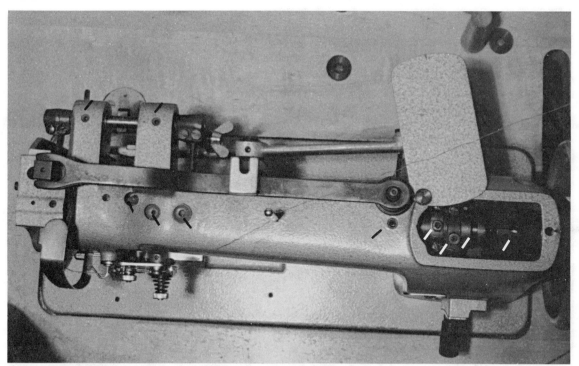

Fig. 7-52. Ten oil locations from top of machine.

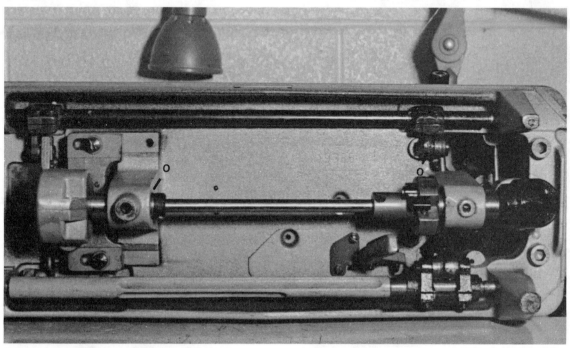

Fig. 7-53. Oil locations in machine base.

Fig. 7-54. Two oil locations in bobbin assembly.

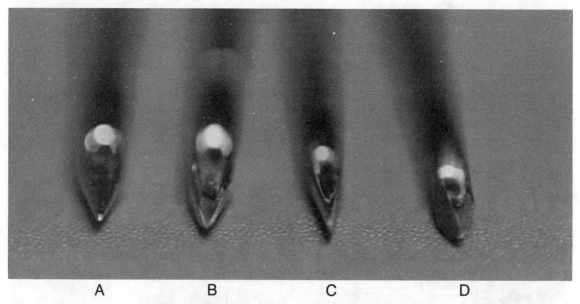

A   B   C   D

Fig. 7-55. Needle points and their purposes: (A) round, for cloth and vinyl fabrics; (B) wedge, for coarse weave tweeds; (C and D) diamond, for leathers. Note: Most upholsterer's use one needle only, for all sewing, a round point, number 135 × 17. Specialty shops or machines used for "special" types of work are about the only ones making use of wedge and diamond point needles.

Fig. 7-56. Throat plates. Keep closed for all sewing! Note 1/2-inch seam guide etched into plate. (Etching done with vibrating carbide tip.)

Cover Plates

Keep them closed when sewing! It is a sad and very memorable experience to have the thread pick tear into a piece of fabric being sewn. Not only is the piece of fabric sure to be disfigured, but of greater consequence, the machine can be severly "wrenched" out of time. One machine required adjustments clear back to the main drive shaft by the handwheel because a fast moving pick rammed into a clump of fabric. Such an unusual adjustment is not only difficult to find, but is also very expensive in time. The simple solution is to keep all cover plates closed, especially those over bobbin (Fig. 7-56).

Consistent Seam Allowance

One of the best aids, especially to the novice, is to establish a consistency for ALL seam allowances. A popular allowance is 1/2". If *every* seam is given a 1/2" allowance, patterns, cutting,

and sewing is greatly simplified (the math is easy too!). The "best" (according to the author, at least!) way to maintain a 1/2" sewing allowance is to etch a line in the cover plates on both sides of the needle. Figure 7-56 shows a machine having the right cover plate etched, the left one unetched. A permanent marking like this can be done by sand blasting, chemical etching, or as in the photo, mechanical engraving. A popular, "quick and dirty" alternative to the permanent etching is the simple application of a piece of masking tape as illustrated in Fig. 7-57. The inside edge of the tape should be 1/2" to the tip of the needle point.

Avoiding Visible Stitches

Most machine sewing is designed to have the stitches invisible. *Only the top stitch is the exception.* Therefore, a little thought must be given to some work to avoid earlier stitches being seen. For instance, on some work one piece of material may be sewn as many as three times before that particular sewing task is complete. One such case, and

Fig. 7-57. 1/2" seam guide—masking tape.

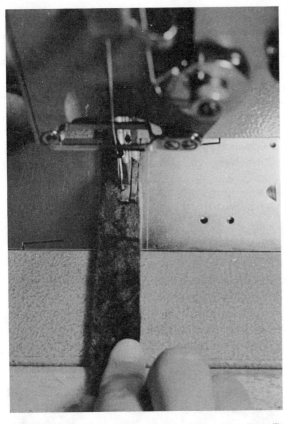

Fig. 7-58. Sewing a welt. (Stitch is not tight against welt cord!)

a very popular one (except for the very experienced upholstery "tailors"), is sewing up a welt (Fig. 7-58). Many times the welt cord is sewn into a strip, as in this illustration. Then, the welt is sewn onto a cushion panel, and finally, the boxing and zipper panel are sewn to the welt and cushion panel, making three times that the welt fabric is actually sewn. If the first stitch were tight, which occurs frequently with beginners, the first stitch would be objectionably visible. That's a "no, no!"

Notice that in Fig. 7-58 the walking foot is not riding tightly against the welt cord, which is to the left of the needle. The welt is sewn loosely at this point. The next sewing, to the cushion panel, will also be done a bit loose (Fig. 7-59). In this photo the operator is shown preparing to make a "square" corner. The purpose of the notch in the welt will be explained below. With the welt securely in place on the cushion panel, the boxing and zipper panel can be sewn to them with greater ease than if all three components were still free to move with respect to each other, especially with napped fabric!

Figure 7-60 shows the boxing being sewn to a cushion panel with attached welt. Notice that the operator now is pushing the welt tightly against the left side of the walking foot. This creates a tight seam and conceals the previous stitches. Notice also

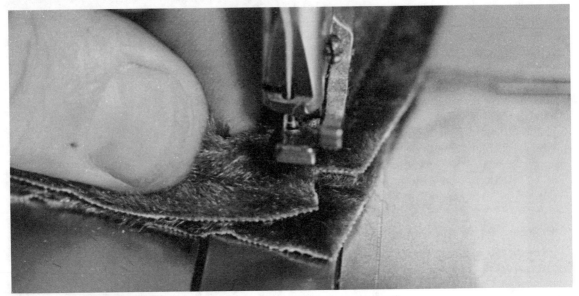

Fig. 7-59. Sewing welt to cushion panel. (Stitch is still not tight against welt cord!)

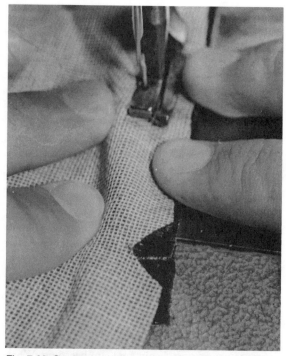

Fig. 7-60. Sewing boxing to welt and cushion panel. (Now, make stitch tight against welt cord!)

that it appears that very short "runs" are being taken. This becomes increasingly important as the nap length increases (Napped fabric, like a tiny child, crawls all over the place unless it is held so it can't!).

Keeping Things "Square and Aligned"

The universal way to assure alignment of matching panels is through the use of "notches." These may be made in numerous shapes and combinations, the most popular being a single "V." In fabric having a plaid or floral pattern, the pattern can be used for alignment, but that takes time to keep opening the fabric to check. So? Put in alignment marks or notches. In Fig. 7-61 the operator is shown clipping off the corner of a boxing which has been folded in half lengthwise. This will mark the center, and is to be made on both sides. A corresponding notch will be made in the front, center of the cushion panels. These two marks, when aligned, will assure that the centers will line up properly. Other notches are made to permit a periodic check on tensions and spacing, such as

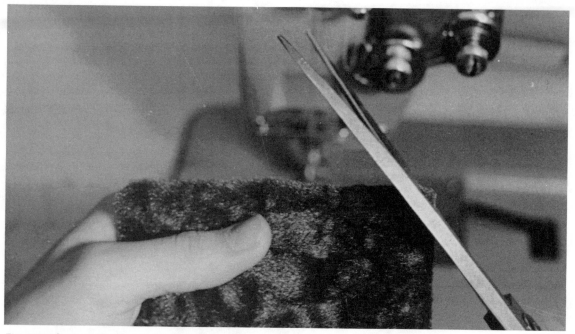

Fig. 7-61. Cutting alignment notch in folded boxing.

where the welt or boxing must bend at the corner (Figs. 7-59 and 7-60 respectively). When the alignment notches have been cut into one side of a panel (boxing in this case), fold the panel in half lengthwise and cut corresponding notches in the other side (Fig. 7-62). This will assure that the two cushion panels, for example, will have their corners located at exactly the same spot along the boxing. Figure 7-63 shows a demonstration boxing panel with a double "V" center notch and periodic alignment notches along both sides.

Elimination Of "Puckers"

My, but it is disconcerting to sew up a cushion only to find that the corners are two inches out of square, and that either the main panel or the boxing has a series of unintended puckers and wrinkles. To eliminate such unsavory occurrences, keep an even, restraining pressure on all pieces as they are fed into the needle. Simple to say, but sometimes not so simple to do. For example, maybe the pieces being sewn are very heavy and cumbersome. What happens? The material has to be almost "pulled" from the rear of the needle because the "walking"

Fig. 7-62. Making matching alignment notch on opposite side of boxing.

Fig. 7-63. A demonstration boxing panel showing double-V center and single-V alignment notches.

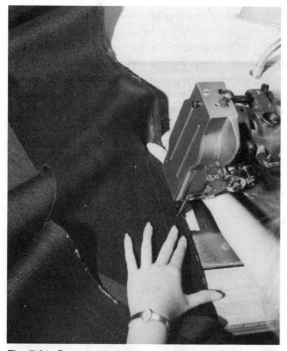

Fig. 7-64. Operator assisting to outfeed large panels. (An aid to even stitch length and reduction of "puckering.")

action can't pull all that weight and bulk. So? Puckers! Ah, but there are ways! Two of the best ways to reduce or eliminate completely this all-too-frequent malady of the beginner are:

1. Help the material feed through the machine. It must be "pulled" through, not pushed! While applying the same restraining tension to both (all) panels being sewn, offset that restraining pressure by pulling on the rear of the sewn materials, as shown in Fig. 7-64. This approach has several immediate benefits: it greatly reduces the affect of any differential in feeding that may occur between the table and the foot, it offsets excessive drag created by the restraining tension or the heavy weight of large pieces, and it facilities more even stitch lengths.

2. Take short "runs." Sew a few inches at a

Fig. 7-65. Sewing fabric with nap. Take short runs; the longer the nap, the shorter the run!

Fig. 7-66. Sewing fabric without nap. (Longer runs, up to several feet, are possible.)

167

time, stop the machine, relocate and retension the ingoing material, and sew a few more inches. This takes more time than sewing several feet each time, but it surely helps in reducing the pucker problem. If the fabric has a nap, take very short runs! The longer the nap, the more critical short runs become as the nap seems to make the material wander all over the place. The operator in Fig. 7-65 is taking a short run with a crushed velvet. On fabrics with no nap, longer runs can be taken, but if puckering seems to be a problem, keep those runs under control at all times. Figure 7-66 shows an operator maintaining positive control of a long run of the in going alignment with the right hand, while assisting with a side-feed and stabilization with the left hand.

Chapter 8

Buttons, Channels, and Tufts

This chapter deals with ways to finish a piece of furniture with buttons, with channels, and with tufts. Shown and discussed will be procedures for making the covered button, tying the upholsterer's knot to secure the buttons, making shallow channels with 1″ foam, and creating a diamond tuft pattern using the sewn-in method.

COVERED BUTTONS

Covered buttons are used extensively in upholstering as well as reupholstering. Several features contribute to their popularity. They add character and style to the furniture, are extremely easy to make, have diverse applications, and are inexpensive and easy to install.

Procedure

1. Insert button base into button base retaining die (Fig. 8-1).

2. Place loaded button base retaining die into the machine, Fig. 8-2.

3. Cut out covering fabric with the cutting die; place button cover on top of the cap retaining die, finished side down; place button cap, curved side down, on top of fabric (Fig. 8-3).

4. While holding the cap retaining die suspended so the bottom section is free to drop down, force the fabric and button cap down into the die with the wooden plunger (Fig. 8-4). With heavier fabrics, this takes considerable pressure, so be prepared for a good push!

5. Place loaded cap retaining die on top of the base retaining die in the machine as illustrated in Fig. 8-5.

6. Pull the lever down until it seats firmly. Raise the handle slightly and bring it down again with a quick motion to clinch the cap to the base securely.

7. Remove the two retaining dies from the machine and separate them. The covered button will usually drop out. If it should stick in the cap retaining die as shown in Fig. 8-6, right, merely squeeze the top and bottom of the die between the fingers and the button will pop out. The now empty

Fig. 8-1. Placing button eye back into button back retaining die. The back could also be a double prong or a nail style.

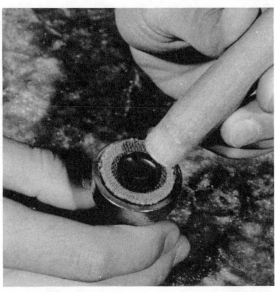

Fig. 8-3. Fabric disc (outer side, down) and button cap in place ready to be pushed into button cap retaining die.

dies, ready for reloading, and finished button (shown top up) are pictured in Fig. 8-7.

Uses

One of the popular uses of the covered button is to add contour and styling to backs, seats and arms of upholstered furniture. A worker is measuring and marking the locations for buttons on a two-cushion sofa in Fig. 8-8. One of the most popular positions for back buttons is very close to the level of the arm rest, as can be seen by the position of the steel rule. Another way to determine back but-

Fig. 8-2. Button back retaining die in place in base of machine.

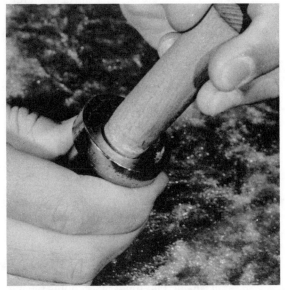

Fig. 8-4. Fabric and button cap in place in button cap retaining die.

170

Fig. 8-5. Placing button cap retaining die on top of button base retaining die.

ton position, assuming that they are installed in-line and not in a diamond or other pattern, is to either measure up from the cushions, or down from the top of the back. Figure 8-9 shows the craftsman locating the buttons 9″ from the top of the seat cushions.

Wherever buttons are used, one of the prime concerns for many upholsterers is to make it easy for the button to be secured, adjusted and even to be replaced (occasionally the cap will pop off, leaving the somewhat less than attractive button back to decorate the unit). To make this adjusting and replacing work possible, two methods are used (1) slip a single strand of the tufting twine through the eye of the button back or (2) make a sliding loop around the eye as illustrated in Figs. 8-10 and 8-11. Caution: *Do not* let the loop move off from around the eye as shown on the left of Fig. 8-11.

To be able to slide freely, the loop must be kept around the eye, as illustrated on the right (Fig. 8-11). This means of attaching the button makes it very easy to replace a "popped cap." All that is required is to make the new button, depress the padding and suspension while pulling outward on the old button base. Then, slip the loop from around

the old base, out of the eye, through the eye of the new button, and around the cap. Releasing the depressed padding and suspension will usually pop the new button back into place as if it had never been missing.

Another of the frequent uses of the covered button is for emphasizing the cushion retaining groove. Figure 8-12 shows a worker starting a button with the tufting needle. All strands of the tufting twine will be held between the thumb and fingers until they begin to penetrate the fabric at which time the worker will release the twine and work the needle with both hands to force it all the way through all padding and stuffing until the needle has either gone the full length or until it can be felt that the twine has been pulled free from the needle's eye. The button will then be tied to the desired depression of the seat and deck joint. This procedure is becoming more and more popular, replacing the practice of sewing the cushion retaining groove to the springs and burlap base.

A third and very popular use of covered buttons is to create the desired depressions in the tufting and channeling processes. This will be illustrated later in the chapter.

Fig. 8-6. View of button base retaining die (left) and covered button still in button cap retaining die (right) after processing.

Fig. 8-7. Top view of completed button and empty retaining dies.

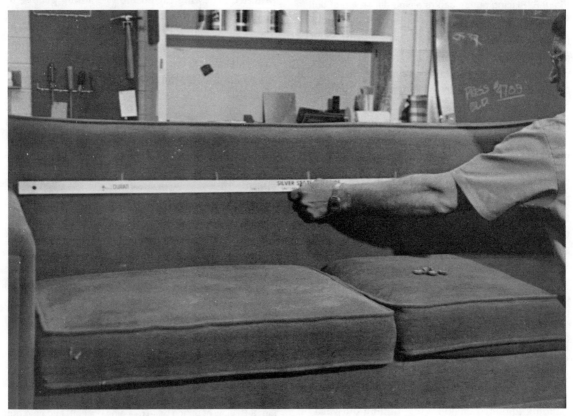

Fig. 8-8. Locating and marking sofa for button placement using top-of-arm method. (Notice bottom edge of steel rule.)

172

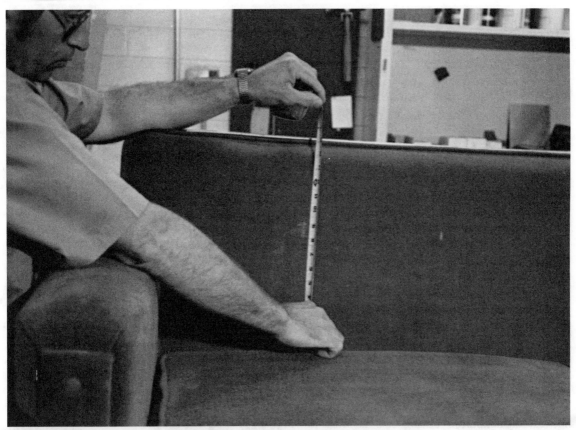

Fig. 8-9. Locating and marking sofa for button placement using vertical measuring method. (This could be taken either up from finished cushion or down from top edge of unit.)

Securing Covered Buttons

One of the methods for securing the covered button is shown in Fig. 8-13. This method is used when more depression is wanted than can be achieved by the "normal" procedure shown in Figs. 8-24 through 8-26. In this application, the loop formed after the upholsterer's knot is tied is hooked around a number 12 tack that has been driven in most of the way. Tension is adjusted by pulling on the "slipping" strand of the twine. In Fig. 8-13, the operator is holding the outside back panel and foam padding out of the way for clarity. (Someone got ahead of themselves and had to tie the buttons after the outside back panel has been attached to the top rail.)

Tying the Upholsterer's Knot

The most practical and versatile way to secure

Fig. 8-10. Looping tufting twine around covered button to facilitate easy replacement.

Fig. 8-11. Left—twine will not slide through eye (Undesirable). Right—proper orientation of twine loop.

buttons or nonbutton tufting ties is with the upholsterer's knot. This knot is easy to tie, forms a one-way slip knot that is ideal for adjusting tension on the ties, and is secured permanently with a simple overhand knot when desired tension is achieved.

After all buttons to be tied have been installed, refer to Fig. 8-12, following the sequence below will almost guarantee success in tying them off.

1. Grasp a strand with each hand and pull alternately to assure that the twine will slip freely through the eye of the button (Figs. 8-14 and 8-15). Also, pull both strands firmly and simultaneously to assure that the eye of the button has penetrated the cover fabric. If it appears difficult to penetrate the cover, pull the button free just enough to get to the hole easily, and carefully enlarge the opening by cutting a tiny slit with a knife or shears. A pull on both strands of the button tufting twine should be sufficient to slip the eye of the button through the fabric.

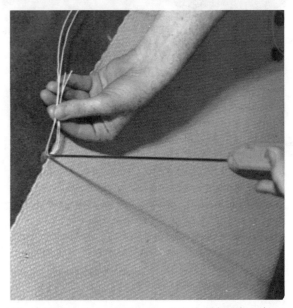

Fig. 8-12. Inserting tufting twine at desired location along a cushion retaining groove on couch that received a new decking.

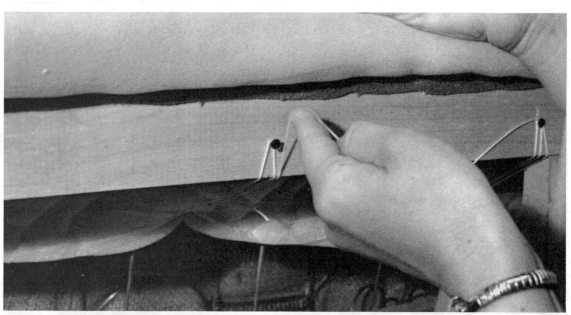

Fig. 8-13. Attaching tufting twine loop formed with upholsterer's knot to tack or nail in frame member to anchor covered button. (Operator is preparing to make a double-wrap with long end of twine to prevent cutting main loop when tack is driven in.)

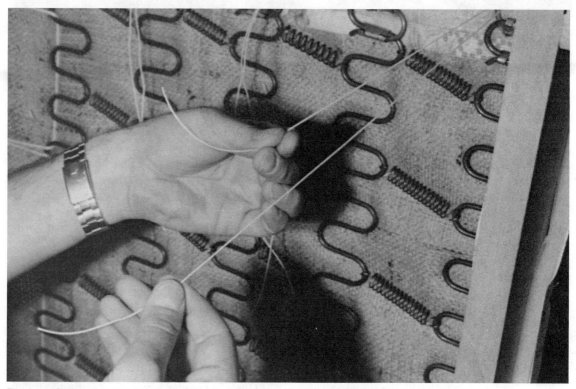

Fig. 8-14. Sliding tufting twine through button back eye to assure free movement.

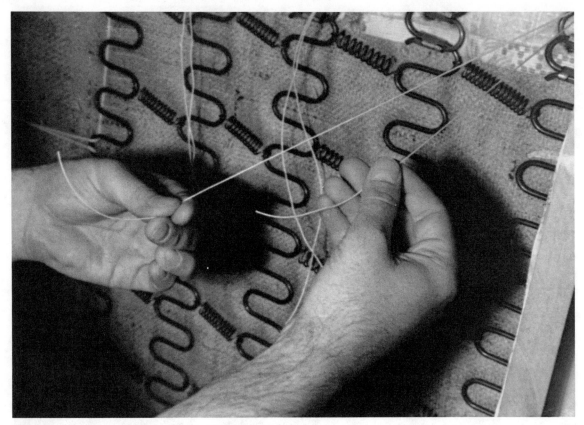

Fig. 8-15. Adjusting tufting twine for tying upholsterer's knot.

2. Grasp the "slipping" strand (which I prefer having the longer of the two) between the third and fourth fingers and the palm of one hand. Drape the "tying" strand over the top and around the fingers, and reach under to grasp it with the right hand as shown in Fig. 8-16.

3. Pivot the hand toward the "holding" hand as shown in Fig. 8-17, while at the same time still holding the "tying" strand (which is the shorter of the two) to the side. Notice the opening that has been purposely formed by the first and second fingers of the left hand? That is essential! Note also that the right hand, still holding the tying end has been raised a little.

4. Thread the free end of the tying strand through the opening just in front of the first and second fingers of the left hand, Fig. 8-18.

5. Reach underneath with the right hand and

pull the free end through, Fig. 8-19.

6. Rotate the left hand back so the palm is up. The view should appear as Fig. 8-20. If it does not, undo the knot and begin again with step two above.

7. Tighten the knot slightly by pulling on the "tying" strand (arrow) and a clearly defined "figure eight" will appear, as illustrated in Fig. 8-21. The "slipping strand" is merely held taut.

8. Finish tightening the knot, Figs. 8-22 and 8-23. Do not tighten the knot so much that it makes sliding very difficult. Figure 8-23 depicts the operator pulling on the slipping strand (arrow) to reduce the length of twine that will exist between the knot and the back or bottom of the furniture piece.

Securing the Upholsterer's Knot

One of the popular ways to secure the uphol-

176

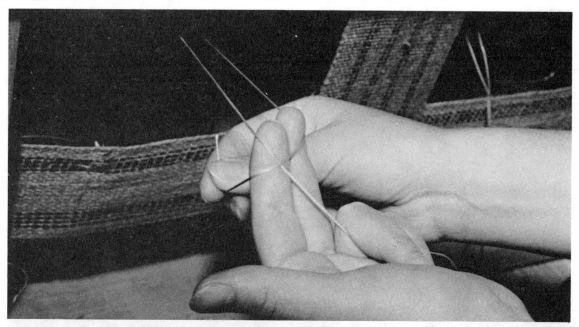

Fig. 8-16. Forming loop around fingers with short end of twine.

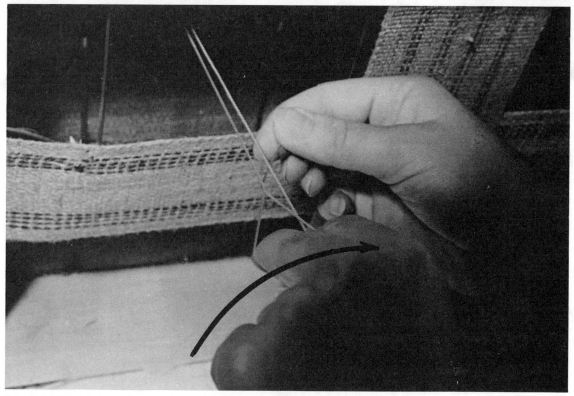

Fig. 8-17. Rotate loop—rolling hand toward the hand holding short end of twine.

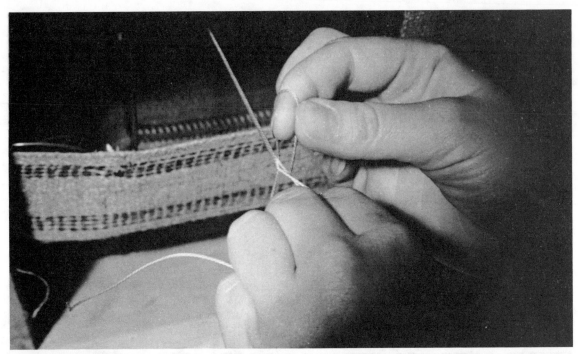

Fig. 8-18. Thread short end of twine through loop.

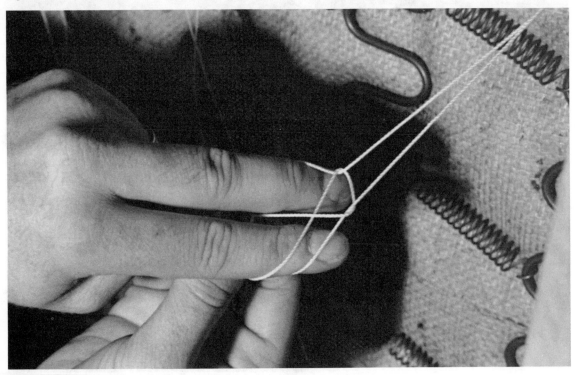

Fig. 8-19. Reach under, grasp short end and still hold on to longer end.

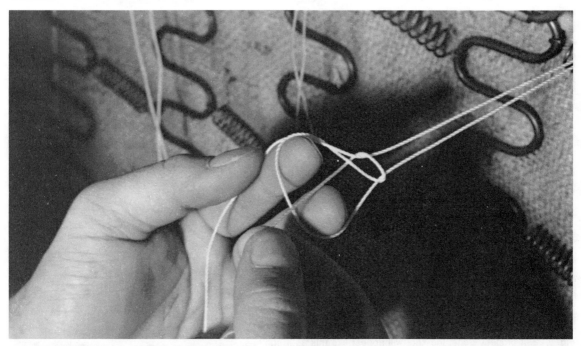

Fig. 8-20. Rotate hand back under, slip fingers out and begin to tighten knot.

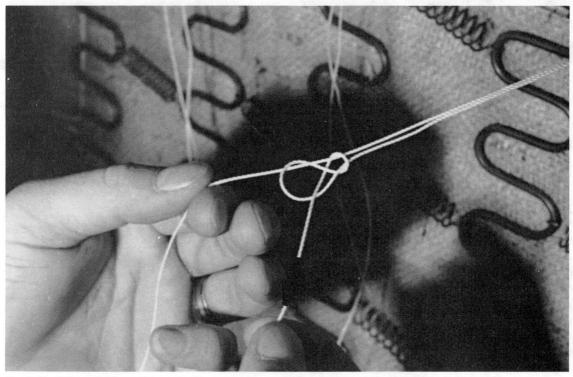

Fig. 8-21. Pull on shorter end (arrow) will reveal a figure eight around the sliding strand.

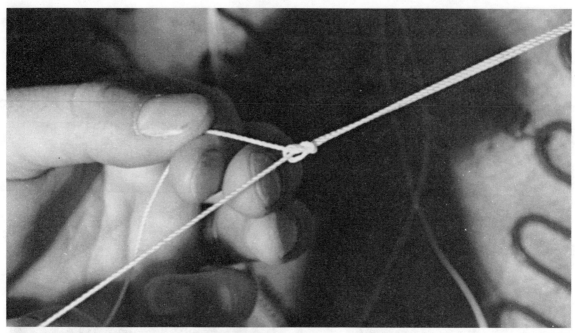

Fig. 8-22. If properly done, the knot will appear like this as it tightens.

Fig. 8-23. Once snug, pull on the sliding strand (arrow) to slip knot closer to foundation.

180

sterer's knot is to place a wad of cotton scrap or rolled fabric between the strands (Fig. 8-24) and slipping the knot to create tension (Fig. 8-25). Snug all buttons about the same and go around to the front side to see if the tension is as desired. If more depression is desired, increase tension. Because the knot is a one-way slip knot, it will retain the tension as applied. If the tension is too great, hold the "slipping strand" firmly beneath the knot and pull backward on the knot itself. Pulling on the "tying strand" will only tighten the knot and make it more difficult to slide it backward.

Once the desired tension has been achieved for all buttons, secure the knot by (1) holding the fingers of one hand against the outside of the knot while tightening the tying strand further, then (2) make an overhand knot (that's the kind that is used to start tying shoe laces) and tighten this against the upholsterer's knot. That's what the craftsman is doing in Fig. 8-26.

Note: The strands shown dangling vertically from the top of the photo in Fig. 8-26 are remnants of the alternate way to secure buttons. Figure 8-13 illustrates that method of securing buttons, anchoring them to a frame member. Some upholsterers have achieved such an accurate feel for the desired tension that they will pull the strands both at the same time and staple them to the frame. No adjustment is possible, and usually not necessary because of the skill they have developed. The later method for securing buttons is usually identified by the strands being stapled, folded over and stapled again to prevent any slippage as the spring action takes place.

CHANNELS

Channeling adds an air of elegance (according

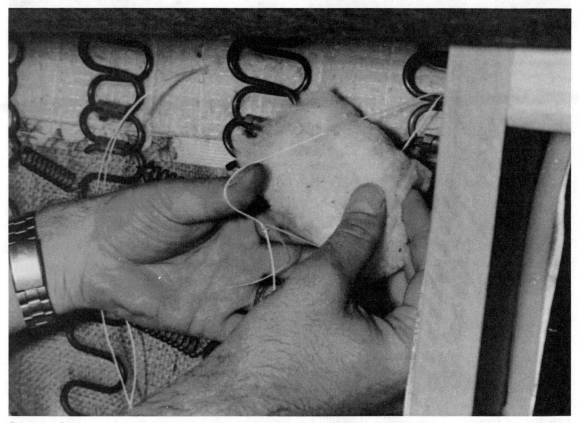

Fig. 8-24. Open loop, insert scrap cotton, fabric, or dacron around which to lock the knot.

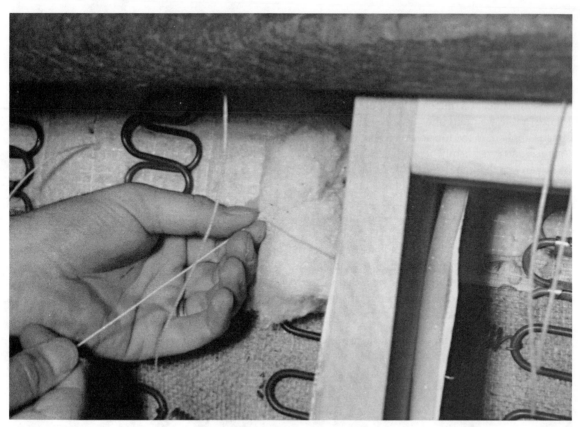

Fig. 8-25. Snug knot against stuffing, adjust all buttons evenly before securing knot.

to me anyway!), beyond buttoning alone. Figure 8-27 shows a couch with a plain buttoned back, ready to be reupholstered. The same unit with a buttoned channel back is shown in Fig. 8-28. Now really, which looks more elegant?

There are differences in shapes, widths, depths, construction methods, stuffing techniques, and materials from which channels are made. In times, for the most part now past, loose stuffing materials were packed into sleeves sewn of a cover fabric and a less expensive backing material. Stuffing materials were of hog hair (off the hoof!); cotton (shredded or rolled); chopped foam, dacron, excelsior (woody fiber), and sometimes paper; or a combination of the above. However, most channels constructed now are being made from flat foam sheets—the process described herein.

Channels are most often used on the backs of upholstered furniture. Occasionally, they will be used on inside arms and less frequently on seat panels and cushions. For this reason, the discussion on channels will deal with a back section.

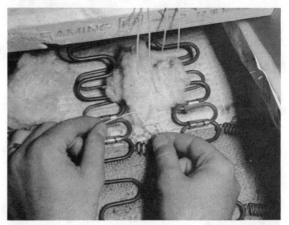

Fig. 8-26. Tie an overhand knot to lock upholsterer's knot securely.

182

Fig. 8-27. View of buttoned, plain-back couch prior to reupholstering.

Fig. 8-28. Reupholstered couch with buttoned channels in 1-inch foam.

183

Elements Of a Channel Sandwich

A channel unit usually consists of the following three parts which are bonded and sewn together, hence the term "sandwich": (1) a light weight, inexpensive backing fabric, (2) the foam padding, and (3) the cover fabric. One of the more popular ways to create this sandwich is by using 1″ or 1 1/2″ foam, between the backing and cover.

Padding For the Channel Sandwich

The first essential step toward creating a channel unit or sandwich is to obtain the major measurements, width (side to side) and depth (top to bottom) from an adequately padded unit (refer to Chapter 4). Because a channel sandwich is in itself a bit of padding, Table 8-1 may be used to determine just how much padding should be applied to a back before the measurements are taken. To make this determination, touch the tips of the thumbs together, fingers spread wide, and press the hands onto the padded back section. Then use the described conditions in Table 8-1 to determine if sufficient padding has been applied.

Determining Size Of Channel Elements

1. Foam Filler. Determine the size for the sheet of foam of the desired thickness and density for your particular application. Normally it will be a bit OVERSIZE, the amount being dependent upon the styling desired and the thickness of the foam to be used.

a. Record the greatest straight-line measurements of the width and depth of the area that is to be channeled (which is the crown-to-crown dimensions of the "adequately padded" section).

b. Take a scrap or section of the same foam that is to be used in the channel and using a piece of fabric on top of it, form the foam around corners or edges to where it is to be terminated. Make adjustments until it forms the ends where desired. Hold the foam in place against the back and let the rounded portion return to its basic flat position. Measure from the outer edge of the foam to a point in-line with the crown measurement taken in step "a" above. Add double these measurements (one for each end) to the straight-line measurements taken earlier and the length is established.

c. The width can be determined, a mite easier, by measuring with a flexible tape from the tacking point at the top rail down to the deck, allowing a spacing between the tape and the padding approximately the thickness of the foam to be used. Allow extra to form between the bottom of the back and the deck and the width is established.

2. Backing Fabric. This one is simple! Measure and cut the backing two inches longer and wider than the foam.

Table 8-1. Minimum Padding Prior to Measuring for Channel Components.

Foam Thickness	Minimum Padding Acceptable
1/2″	No discernment of foundation elements (springs, etc.)
1″	Springs barely distinguishable, no discernible lumps or depressions
1 to 2″	Springs may be felt but no lumps or depressions should be felt
2″	No "pronounced" depressions or lumps is all that is required

(Pad the "base" until the above conditions exist.)

Fig. 8-29. Spraying foam and backing with adhesive to bond the two together.

3. Cover. The width (depth) of the cover panel is a simple one too! Make it 2″ wider than the foam. To this may be added either a stretcher at the bottom to reach the rear seat rail, or, enough extra cover to reach it. The choice is a matter of economy. If sufficient cover fabric is available without creating problems in cutting other panels use it and avoid the additional, though minor, sewing of the stretcher. The latter choice is quite often preferred when doing single units where yardage has been ordered according to the standard charts.

To calculate the cover length in inches use this basic formula:

$$L = 2'' + F + 1.6dn, \text{ where:}$$

L = total length of cover needed to reach from side to side

F = length of the foam (in inches)

d = depth of each cut (in inches)

n = number of channel cuts

Creating the Channel Sandwich

Now that the component sizes have been determined, proceed with the construction of the chan-

nel sandwich in following manner:

1. *Lay the foam on a flat, clean work surface.* *Tip:* It would be a good idea to have some scrap paper underneath the foam around the edges to protect the work surface from adhesive overspray!

2. *Smooth the backing fabric over the foam so that it overlaps evenly on all sides*, similar to that being shown in Fig. 8-30.

3. *Carefully fold about 1/2 of the backing over and lay it on top of itself*, keeping everything relatively smooth and free of wrinkles.

4. *Spray the exposed underside of the backing and the foam with a fabric and foam adhesive.* With the backing folded over itself, the full half of the backing and one half of the foam can be sprayed in one step as illustrated in Fig. 8-29. Let the wet look disappear from the adhesive. (See why we need the paper under the foam?)

5. *Adhere the backing to foam.* Carefully suspend the sprayed half of the backing over the sprayed half of the foam. This is best done by grasping one corner of the backing in each hand and pulling it straight out over the foam without letting any portion of the sprayed half touch until it is all straight. (There is usually enough frictional resis-

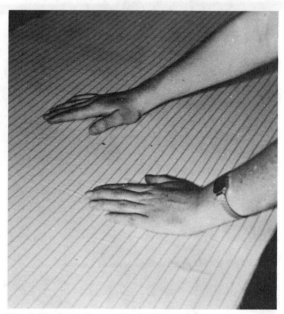

Fig. 8-30. Smooth out all wrinkles and bond backing and foam firmly.

tance of the unsprayed half to keep the fabric from moving, unless one sneezes at that critical moment or a "tug-of-war" is on-going.) Then, let the backing slowly down to contact the foam, beginning at the center and progressing outward. If done carefully, the backing can be smoothed against the foam with very small or no wrinkles. That is what is actually being shown in Fig. 8-30. A light rubbing action seats the two together. Any attempt, at this point, to move the fabric with respect to the foam will probably result in tearing the foam, so don't try it!

6. *Fold over the second half of the backing and repeat steps 4 and 5.*

7. *Lay-out and mark the foam for the channels.* Turn the backed-foam sandwich over so the foam is up. Determine the width, number and location of channels. The width and number of the channels is a matter of choice, and both depend somewhat on personal preference and the width of the unit. Those pictured in Fig. 8-31 are nine inches wide. Centering is also a matter of choice. At times, one of the channel seams will be at the center of the unit. The other alternative is to center the channel itself along the centerline of the unit. Mark the foam with a felt tip marker.

8. *Cut the channels.* A steel rule and a *sharp* razor-blade cutter are the best tools to use for this operation. The first cut is made using the steel rule as a straight edge and cutting along the lines marked (Fig. 8-31). Make no attempt to cut deeply with the first pass. The second cut is made by slightly opening the first cut, and *not* using the straight edge. This is done by pressing and pulling the top of the foam to one side *slightly*, as illustrated in Fig. 8-32. Cut the foam to the depth desired (1/2" to 3/4" is the average depth in 1" foam). **Caution:** *Do not* cut all the way through and into the backing!

Fig. 8-31. Use steel rule to make first channel slit.

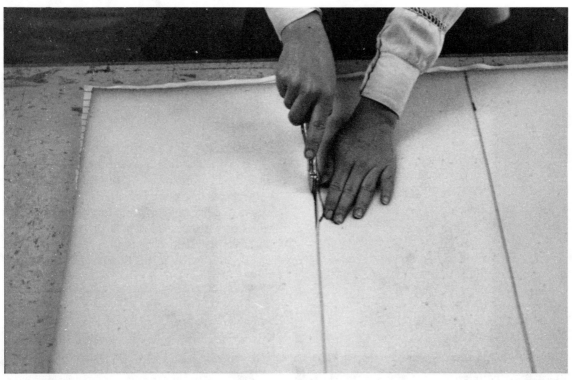

Fig. 8-32. Open cut to continue slicing to desired depth. (Multiple shallow cuts are much better than trying to achieve full depth with one cut!)

9. *Form the cover to the channels.* Start the forming process with the center channel and move alternately outward to the ends. Fold the cover in half, face side to face side, and locate the center fold along the edge of the center channel cut as shown in Fig. 8-33. Open the cut and press the fold of the fabric into the cut as shown in Figs. 8-34 and 8-35. When the folded fabric is pressed into the cut, let the foam come back into place. This will hold the fabric in place, as can be seen in the upper portion of Fig. 8-35.

10. *After the entire length has been put into place, open the cover fold and increase the depth of the fold by smoothing the fabric into the cut foam with the sides of the fingers,* Fig. 8-36. The finished crease should appear similar to Fig. 8-37.

11. *Pin the crease of the channel in place before moving to the next one.* Insert a skewer along the centerline of the crease so that it will hold the cover securely to the backing strip, Fig. 8-38. *Tip:* Lift-

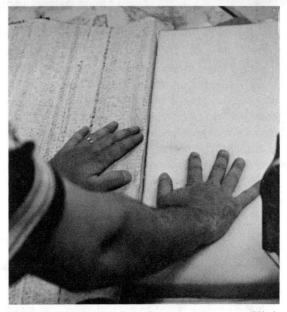

Fig. 8-33. Fold cover to channel cuts to create crease. (Work from center out!)

187

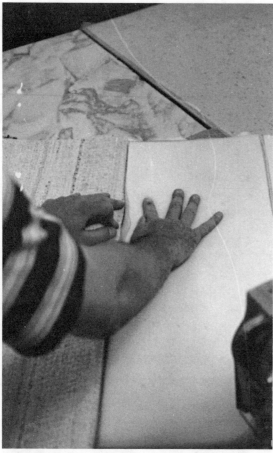

Fig. 8-34. Open cut and press folded cover into it.

ing the channel sandwich from the bottom to create a slight convex curvature along the seam line will make it much easier to get the skewer to catch all components. Place the outside pins 2 1/2" to 3" from each edge. Three to four pins are required for each crease. Do not try to smooth the crease at this time; it hurts!

12. *Sew the channels*. Beginning with the center crease, sew the sandwich together along the centers of each crease. Just after starting the stitch, pull out the end pin. Sew along the crease to within a couple inches of the next pin, then remove it. Warning: Sewing over the skewers could be dangerous! Broken needles sometimes fly with *blinding* speed. Be careful! The crease being sewn in Fig. 8-39 is the last one on one end, otherwise there would be a large roll of material being forced

through the throat of the machine to the right of the needle. (We wanted to make it look simple!) *Tip*: Opening the fabric sideways slightly, as depicted in Fig. 8-39, helps in keeping the needle and the walking foot from catching the sides of the channel material, thus aiding in a straight seam.

TUFTING

There are three major ways to create tufts using foam. The first is to cut the desired pattern into "backed" foam, using the same principle as with channeling described above. Then sew the seams to a backing strip and button the junctions when fitting the sandwich to the unit. This emphasizes the junction points.

The second is to cut the desired pattern and

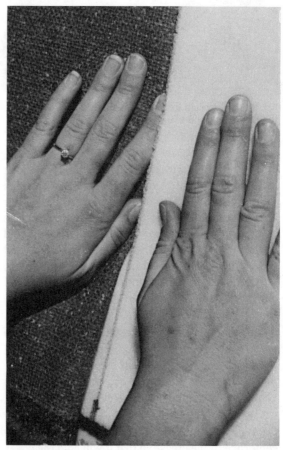

Fig. 8-35. Let foam relax against tucked-in fabric to hold in place.

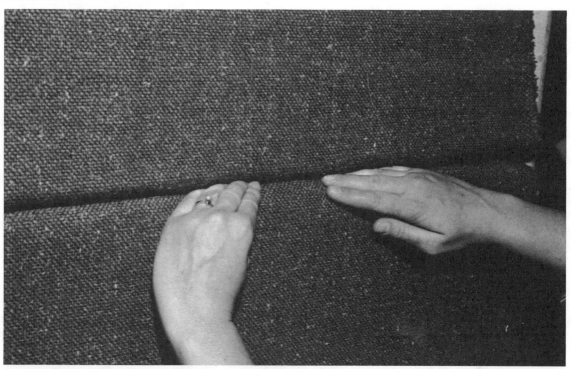

Fig. 8-36. Lay cover open and smooth fabric deeper into slit.

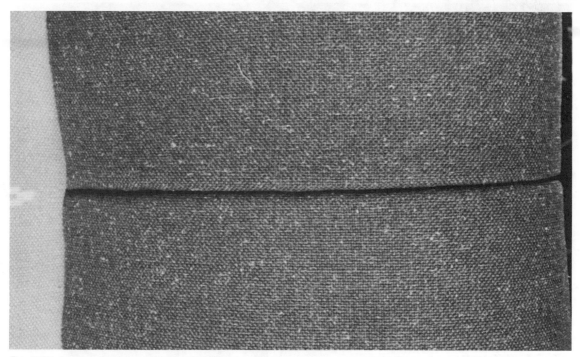

Fig. 8-37. A properly prepared channel in 1″ foam prior to pinning and sewing.

Fig. 8-38. Pin each channel before tucking-in next one.

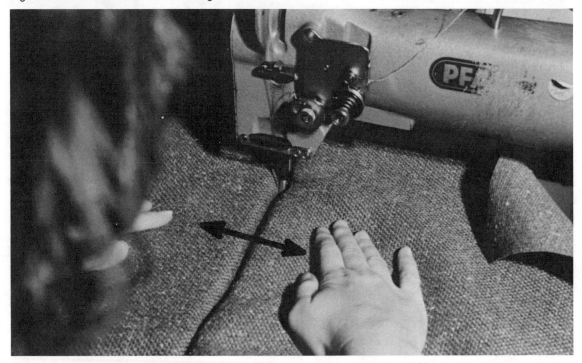

Fig. 8-39. Sewing channel seam (slight opening pressure aids in making straight stitch).

190

drill holes at the intersections partially through un-backed foam. The cover, cut oversize according to the formula (see page 185), is then buttoned onto the unit beginning with the center and progressing outward in all directions. The fabric is folded between each button, or tucked into the cuts in the foam. *Tip*: Make all angular or horizontal folds so they face downward to eliminate the "dust catcher" property. Make vertical folds all one direction or so they face either outward from the centerline or inward toward it.

The third is to sew the pattern into the cover in such a way that when buttons are installed, a natural pocket or recess is formed to permit the buttons to be depressed significantly into the padding. Figure 8-40 shows the inside of a vinyl fabric with a sewn diamond tufted pattern that has been removed from a recliner. Notice how the previously buttoned locations protrude upward? This style is especially suited for pillow backs and arms that are stuffed with chopped materials, foam, foam and cotton, down, or other loose fillers. The following procedure is an easy one to establish the pattern for diamond tufting:

1. Layout desired pattern on the back side of the panel. Figure 8-41 shows two workers completing the markings for a diamond pattern.

   a. Make the horizontal and vertical centerlines. (Notice the vertical lines extending from top to bottom, even through the centers of the diamonds. The horizontal centerlines are very difficult to see.)

   b. Draw in the diagonal centerlines that will create the desired diamond pattern.

   c. Scribe circles at the junctions where the

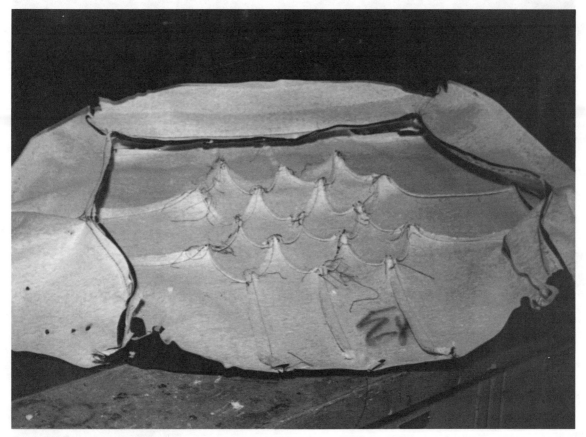

Fig. 8-40. View of underside of diamond-tufted back stripped from a recliner.

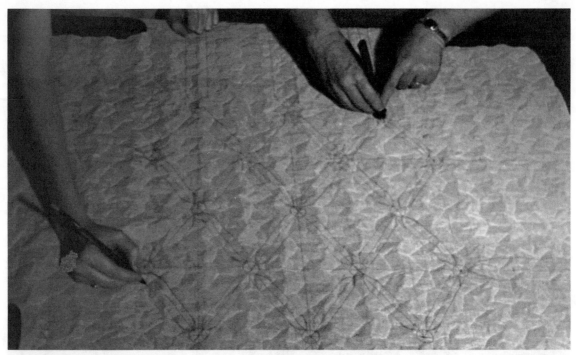

Fig. 8-41. Laying-out and marking new IB panel for diamond tufting.

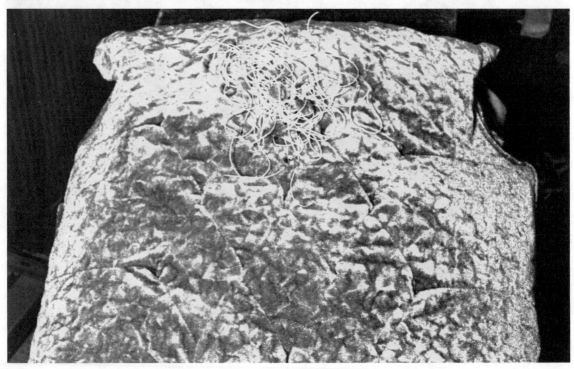

Fig. 8-42. Filled sewn diamond-tufted back prior to attaching buttons.

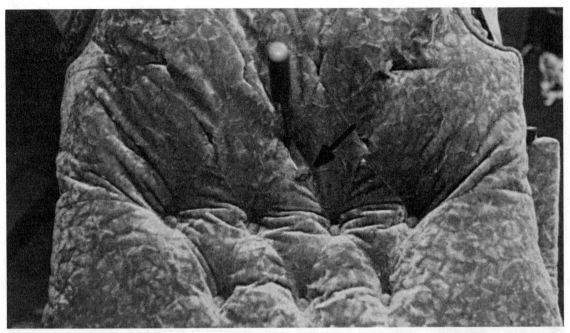

Fig. 8-43. Installing button (indicated by arrow) for diamond tuft.

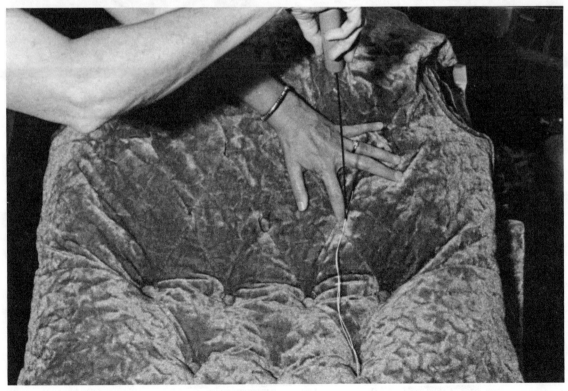

Fig. 8-44. Stretching and locating centers for next button.

Fig. 8-45. Sewn diamond tufts equally spaced.

ton spots to the edges of the panel). This makes it easier to establish the diagonal folds that will be done next.

b. Sew the diagonal seams.

After the tufting seams have been completed, sew all of the panels for the complete pillow back together, except for the bottom where the filling material will be blown or stuffed in. Then, after all stuffing is in, sew up the bottom. This can usually be done on the machine. Some, however, are sewn by hand. Figure 8-42 shows the back filled with a combination of chopped foam and shreaded cotton along with the buttons and twine ready to be attached to a recliner.

Because loose stuffing was used in this unit, the button process was done with the unit laying on its back. This helped keep the filler from settling to-

buttons will be placed. A template is handy, like the quarter being used by the worker at the upper right of the photo (Fig. 8-41).

d. Mark the sewing lines, parallel to the diagonal centerlines, and round these to a point at the circles, shown in process at the lower left in Fig. 8-41.

2. Sew the tufting pattern. Fold along the centerlines and sew along the sewing lines. If done properly, the sewing lines will actually be in line with each other. *Tip*: Lock stitch or tie the endings of every sewn section to prevent the seams from loosening with service.

a. Sew the horizontal and vertical sections first (those that go from the outside but-

Fig. 8-46. Diamond tufts of varying size, top tucks only are sewn.

ward the bottom. Also, because a softer head rest and a more firm kidney roll were desired, buttoning was started at the top center and progressed toward the bottom (Fig. 8-43). This procedure tends to hold the softer stuffing in place at the top while at the same time pushes and packs the remaining filler downward to create a more firm bottom. "Easy chair" comfort can thus be tailored in. As each button is placed and snugged down, the next spot must be stretched out and the center located rather precisely. Figure 8-44 shows a worker stretching one of the diagonals and at the same time locating the precise center with the forefinger. With the center thus located, the tufting needle, with

both strands of twine threaded about 3″ through the eye, is carefully placed and then forced through all stuffing materials and the burlap until the twine slips free from the needle eye. Snug up each button as it is placed using the upholsterer's knot shown earlier (Figs. 8-14 through 8-26). Two diamond tufted units are pictured in Figs. 8-45 and 8-46. In Fig. 8-45 the tufting is of the sewn variety, with equal spacing for each tuft. Figure 8-46 displays a tufting style with the diamonds increasing in size downward. The top row of four tufts is the only row that involves sewn tucks (four from the top edge, to each button, and one from each side to the side buttons).

Chapter 9

Installation of Inside Panels

One of the major hazzards for the novice when it comes time to recover a unit is the tendency to think of saving time by anticipating and cutting the contour, size, and fitting cuts (diagonal cut, Y-cut) in a panel before actually putting it onto the unit. Slight differences in padding and even in stretching tensions can make significant changes in exact location cuts and contour cuts. Sometimes, even anticipating contours and rough cutting them before fitting can result in erroneous contours being cut. Our cougar friend on page 197 is a bit concerned about an improper rough cut made on the outside arm panel. But, the consequence of a ruined panel applies to all locations. The best practice is to do the fitting to the unit and not to a supposition.

INSTALLATION STEPS

The first panel to be installed on any completely reupholstered piece of furniture of integral frame construction is the deck or seat and deck combination. Only a few of the numerous types of seat assemblies will be covered (that's a pun!) in this volume.

The Hard Edge Style

The hard edge seat assembly is usually styled such that the deck and the seat panel are separate entities. The decking is the first panel to be attached after burlap and basic stuffing have been applied to the seat area. Installation is almost identical to the burlap, with the main difference being that folding a flap over or under to avoid tear-out is not considered. It is tacked straight to the frame.

Deck Installation

Figure 9-1 illustrates the beginning of deck installation. After stapling the front edge to within a couple of inches of the arm post or stump, stretch to the rear, seat rail and staple the center, Fig. 9-2. Fitting proceeds the same as burlap installation, Figs. 4-39 through 4-44, including the Y and diagonal cuts. Figure 9-3 shows the decking marked for making the diagonal cut for the back post on a sofa. Figure 9-4 shows the first tuck folded with the second to be fitted. The deck should fit snugly against any uprights around which it is to be fit, Fig. 9-5.

Never contour panels before fitting to the unit.

To fit around the center upright of a couch having a triangular brace (best shown in Fig. 9-9) requires a slight modification to the diagonal cut. In Fig. 9-6 a mark has been projected from the center of the rear upright, then angles over to the front of the brace (Fig. 9-7). This creates a flap for both sides which will be folded under to give as straight a pull on the decking as can be arranged. Each side should be fastened snug to the upright as shown in Figs. 9-8 and 9-9.

Installing the Seat Panel

With the deck in place, Fig. 9-10, the hard-edge seat panel is ready to be installed. For specifics on how the hard-edge is usually constructed, refer to Fig. 3-20 through 3-23. With the seat panel attached to the wider plywood strip, nailed in place, and the second or elevator strip also in place, pad the hard edge as desired. In all padding, the outer layer should be completely smooth and thus must be the layer that covers the full area in one piece, if possible. If padding that is wider than normal is required,

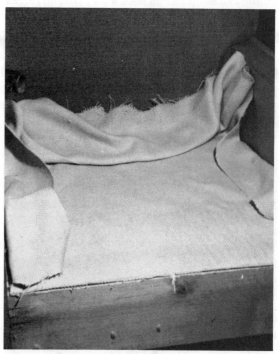

Fig. 9-1. Stretch and attach decking along front edge.

Fig. 9-2. Stretch and attach center at top of back seat rail.

cotton can be spliced in such a way that no ridges will be perceivable (Figs. 13-16 and 13-17).

Figure 9-11 shows a narrow layer of cotton felt that will just cover the hard-edge strips and rail edge. At least one more layer of cotton is necessary, and, if it is to be the last layer, it should be wide enough to cover the entire rail as depicted in Fig. 9-13. In this installation, three layers of cotton were

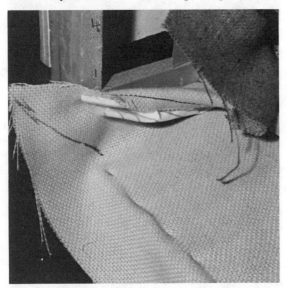

Fig. 9-3. Back of decking attached, corners marked for diagonal cut.

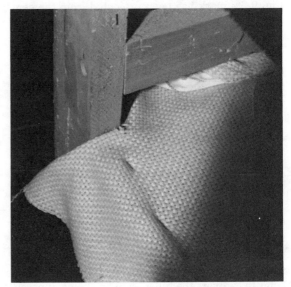

Fig. 9-4. Fold flap under and form tight to upright.

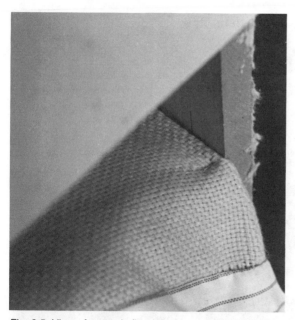

Fig. 9-5. View of properly fitted decking at right, rear post.

desired, in which case the second or intermediate layer is not full length (Fig. 9-12). The outside and final layer is tucked under the cover at the rear of the hard-edge strip and laid extending toward the rear of the chair. The other two layers (in this case) are then placed on top of it at the front edge, as shown in Fig. 9-13 (It is very difficult to see the separations of cotton layers, isn't it?). The seat panel with the cotton is rolled forward and pulled over to be stapled in the center of the bottom front rail.

Figure 9-14 shows a completed chair with the hard-edge construction and recessed arms. This style will require a T-cushion. The unit pictured in Figs. 9-11 through 9-13 has flush arms and will accommodate a standard rectangular cushion.

Regardless of the style or arms and whether it is a hard or soft edge, all units that utilize removable seat cushions will require some means of retaining the cushion in place—the cushion re-

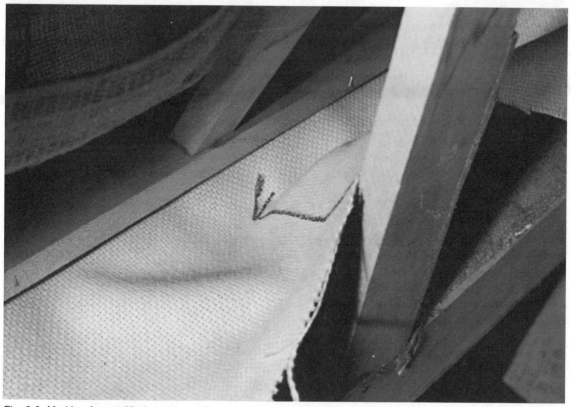

Fig. 9-6. Marking for modified cut around braced center upright of a sofa.

199

Fig. 9-7. Appearance of modified cut prior to fitting.

Fig. 9-8. Properly fitted decking around center upright.

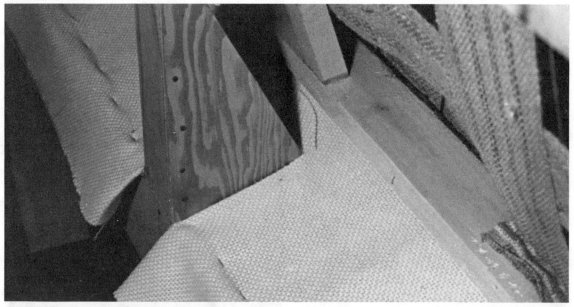

Fig. 9-9. Finished edge of decking along side of back plywood brace.

Fig. 9-10. Finished decking on a hard-edge construction.

Fig. 9-11. Narrow, first layer of cotton for padding hard-edge.

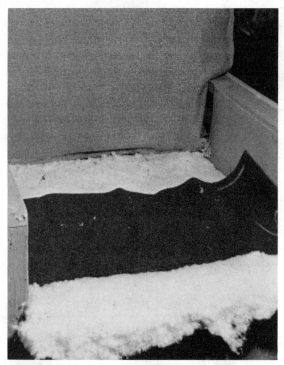

Fig. 9-12. Second layer of cotton, wider than first.

Fig. 9-13. Third and final layer of cotton to pad hard-edge. (All three layers have been layed back, revealing hard-edge strip.)

Fig. 9-14. View of a finished hard-edge with sewn cushion retainer groove.

taining groove. This is actually an elevation at the front of the seat. One way to achieve this elevation is with the two plywood strips and padding as indicated above. Another approach is to establish the *cushion retaining groove*. This can be done by sewing the seat-deck seam to the burlap and spring assembly as illustrated in Fig. 9-15. Sew all the way through any padding, the burlap, and wherever possible, around spring wires. Make the stitches tight and straight. A double-pointed, straight needle is usually used to make a running stitch along the seam. The finished groove is shown in Fig. 9-16.

Figures 9-17 and 9-18 show another style of sewn cushion retaining groove utilized on an executive chair. Yet another popular means of establishing the retaining groove, and one that is gaining popularity because it reduces hand sewing time, is through the use of covered buttons. Figures 9-19 and 9-20 show the previous style executive chair being prepared using the button method. The finished products are shown, side by side, in Fig. 9-21. One has the buttoned groove, the other has the sewn groove. At this point, no one can distinguish the difference without lifting the loose T-cushion.

Occasionally, a deck may become excessively soiled or otherwise damaged with no other damage occurring to permanent cover panels. In such cases, replacing the decking is the only job to be done. With the least time possible, and disturbing only the outside arm and back panels, a new deck can be installed by using the blind stitch along the deck-seat seam. Because the blind stitch is so valuable in many circumstances in upholstering, detailed in-

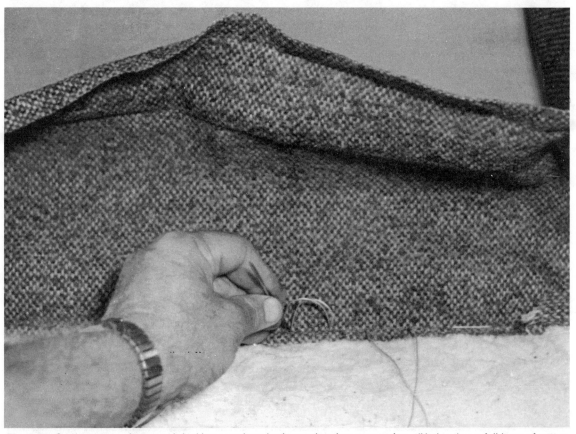

Fig. 9-15. Sewing seam of seat and decking panels to burlap and spring suspension. (Notice that a full layer of cotton covers the hard-edge.

Fig. 9-16. Top view of sewn retainer groove for one style of hard-edge.

Fig. 9-17. Top view of modern style of sewn cushion retainer groove.

Fig. 9-18. Executive chair using sewn cushion retainer groove.

Fig. 9-19. Using buttons to establish a cushion retainer groove.

Fig. 9-20. Modern styling created on executive chair with buttoned retainer groove.

Fig. 9-21. Two executive chairs, one with sewn, one with buttoned retainer grooves. (Notice the slight difference in the cushion and arm styling?)

Fig. 9-22. The blind stitch to attach a new decking to existing cover. (Notice the skewer holding the folded decking in place.)

structions are given so even the beginner can be totally successful with it.

THE BLIND STITCH

The blind stitch is used anywhere (1) machine sewing is impractical or impossible, (2) on-the-unit repairs are to be made, or (3) closing of tuck and pleat folds on the unit is desired. The attaching of a new deck to the seat panel is shown in Figs. 9-22 through 9-26. Notice in Fig. 9-22 that a good portion of the seam has already been accomplished. Also, note the skewers holding the folded front edge of the deck panel in place. This step is a great time saver and aids in assuring a straight seam.

The principle of the blind stitch is to make square (90 degree), alternating stitches across the seam which will permit tightening the folded edges of the two pieces of fabric together. This stitch is always done with a curved needle! *Note:* Any deviation from the 90 degree stitching will result in undesirable puckers and gathers. (Additional instructions and illustrations on the blind stitch are given in Chapter 12, Figs. 12-21 through 12-26.)

1. Start the stitch in a location where the knot will not be visible when the unit is finished and in normal use.

2. Exit the cover from the underside near the seam to be created.

3. Make the first stitch by moving the thread straight across the seam to the fold of the adjoining panel, enter that side exactly beneath the thread, Fig. 9-22.

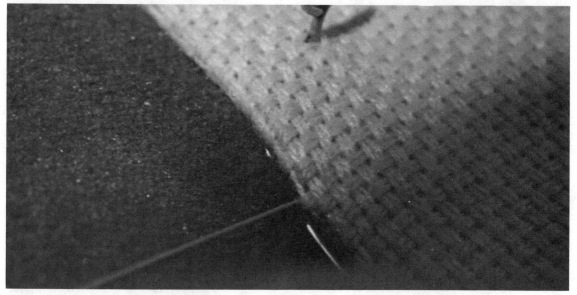

Fig. 9-23. Blind stitch is made parallel and close to the seam. (Notice the tip of the needle just emerging?)

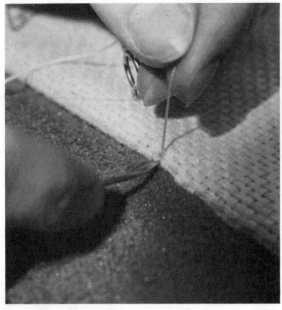

Fig. 9-24. Stitches are made "square" to the line of the seam.

4. Rotate needle parallel to seam and exit fabric the desired stitch length (usually from 1/4″ to 1/2″) as shown in Fig. 9-23. Tighten previous stitch.

5. Cross the thread, while holding the stitches taut, over to first fabric, again at 90 degrees to the seam, and enter needlepoint exactly beneath thread, Fig. 9-24.

6. Rotate needle parallel to seam and exit first fabric at stitch length, Fig. 9-25. Continue to end of sewing. Secure last stitch somewhere beneath or inside of seam so thread knot will be secure and hidden from view. Figure 9-26 shows a couch with new decking partially sewn in place (at both ends) to a previously upholstered seat panel. Additional material on the blind stitch will be found in Chapter 12, Figs. 9-20 through 12-26.

THE SLIP SEAT

Covering a slip seat is a straight forward process with just a few "tricks" that will make the process easier. The seat illustrated in Figs. 9-27 through 9-31 has sewn front corners and tucked rear corners. To install the sewn seat panel:

1. Slip the cover over the frame and padding. Then, open a portion of the corner seam to the point where it just meets the bottom edge of the frame.

2. Snug the side panel into the frame, tightening the fabric on an angle toward the front as indicated in Fig. 9-27. Make any adjustments nec-

Fig. 9-25. View showing constant parallelism of blind stitch to seam.

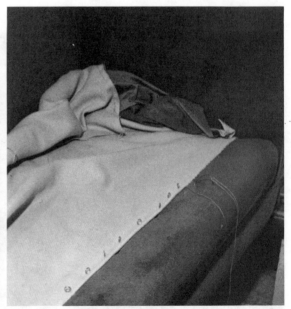

Fig. 9-26. Blind stitching new decking to good cover requires loosening only the OA and OB panels.

Fig. 9-27. Opening and fitting side, front corner seam of a slip seat.

essary to assure that the seam is right at the corners of the frame.

3. Snug the front portion of the opened seam such that the folded edge will lay at a slight inward angle while taking up the excess material along the front edge. Figure 9-28 shows side panel stapled in place and the operator beginning the front fold. Fold additional material under, if necessary, to permit tightening the front panel sideways and still not let the fold extend beyond the edge.

4. Stretch and tack the front edge in place, then go to the back. Stretch and tack the center in place.

5. Stretch and tack both sides, working from the centers toward the corners, leaving about four inches free from each corner as shown to the right of Fig. 9-29.

6. Fit each of the rear corners by starting at the side, taking small tucks and stapling each as progress is made around the corner to the back side.

Continue around the rear corner to a point where, by taking up the excess material, a fold will be made that finishes a neat corner, Fig. 9-30.

7. With the exact location of the fold identified, cut out the excess material, to allow a 1/2″ tuck, Fig. 9-31. Complete the seat by stapling around the edges and trimming the excess as is illustrated along the back and sides of Fig. 9-30.

FITTING THE INSIDE ARM (IA) PANEL

Hint: If you haven't already planned the orientation and layout of every panel for your unit, review Chapter 7 before doing any cutting!

Place the rectangular IA panel over the padded arm. For ease and speed in fitting, the four-point stay procedure is suggested.

1. Stay tack the front top in place as shown in Fig. 9-32. This is the *first* of the four-point stay. Smooth the cover to the rear and fold over at the

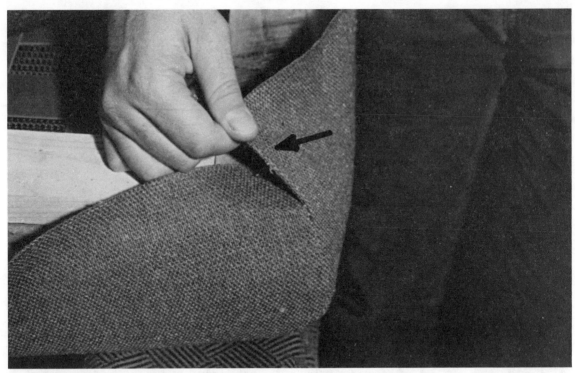

Fig. 9-28. Fitting front corner flap over stapled side.

Fig. 9-29. Fitting a rounded corner to a slip seat.

210

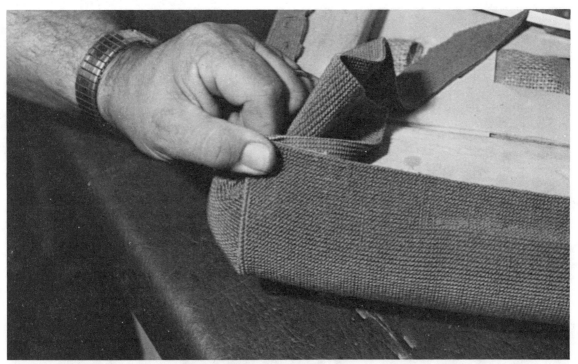

Fig. 9-30. Locating fold for a tucked edge along rear of slip seat.

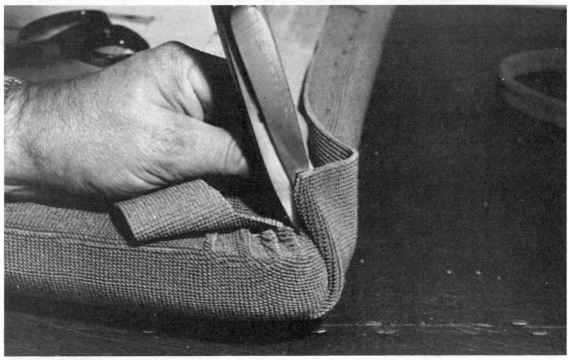

Fig. 9-31. Cutting our excess fabric to make low-profile tuck.

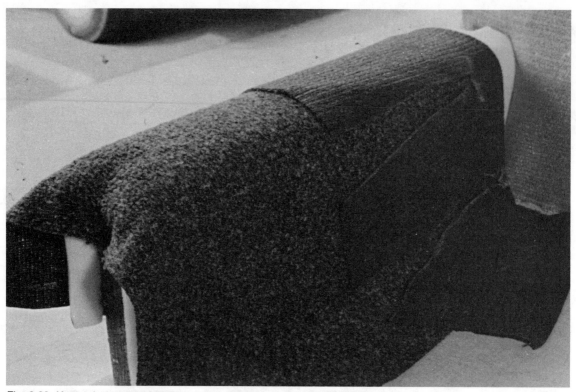

Fig. 9-32. IA panel stay tacked at front, Y-cut to fit at crown and lower back rail.

very front edge of the bottom back rail. Mark and make the Y-cuts (refer to Figs. 4-38 through 4-41 if necessary) that are necessary to fit the cover to the bottom, back rail, and along the crown of the arm as illustrated (Fig. 9-32).

2. Roll the top portion of the IA not quite half way under the back extensions as shown in Fig. 9-33. The extension is usually cut to leave 1/2" to 3/4" gap above the arm itself. Make the Y-cut so the legs end about 3/16" short of the front of the extension. This will result in four "strips" that are to be pulled and stapled to the back upright. Pull the top, outside portion of the panel back, smoothing with the one hand (Fig. 9-34) as you do so, to get it quite snug. Stay tack to the back of the rear upright. This creates the *second* of the four-point stay.

3. Go to the inside, bottom of the IA to fit it around the bottom back rail. Notice the tab ready to tuck under at the front edge of the rail, Fig. 9-35. Slide the remaining strips through the opening; one

beneath the bottom, back rail (the one that is shown still laying on the deck in Fig. 9-36). Tuck a small portion of the rear of the IA panel between the deck and the arm as the operator is doing in Fig. 9-36—just enough to hold it in place, temporarily.

4. Fold the bottom, front portion of the IA panel up, over itself to locate the Y-cut for the inside of the arm stump or post. *Cautions:* (1) Allow enough material so that the legs will tighten against the stump when the panel is pulled tight. (2) If the front of the seat depresses (spring loaded) instead of being rigid, make sure that the cuts will be concealed when the seat is depressed to its bottom-most position.

5. Finish tucking the bottom inside flap of the IA panel between the deck and the lower arm rail. When properly done, it will look like that shown in Fig. 9-37.

6. With all of the cuts made and the flaps tucked in their proper direction, it is time to fit the panel. Smooth the fabric so that the pattern or

212

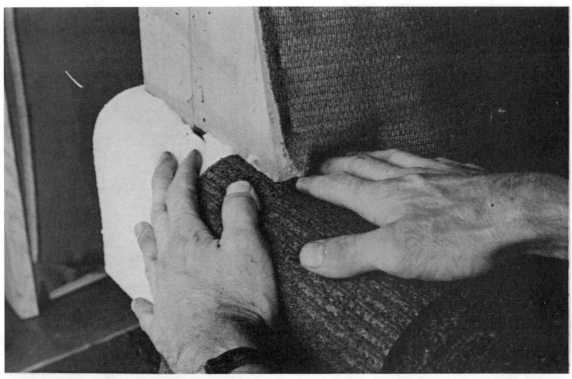

Fig. 9-33. Rolling top of IA half-way under back extension to locate Y-cut.

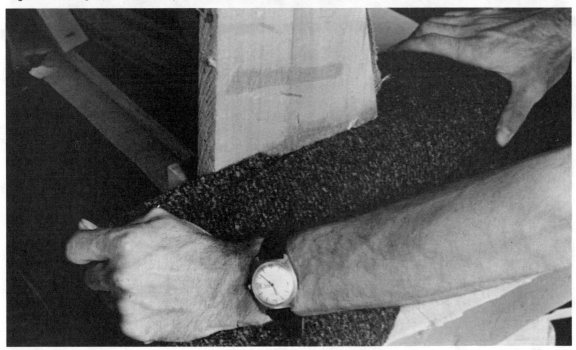

Fig. 9-34. Smoothing IA panel toward back for the second of the four-point stay tacks.

Fig. 9-35. Tab at bottom back rail ready to tuck under.

Fig. 9-36. Wedging IA panel prior to locating stump Y-cut.

214

Fig. 9-37. Inside arm panel tucked in, ready for 3rd and 4th stay tacks.

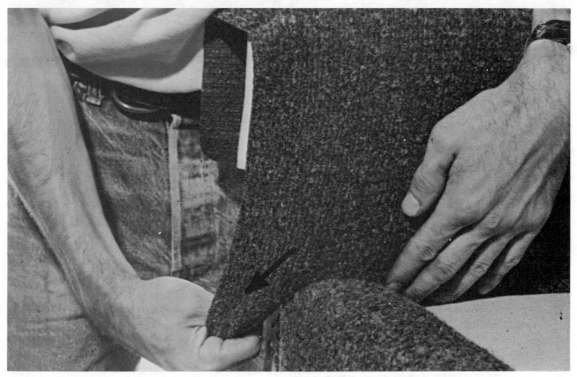

Fig. 9-38. Smoothing and fitting inside front for third of four-point stay.

weave will be oriented vertically and not at an angle. Figure 9-38 shows the operator pulling the fabric diagonally downward and forward with one hand while the other is "smoothing" the fabric forward. This smoothing action greatly reduces the effort needed to get a snug fit. Notice that although the "weave" seems to be angling forward at the bottom, the pattern will line up when the center portion is fitted. A little care at this point pays high dividends in the end. Figure 9-39, with the pronounced plaid pattern, vividly illustrates the vertical orientation concept that is so essential to quality work. Notice that the decking is the same fabric as the cover. Seldom is any effort made to match the pattern of a deck to the arm, back or seat panels. This is rather obvious in this photo.

7. Stay tack the bottom, front in place. This is the *third* of the four-point stay (see Fig. 9-40 for positioning).

8. Complete the last of the four-point stay by tacking the outside front, also indicated in Fig. 9-40. Notice how the downward stretch on both inside and outside has almost formed the rounding for the top of the arm. With the four-point stay in place, final fitting and tacking is greatly simplified.

Go to the rear of the unit and snug the bottom strip, assuring that the tab seats against the bottom, back rail. Staple in place, Fig. 9-41. Next, tighten and staple the middle strip in place as indicated in Fig. 9-42. Complete the inside portion of the rear IA by tacking the top strip as shown in Fig. 9-43. Remove the second stay tack at the outside rear of the arm, if necessary (and it usually is!), tighten the outside bottom of the panel and

Fig. 9-39. Vertical orientation of IA pattern or weave is essential.

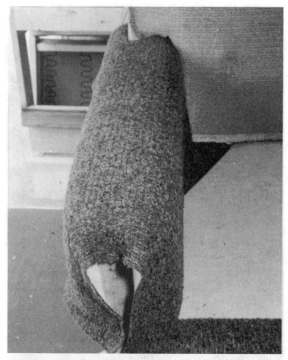

Fig. 9-40. Fourth of four-point stay in place.

staple in place at the rear of the back post as shown in Fig. 9-44. Notice the staple holding the panel just beneath and to the left of the staple gun? This staple *must* be below the level at which the outside arm panel is to be attached in order to conceal the staple when the OA panel is fitted.

Finish stapling the rear of the panel in place. By folding any excess underneath all wrinkles and looseness in the fabric can be removed. Snug and staple the outside portion of the panel in place, making sure that all staples will be below the line where the top of the outside arm is to attach. Return to the front and form and staple both sides to the stump. Notice that stapling of the inside portion proceeds from the bottom toward the top (Fig. 9-45) but does not go all the way. Leave about 3 inches to finish later. The top is the *last* portion to fit and contour. Figure 9-45 also shows the operator making the last angular fit to smooth the outer portion of the panel. Notice the direction of tension (shown by arrow), down and inward, keeping all wrinkles out. When the precise position of this last fold has been identified, as shown in Fig. 9-45, lift the folded

Fig. 9-41. Fitting and stapling bottom, rear strip of IA panel.

Fig. 9-42. Attaching middle strip of the IA panel.

Fig. 9-43. Snugging and attaching top strip of IA panel.

Fig. 9-44. Fitting and tucking rear, outside portion of inside arm.

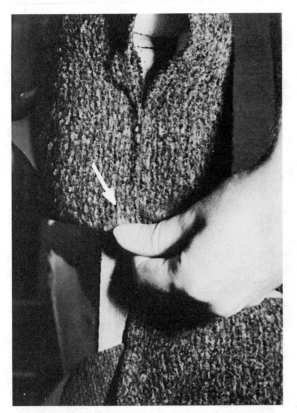

Fig. 9-45. Final fitting of front, outside IA panel at arm stump.

material to staple the bottom edge in place, Fig. 9-46. Return the fabric as shown in Fig. 9-45 and staple.

Now, go to the top and start the problem-solving process to determine exactly where the tucks are to be made. This is done by "experimenting" to see what looks good to *you*. There is no "absolute" in this case, it is a matter of preference. Whatever is done, be sure that all tucks will result in the folds facing downward so they do not create "dust catchers". Figure 9-47 shows the top being formed. In this case, there were to be only two tucks to form the top. This gives a mildly "squared" or flat-top look to the arm.

Figure 9-48 shows an arm that will have a more rounded top. The operator is adjusting the inside, front of the panel to make the *second* stay tack. The *first* stay on *this* arm was made near the top of the outside, front, just beneath the foam, Fig. 9-48. In this case, the operator is "smoothing" the fabric up the outside, around and over the top, and is pulling straight down to assure alignment of the stripes. Angled stripes at this point will destroy the final appearance. The same down-and-in diagonal snugging into the seat panel results in a smooth, tight appearance, Fig. 9-49. Smoothing toward the rear is being done in Fig. 9-50 to assure a tight fit as well as straight pattern alignment.

A rolled front edge of the arm stump is being finished in preparation for a narrow panel that will be used to finish the front of the arm stump (Fig. 9-51). Notice also that the top is still the last portion to be finished? Final tacking of the outside bottom of the arm is shown in Fig. 9-52. To finish off the arm front with a rounded top, multiple tucks are taken, close together, and stapled in-line or at a slight angle as illustrated in Fig. 9-53.

INSIDE BACK INSTALLATION

The couch shown in Fig. 9-54 has been reupholstered from the frame out with all new materials. It is of the hard-edge design and is now

Fig. 9-46. Making the under-tack to hold front, outside, bottom of IA panel in place.

ready for the installation of the inside back panel. A 9-inch wide channel construction, made with one inch foam was chosen. (How to make this kind of channel is discussed in Chapter 8.)

When it comes to installing an inside back panel, one of the handiest "tricks of the trade" is to lay the unit on its back so the panel will lay naturally on the padding, Fig. 9-55. (The centers of the top and bottom back rails should have been marked before putting that unit on its back.) The center of the back panel should also be marked (or at least identified for sure) to assure alignment of the panel to the frame. With the above details taken care of, proceed in the following manner:

1. Lay the panel on the back, as illustrated in Fig. 9-56, so the foam just reaches the back edge of the top rail. Make sure that the centers line up by rolling the top of the panel back to the mark on the frame. Establish sufficient material to tack at the top and tuck the center portion of the bottom in, as illustrated in the photo. Notice the chalk mark on the decking? That is the center mark and helps in aligning the back panel.

2. Tuck the bottom in, progressing from the center toward the ends, leaving a foot or so free for fitting to the arms. Cut the foam approximately an inch oversize so that it will press against all parts

Fig. 9-47. Making the final tucks to form top section of the inside arm.

Fig. 9-48 Assuring alignment of pattern for rounded inside arm.

Fig. 9-49. Angular pull to form and tighten inside, bottom portion of IA panel.

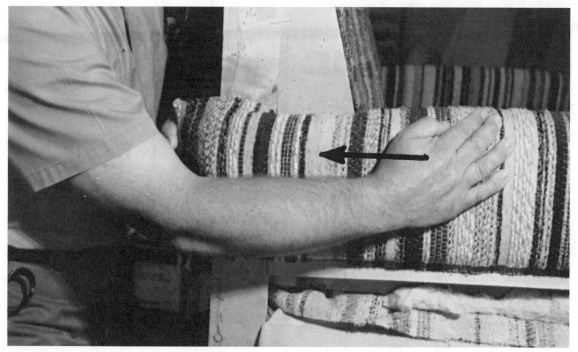

Fig. 9-50. Smoothing for the final adjustment for tacking outside, rear portion of IA panel.

Fig. 9-51. Forming rolled edge at front of arm stump.

of the arm as shown in Fig. 9-57. Note that the backing is cut out along with the foam. (The piece laying on top of the back panel in this Figure is the cut-out.)

3. Make the Y-cuts as illustrated in Fig. 9-58. The two cuts shown are to provide a pulling strip (A) along the inside of the arm, (B—marked with chalk) to cover around back above the arm to the back post, and (C) a strip that goes beneath the bottom back rail. The top cut is located so that it leads directly to the crown, if it were to be projected all the way. Notice that the cut **does not go all the way to the arm**. This is essential to permit the fabric to tuck beneath the back foam and be totally concealed from view, even when the back is depressed. The bottom cut is made such that the tab will meet the front of the bottom, back rail when pulled taut. (*Tip:* Tuck the cover in to identify where it meets the rail, then pull it out again to make the cut.)

4. Tuck the pulling strips ("A" and "C", Fig.

Fig. 9-52. Working from bottom, outside to form rolled edge.

222

Fig. 9-53. Rounded arm is formed with multiple tucks and stapled diagonally as shown.

Fig. 9-54. Back padded and ready for inside back panel.

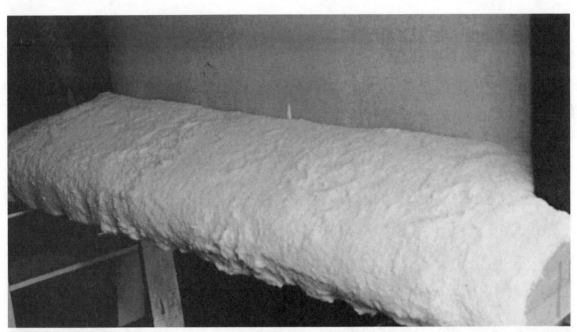

Fig. 9-55. To make fitting of IB easier, lay unit on its back.

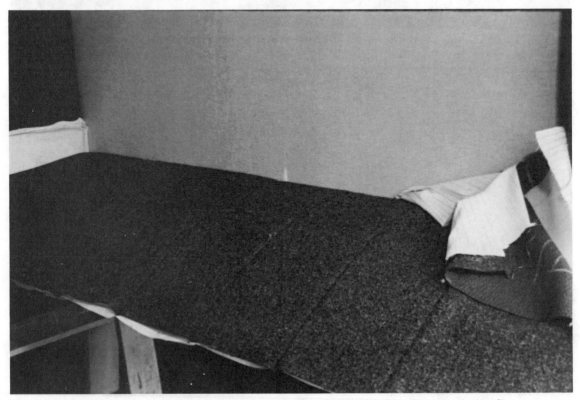

Fig. 9-56. Laying and tucking a channeled back in place. (Notice the chalked center mark on decking?)

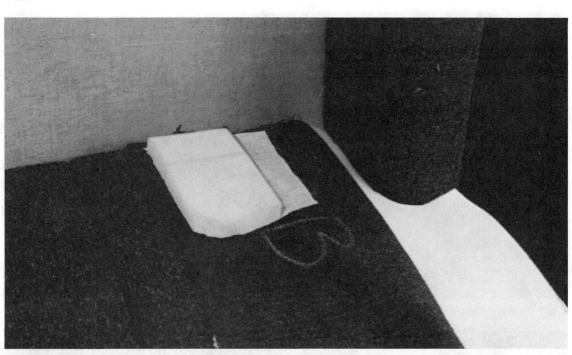

Fig. 9-57. Corner of padding and backing fabric cut out for arm.

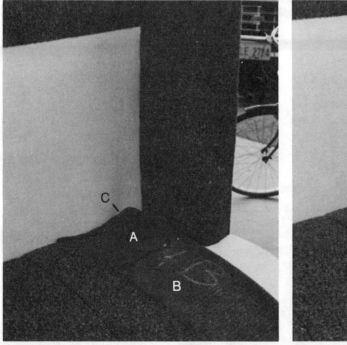

Fig. 9-58. Y-cuts made in IB panel to fit at IA crown and bottom back rail. (Flap (C) goes under rail, (A) along inside of arm (B) around outside to back post.)

Fig. 9-59. Inside back fitted to arm, bottom tucked in and is ready to fit along top.

Fig. 9-60. Stay tacking channel seams to marked top, back rail.

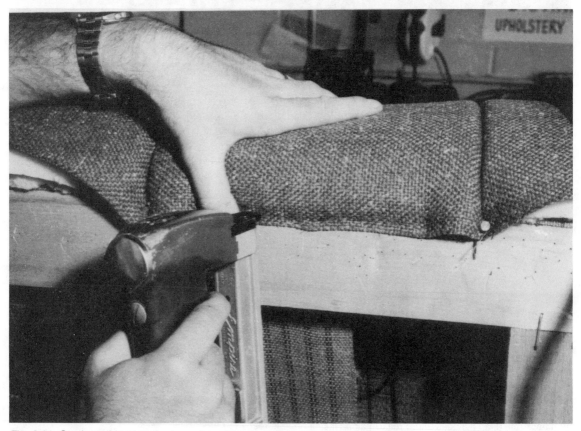

Fig. 9-61. Staple and level each channel, working from the center toward the seams.

Fig. 9-62. View of back ready to fit channel seams.

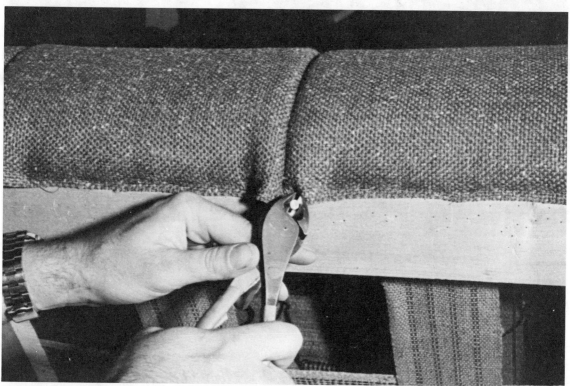

Fig. 9-63. Removing stay tacks.

Fig. 9-64. Channel seam ready to be fitted.

Fig. 9-65. Folding excess fabric from one side over to meet at seam mark (not visible).

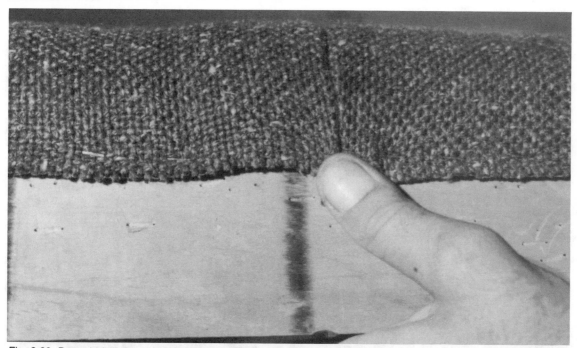
Fig. 9-66. Properly fitted channel back seam ready for stapling.

Fig. 9-67. Finished channel seam.

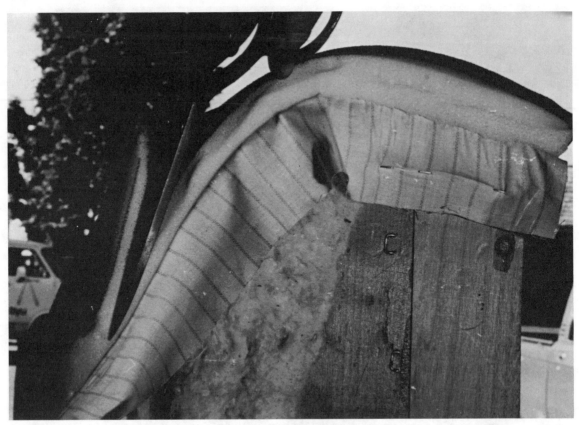

Fig. 9-68. Trimming outer edge of foam at a 45 degree angle to make rounded edge.

9-58) through their appropriate spots at both ends to continue fitting the back. It will appear something like Fig. 9-59. Then place the unit on its base (the legs have probably been removed) to attach the top.

5. First, stay tack the center, identified by the "C" with the letter "L" going through it. In this case a channel seam was selected as center. Marks have been made on the frame for each of the other channels, stay tack each channel seam in place as shown in Fig. 9-60.

6. Start in the center of each channel and, forming the top to a consistent height, staple to within one inch of each stay, Fig. 9-61. Repeat this process for all channels, Fig. 9-62.

7. Now, go back and remove all the stays, Fig. 9-63. The channel back will appear as Fig. 9-64.

8. Fold the excess fabric from one side so the outer fold will lie on the mark, Fig. 9-65. (Alas, the mark is not visible in this photo. Sorry!)

9. Fold the opposing side in like manner, Fig. 9-66, and staple in place. The finished channel will appear as Fig. 9-67.

10. Go to the extreme sides and trim off the outer edge of the foam at a 45 degree angle. See Fig. 9-68. This will give a feathering effect and a smooth rounding as the cover is pulled around and tacked to the back post. Follow fitting procedures much the same way as done for the IA panel.

Chapter 10

Installing Outside Cover Panels

The outside panels are among the easiest of all the work in upholstering furniture. This is also the more exciting of the process. It is like putting the capstone on a monumental work (and for the beginner, reupholstering that first unit may seem just that—a monumental work!).

OUTSIDE ARMS

There are dozens of shapes to outside arm panels. But, regardless of the shape, the same principles hold true for all of them. In fastening outside panels the majority of work will be blind tacked. That is, the panels are to be attached, but the means of attachment will not be visible. The three popular blind tacking methods are accomplished with (1) tacking strip, (2) tack strip, and (3) flexible tack strip (see glossary for specific definitions).

Installing Rigid Tacking Strip

Rigid tacking strip is used anywhere an outside panel is to be installed having a straight top edge.

Units with straight arms, straight-top backs, bands with straight edges, and almost all skirts will make use of the rigid tacking strip.

1. The first step is to locate and spot tack the panel along the top edge. For an outside arm this will be just beneath the arm rest. One approach, not the preferred one, is to staple the front first, allowing sufficient for any covering that is to be done on the front of the post or stump (Fig. 10-1). Then, stretch the panel to take out any wrinkles, and spot tack along the edge. *Note*: Keep the staples a little way from the very top where the fabric will be folded down. The tacking strip must conceal all spot tacking, thus achieving a nice, smooth, straight edge.

A second, and preferred, approach is to start at the center of the panel, (Fig. 10-2), and spot tack while stretching the fabric toward each end (Fig. 10-3).

2. Cut an appropriate length of tacking strip. Shears may be used to cut this rather stiff cardboard strip, but dikes work extremely well (Fig. 10-4). (The length should be 3/4" to 1" short at

231

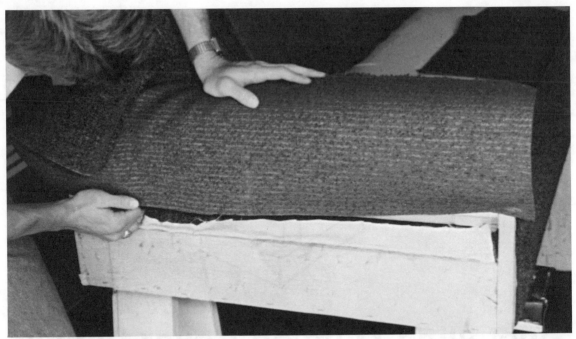

Fig. 10-1. Aligning an outside arm (OA) panel.

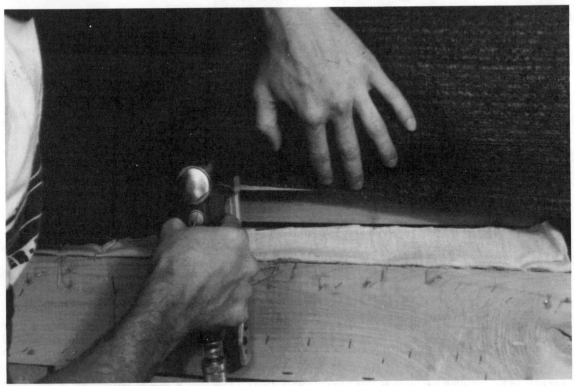

Fig. 10-2. Placing tacking outside arm panel.

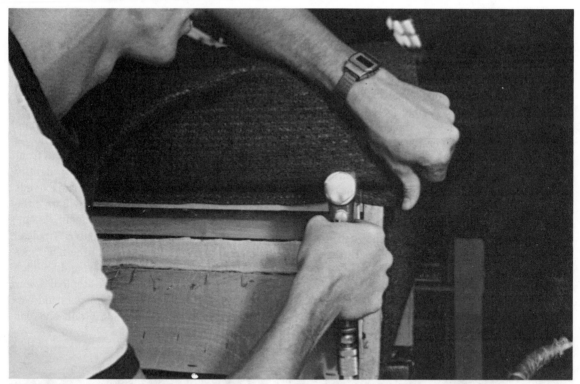

Fig. 10-3. Stretching OA to complete place tack.

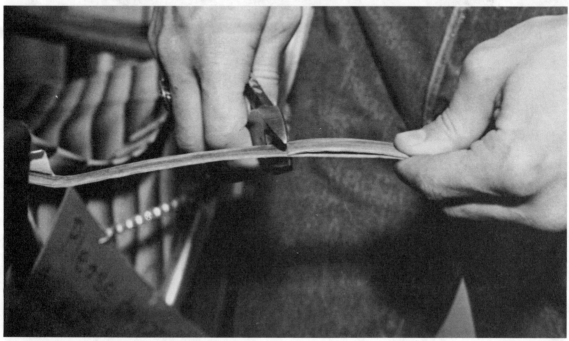

Fig. 10-4. Cutting the heavy tacking strip with dikes.

each end where other blind tacking material is to be used.)

3. Lay the tacking strip along the stapled edge and, working from the center out, staple in place. *Tip* 1: Keeping the staples (or tacks) close to the top edge of the tacking strip will give the best results—keeping that top edge tight against the frame. *Tip* 2: If very heavy, thick fabric is used, or there are multiple layers, (as with a welt, plus the inside panel, plus the outside panel), it is advisable to install the staples at a diagonal, as shown being done in Fig. 10-5. This will prevent the inside edge of the tacking strip from "pooching" out and creating an objectionable ridge in the panel when it is pulled down. Figure 10-6 shows the tacking strip in place, barely visible beneath the OA panel.

Padding the Outside Arm

Frequently, it may be desirable to pad the out-side panels (arm and back). Padding the outsides gives a more plush, softer appearance to the whole unit. On units having a low profile, like the one currently being shown, attaching a layer of 1/4″ or 1/2″ soft foam will do nicely. No additional base is needed because of the narrow span to cover (refer to Fig. 10-6). The foam has been stapled along the top edge (Fig. 10-7), over the top of the tacking strip. Notice that it is stapled sparingly, just enough to hold it in place without sags. (The bottom front corner has been folded under to clearly identify what is happening.) Note also that the foam extends about 1/4″ beyond the bottom. This will give the edge a "soft" appearance. With soft foam, it compresses to the point that no objectionable "ripples" will be created. *Note*: This is one of the few cases where a padding material will go around an edge onto the surface to which it will be stapled! A few staples along the front and back uprights and bottom rail will hold it in place. Spray adhesive can also be used.

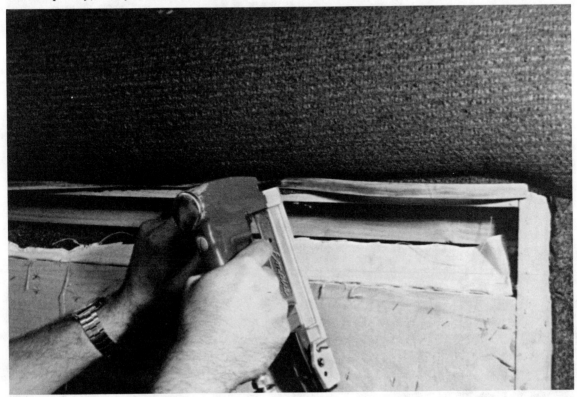

Fig. 10-5. Begin stapling tacking strip at center.

Fig. 10-6. Tacking strip finished for OA. Notice angular placement of staples, panel identification, and orientation mark (chalk mark at extreme top right of panel).

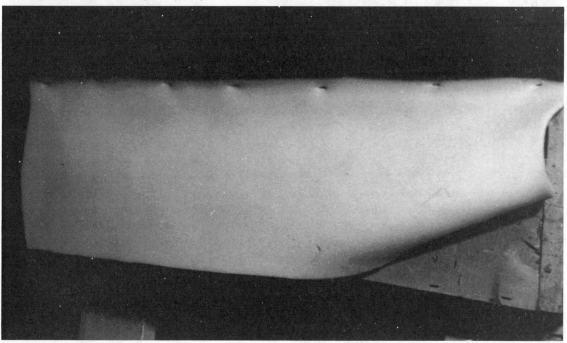

Fig. 10-7. Place tacking a 1/4-inch foam pad for OA.

235

Now, back to finish the outside arm panel. Pull the panel down, near the center, and staple (Fig. 10-8). (Notice abundant material for pulling. This is much better than not having quite enough.) Stretch the bottom, front corner on a diagonal as indicated by the arrow, Fig. 10-9, and tack on the bottom. Pull down the fabric between staples (Figs. 10-8 and 10-9) to align the pattern and staple in place along the bottom of the rail. Figure 10-10 shows the small rolled edge being formed from the OA panel for a narrow panel to be installed on the arm stump.

COVERING A ROLL-OVER SIDE

Although this cannot really be classified as an arm, it comes closer to that than any other part. This is a very low, padded, rather solid end to a bench-type seat having a low, vertical back. In this case, the outside "arm" panel actually starts on the inside, rolls over the top, and finishes off the outside as well. In covering this style, a useful "trick-of-the-trade" is also shown. Figure 10-11 shows a Y-cut made for the back post. *Tip* 1: Note that in this case the tab will remain upright and be stapled to the post rather than be tucked down. This will create a fabric "bridge" that will make it impossible to have frame wood showing when the back panel is pulled down over it. *Tip* 2: The outside flap is also left up and will be stapled in place to create another fabric "bridge."

After the bottom, center is stapled in place, the corners are stretched diagonally and stapled. In Fig. 10-12 the fabric is being stapled to the side of the rear upright because a narrow panel will be installed to finish off the upright. Notice the upward curve to the fabric pattern? This will be taken out when the center portion of the panel, between the staples, is fitted and stapled.

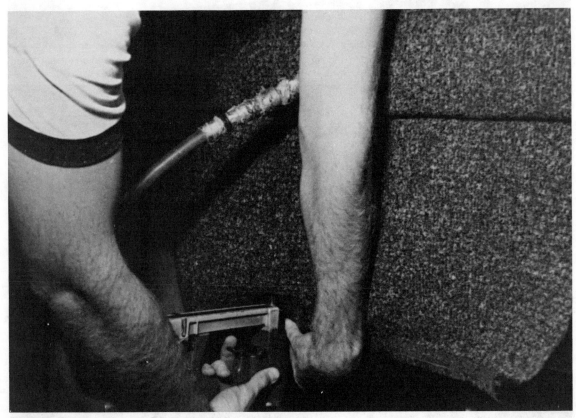

Fig. 10-8. Stretch and staple OA, working from center outward.

236

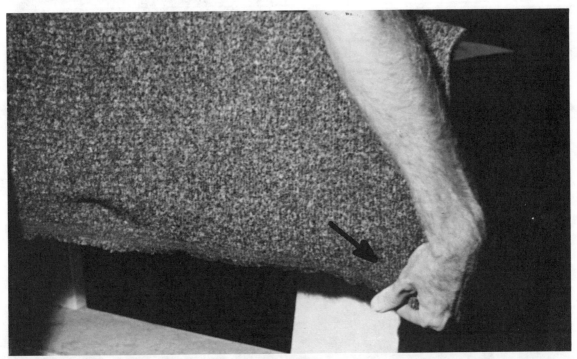

Fig. 10-9. Stretch diagonally (arrow) to fit front and rear of panel.

INSTALLING FLEXIBLE TACKING STRIP

Flexible tacking strip is used to attach panels having curved edges. In the earlier days of the industry all of this type of work was either sewn on with the blind stitch or applied with decorative tacks. All three methods are still in use and each has its specialty. For example:

Blind stitching is about the only method that can be used where there is no frame immediately beneath the locations where the attachment is to be made. It is extremely economical (in materials), requiring only the sewing thread to complete the job. Stitching requires a bit more craftsmanship and time than either of the other two methods.

Decorative tacks are used, as the name implies, to add a distinctive decoration to the installation, and where the presence of the raised heads will not be objectionable. One such objection would be found in using decorative tacks to apply the backs to dinette chairs that will be used near walls or against wood or painted furnishings. The tacks will mar such surfaces significantly! A requirement for using tacks is that there must be framing material

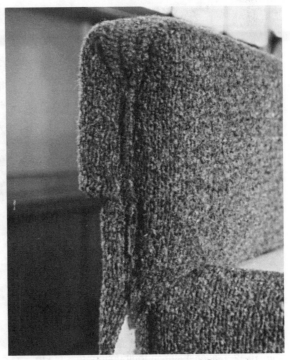

Fig. 10-10. Forming small roll at front of OA panel.

237

Fig. 10-11. Y-cut to fit OA to back post.

Fig. 10-12. Diagonal stretch to fit bottom rear of OA.

238

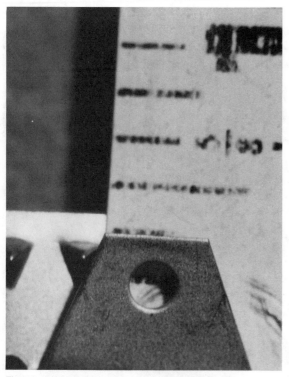

Fig. 10-13. View of flexible tacking strip showing "grippers", attaching hole, folded dimension, and overlap.

in the area of the attachment. Of the three methods, this is the most expensive in materials as the tacks are comparatively costly.

Flexible tacking strip (with brand names of "Curve-Ease" and "Pli-Grip") finds its "specialty" application anywhere curved surfaces are involved and the presence of tacks is undesirable. It can be accomplished with relative speed and ease. Material cost is almost negligible. Like tacks, framing beneath points of attachment is a must! Figure 10-13 shows the back view of the tacking strip with a pronged tab folded over, as it would be in an actual application. Two prongs are visible on the left side, these will grip the fabric as they are pressed toward the frame of the chair. The rear tab (front, Fig. 10-13) has a hole punched in it through which a tack or one leg of a staple will pass, attaching it to the frame. The cloth measuring tape has been inserted between the two tabs to show their dimensions. *Note*: The pronged (gripping) tab is 7/16″, the attaching tab is 3/8″. *Tip*:

Leave a space a little more than 1/16″ between the edge of the attaching tab and where the finished edge of the fabric is to be located. This is to allow for the added 1/16″ length of the gripping tab plus the thickness of the fabric. The following procedure is used when installing flexible tacking strip.

1. Locate the flexible tacking strip about 1/16″ from the edge to be finished. Bare wood was used in Fig. 10-14 to illustrate this concept. The position of the staple gun shown is one way to assure that the staple will go through the hole (Notice the curvature of the outside edge of the hole?).

2. Continue attaching the strip to within 2″ of the point it is to terminate and cut it off with a pair of tin snips. Aviation snips, as shown in Fig. 10-15, are preferred by many operators. Figure 10-16 shows the flexible tacking strip applied to an outside arm of a recliner.

3. Align, mark, and trim the panel. Figure 10-17 shows a panel that has been stay tacked to the bottom (Notice the very bottom of the photo.), stretched and stay tacked at both front and back

Fig. 10-14. Attaching flexible tacking strip. (Note particularly the position of the attaching tab and staple gun.)

239

Fig. 10-15. Cutting flexible tacking strip to length with tin (aviation) snips.

Fig. 10-16. Flexible tacking strip in place on OA.

Fig. 10-17. OA panel pinned (top), stay tacked (ends and bottom), tucked behind flexible tacking strip, and marked for trimming to contour.

(not shown), formed over the projecting edge of the strip (distinguishable by the dark line just above the chalk mark), and marked with chalk. The easiest way to accurately mark the contour is to thus locate the panel, hold it in place, and then rub the side of the chalk along the edge of the metal. It marks the cover extremely accurately. Remove the skewers and trim the fabric about 7/16" beyond the mark as shown in Fig. 10-18.

4. Lock the fabric around the toothed segments (Fig. 10-19). Most of this work can be done by pressing the fabric around with the fingers. *Tip* 1: A skewer is a real handy helper to move around the fabric accurately. *Tip* 2: Keep the panel taut during the tucking under process to eliminate those unwanted guests, the "puckers," that will otherwise surely appear later.

5. Press the gripping tabs over against the frame. *Tip*: Fabric slippage can be prevented by pressing inward just inside the metal edge with one hand, as is being done by the left hand of the operator in Fig. 10-20, and pressing the nearby tabs over with the other thumb. The panel to the right of the operator's right arm has been folded into place.

6. Seat the tabs firmly against the frame. One handy way to do this is to use a piece (about 2 1/2" × 4" × 3/4") of close grained hard wood, like maple, cherry or birch to tap the tabs firmly in place. A short dowel "handle" was added to the one pictured in Fig. 10-21.

7. Restretch the bottom and ends of the panel, if necessary, and staple in place. The finished job will look like Fig. 10-22.

Fig. 10-18. Trimming OA panel to contour (3/8 of an inch beyond chalk mark).

Fig. 10-19. Attaching OA panel to grippers using skewer to help align.

242

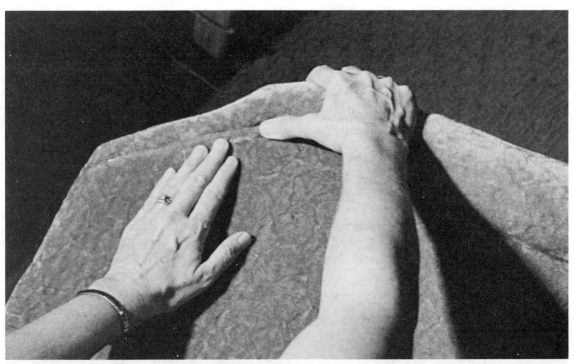

Fig. 10-20. Maintaining tension on panel while folding tabs down.

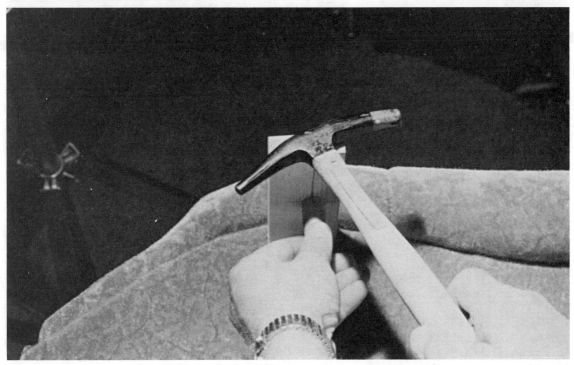

Fig. 10-21. "Setting" flexible tacking strip with hardwood block.

THE OUTSIDE BACK

Outside backs are installed in much the same manner as the outside arm.

1. Start with the top, center the pattern (Fig. 10-23), and spot tack in place. Figure 10-24 shows the center staple being set.

2. Stretch the fabric sideways and spot tack to the sides of the unit. Notice that rather long spans, Fig. 10-25, can be taken when making the stretch. A few staples will be set later between those shown, just to hold the edge in proper alignment.

3. Measure, cut and install the tacking strip as indicated earlier in Figs. 10-4 through 10-6. Figure 10-26 clearly shows the diagonal stapling of one of the heavier tacking strips. (It can be identified as a heavy tacking strip because of the greater-than-normal spacing between the staples.)

4. Measure and cut two pieces of tack strip to length, as indicated in Fig. 10-27. *Tip*: The top of the strip should be in line with the top edge of the tacking strip and the bottom will end 1/4 to 1/2 inch short of the bottom of the seat rail.

5. Position the tack strip. *Tip*: Best results will be achieved if the panel is trimmed so there is about 3/4" to be rolled under. (The "rolling under" will be explained shortly!) Align the inside edge of the strip (with the tacks pointing out) along the inside edge of the welt (if welt is used—and it was in this case!), as illustrated in Fig. 10-28.

6. Set the tack strip. Hold the strip carefully, and faithfully, in position while lightly pulling the

Fig. 10-22. Completed flexible tacking strip application.

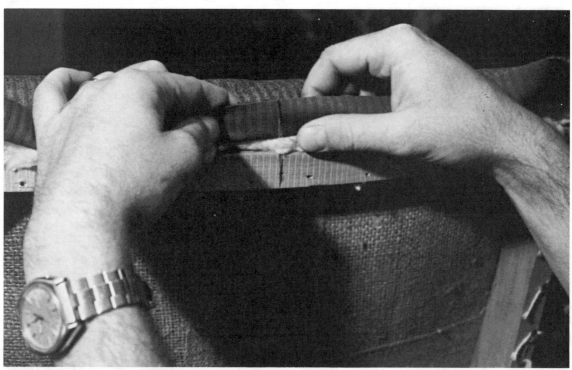

Fig. 10-23. Locating marked centers outside back (OB) panel and top rail.

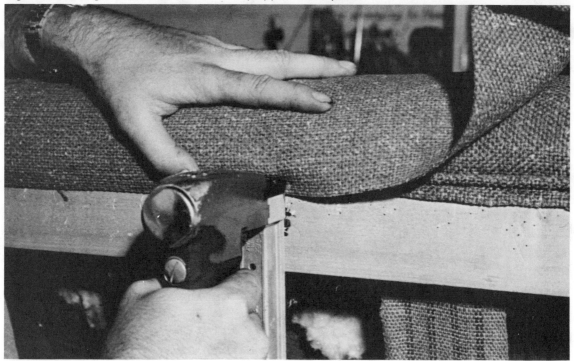

Fig. 10-24. Place tacking OB panel prior to attaching tacking strip.

Fig. 10-25. Example of length of run in place tacking OB to couch. Note center line notation at right.

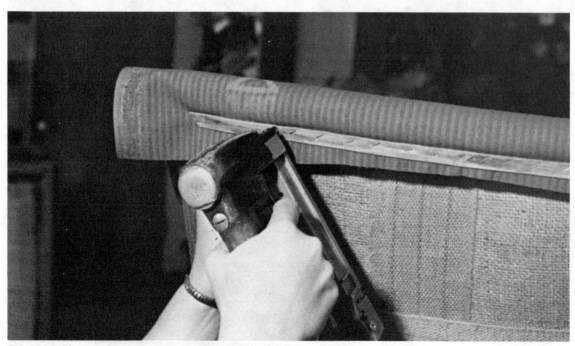

Fig. 10-26. Diagonal stapling of tacking strip on OB panel.

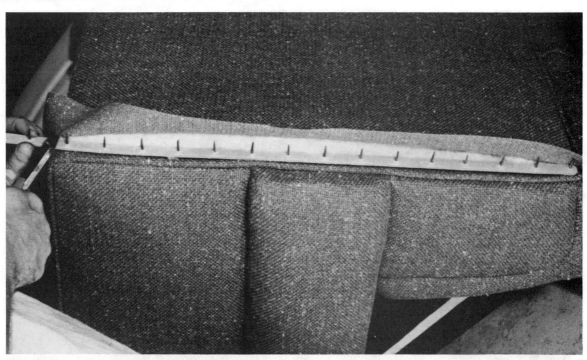

Fig. 10-27. Measuring and cutting tack strip to length.

fabric over the tacks and setting it partially onto the tacks, Fig. 10-29. *Tip*: Push the fabric over **All** tacks, then go back and set the fabric all the way to the strip base. Puckers will be created if you first try to set the fabric all the way down for each tack!

7. Roll the tack strip and fabric inward. It should require a slight stretching to get the, now, *outer edge* of the strip to coincide with the *inner edge* of the welt. If it does not take a little effort to tighten the fabric or if it cannot be stretched far enough, remove the strip and start over, making adjustment as necessary. *The fabric must be taut!* But, not so taut that fingernails are broken trying to put it in place, however.

8. Set the tack strip. Ideally, the tacks will be angled slightly outward so that when the strip is set, it will tend to tighten the fabric just a little bit more. Use the side of the tack hammer (Fig. 10-30), a hard, white rubber mallet, or a rawhide mallet (refer to Fig. 2-13) to set the strip. **Caution**: The major force must be centered over the heads of the tacks (Fig. 10-31), not between them, otherwise the strip will be destroyed and perhaps the fab-

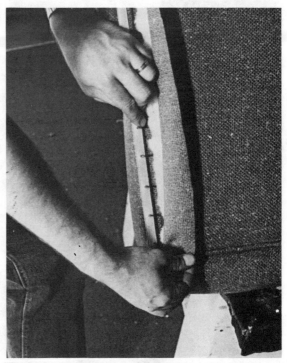

Fig. 10-28. Locating tack strip for OB panel installation.

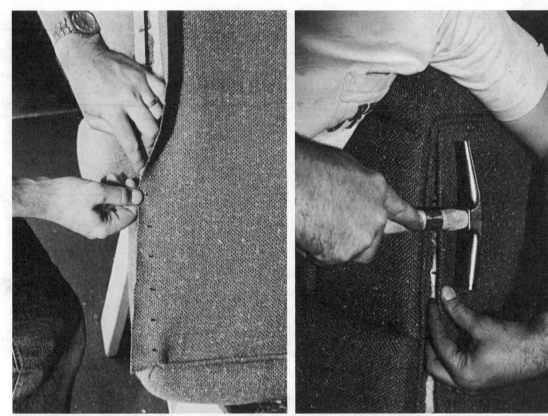

Fig. 10-29. Affixing side of OB panel to tack strip.

Fig. 10-30. Tack strip rolled under ready to set tacks.

Fig. 10-31. Apply driving pressure directly over tack heads (not between them).

ric damaged!

Tip: Occasionally, when using the tack hammer the hard steel side may cut some fabrics due to the pressure needed to drive the tacks into some of the harder woods (like oak). To avoid that cutting action, place a couple layers of scrap fabric over the strip to finish setting the tacks. Figure 10-32 shows a finished outside back.

Offset Backs

Occasionally a unit will have a little jog along the sides of the back, and a single, straight tack strip cannot be used. In those cases use two pieces for each side. A little problem solving is needed for each case, but all cases are rather similar.

1. Cut and install the top tack strips. These should end at the point where the "jog" takes place. *Tip*: It will probably be necessary to make a short diagonal cut into the fabric at this point to permit the top flap to be folded under with the strip, and another flap to fold under to create a finished edge at the "jog." Figure 10-33 shows a back with the top tack strips installed.

2. Cut and install the bottom two tack strips in the same manner indicated above. Figure 10-34 shows the finished back with a jog (Difficult to find, isn't it?).

CAMBRIC

Cambric has a "face side" and a "back side." The face side is the shiny side, the back side, rather dull (Fig. 10-35). The face side goes to the outside, just as with any other fabric. Although rather simple in installation, a few "tricks" may prove helpful.

1. Measure the major dimensions of the bottom (Fig. 10-36) to determine the size to cut. Allow 1/2" to 1" per side to be folded under. Less can be used when necessary as all that is really needed is

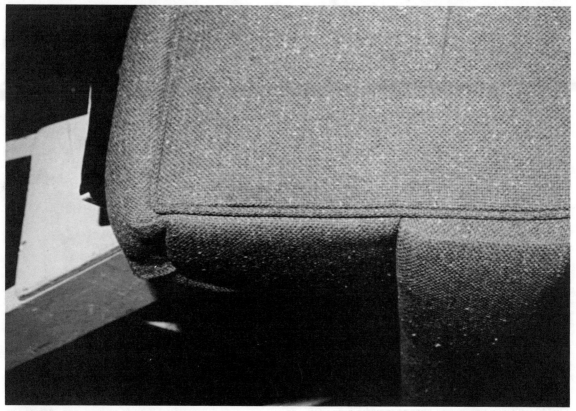

Fig. 10-32. Finished end of OB panel on a sofa.

Fig. 10-33. First steps in installing OB panel with a bottom width wider than the top.

Fig. 10-34. Done properly, a change in width in the OB panel is nearly invisible.

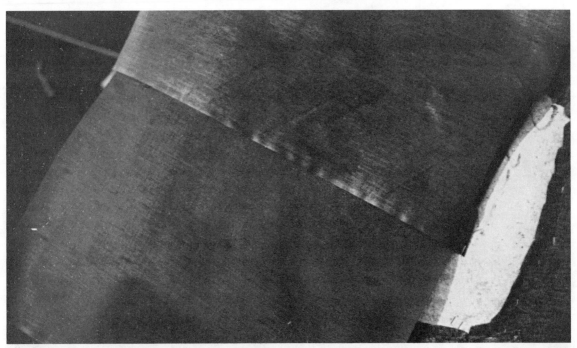

Fig. 10-35. View of cambric showing outside (shiny) and underside (dull) of the fabric.

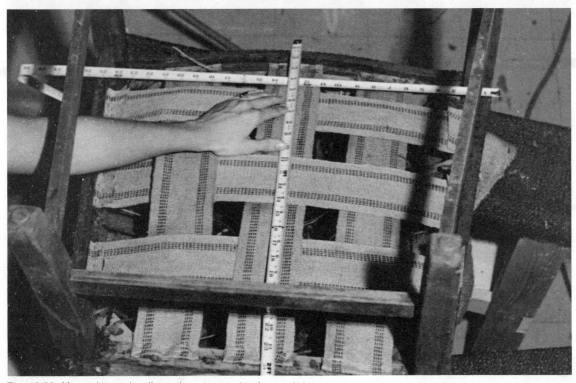

Fig. 10-36. Measuring major dimensions to get size for cambric.

Fig. 10-37. Locate and staple cambric at centers first.

enough to make a finished edge. The allowance suggested is a "quick" way to assure sufficient coverage without taking a lot of time to measure.

2. Anchor front and back centers, tucking a flap under to create a finished edge, Fig. 10-37. Staple near the edge of the fold, within 1/8" is best.

3. Fit around legs and staple to the bottoms of the rails whenever possible. Fig. 10-38 shows an unusual and rather awkward fitting. A better solution is shown in Fig. 10-39.

4. Make a diagonal cut to fit around legs when only two sides are to be finished. Refer back to Figs. 4-42 through 4-44.

5. Fold edges *under* and staple close to the folded edge to create a tight edge that won't be visible from normal sitting positions. Double fold corners rather than take the time to cut out excess.

Fig. 10-38. Improper tacking of old cambric around leg. (Note recessed tack driven into leg.)

Fig. 10-39. A somewhat better fitting of an old cambric around leg.

Fig. 10-40. Trimming cambric to match curved perimeters.

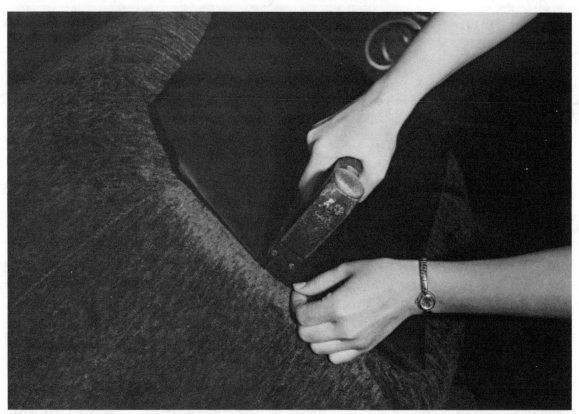

Fig. 10-41. Center stapling of cambric panel having curved perimeter.

When fitting to curved areas, trim the cambric to the outline, leaving the tuck-under allowance on all sides (Fig. 10-40). Tuck and staple the centers of four opposing positions and work around the contour to create the finished edge all around, Fig. 10-41.

Often, with the cambric installed, it is difficult to see or locate the mounting holes for leg brackets, or the t-nuts for the leg bolts. *Tip*: Use a stuffing regulator (ice pick) to prod for the holes. Little damage is done to the cambric and precise location can be achieved rather easily. Cut a " + " in the fabric where bolts must pass through. That eliminates fabric wrapping around the bolt as it is turned into the nut.

Chapter 11

Cushion Construction

This chapter on cushions will deal with those of a reversible or loose styling. No attempt will be made in this unit to cover (no pun intended) the particulars of cushions that are attached directly to the unit. In that light then, let us establish that all styles of cushions are started in quite the same manner, by determining the appropriate size and shape. To do this, one of three basic methods will generally be used whether the cushion is a Box, Knife-Edge, or Waterfall style. These three methods are: (1) patterns, usually most appropriate for producing multiple units of the same style and size; (2) measuring, to obtain length and width for cushions having rather straight, regular sides; and (3) tailoring, the most accurate method to match cushions to irregular or curving perimeters. Patterns are made and measuring and tailoring done after the deck and inside arms and back have been completely padded and covered. That is the only way the proper dimensions can be determined with reliability.

Once the orientation of the nap and cover pattern have been determined, as explained in Chapter 6, a few preliminaries must be attended to before actually getting to the cushion construction phase. These particulars are presented in Table 11-1. The considerations are listed in the left column, and the specific treatment under each cushion style.

The knife-edge cushion is made in two basic styles—(1) the mid-seam is made on the front and sides (for seat cushions) or top and sides (for back cushions), (2) the mid-seam is made only on the front seat or top back of the cushion. The two styles are specified in Table 11-1 for this style.

TAILORING

With all three cushion styles, one thickness of the main panel is smoothed onto the deck area, face side up, as shown in Fig. 11-1, with the front oriented properly. Smooth out the panel so that the back and sides are tucked under about even distances and let the excess extend over the front crown. Now, the tailoring process can begin.

1. Mark the perimeter with chalk (Fig. 11-1). This is done by holding the chalk vertical with the

Table 11-1. Preparations and Considerations for Tailoring Three Popular Cushion Styles.

Preparation & Consideration	Box Cushion	Waterfall Cushion	Knife-Edge Cushion
Number of Main Panels and Pattern Orientation	2 Panels Pattern or nap forward on both	1 Panel Pattern or nap forward on top, (will be reversed on bottom)	2 Panels Pattern or nap forward on both
Rough Cut Size of Cushion Panels	Max. width +2″ Max length +2″	Max. width +2″ Max. length +2″ +boxing thickness	Max. width +2″ Max length + boxing thickness
Boxing Style	Seams parallel to top and bottom (all 4 sides)	Seams parallel to top & bottom at sides & back (Rounded nose at front of sides)	TWO STYLES: Notched Corners No boxing Seams and welt at middle of sides Tucked Corners Seams parallel to top & bottom at sides & back (Rounded nose at front of side boxing)
Seam and Side Allowances	Back, sides & Front: 1/2″	Back and sides: 1/2″ each Front: width of finished boxing	TWO STYLES: Notched Corners— Front, back and sides: 1/2″ + 1/2 cushion thickness Tucked Corners— Front: 1/2″ + 1/2 cushion thickness Back and sides: 1/2″
Special Tucks	None	TWO STYLES: Square Corners— No tucks Rounded Corners— 1/4″at front seam lines	TWO STYLES: Notched Corners— No tucks Tucked Corners— 1/4″at front seam lines

back or arm and marking on the FACE side of the cushion panel as shown. *Tip:* The side of the chalk should be in line with but not pushing into, the padded back and inside arm at a point approximately half the cushion thickness from the deck level.

2. Mark the centerline or cushion line, whichever is appropriate, on the cushion panel to be in line with locating marks made on the unit. (Refer to Fig. 11-1, far right side.)

3. Mark the seat crown at both sides, Figs. 11-2 and 11-3. If a waterfall cushion, layoff two additional marks from the crown mark that measure 1/2 the cushion thickness each. Figure 11-4 shows these markings for the standard 3 1/2″ cushion. Fold the panel on the centerline aligning the weave or pattern and staple together inside the seam lines (Figs. 11-5 and 11-6). CAUTION: Be sure to not fold the panel at the seat crown mark!

4. Trim to seam allowances as indicated in the Table 11-1. Refer to Figs. 11-7 and 11-8.

5. For waterfall cushions, make tucks at crown marks (6 1/2″ and 10″ markings, Fig. 11-4) so the fold faces toward the centerline mark as

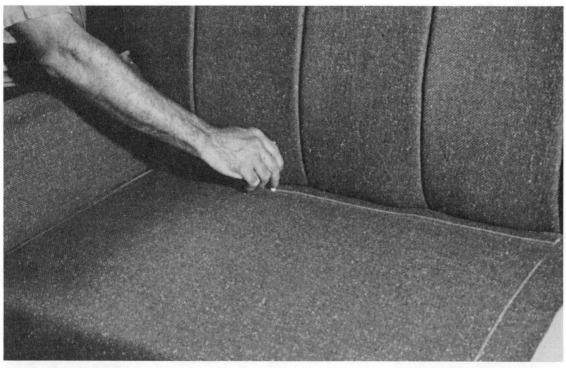

Fig. 11-1. Tailoring operation: marking centerline and perimeter for one of two waterfall couch cushions.

Fig. 11-2. Marking seat crown at end for waterfall cushion tailoring operation.

Fig. 11-3. Marking seat crown at center for one of two tailored waterfall cushions.

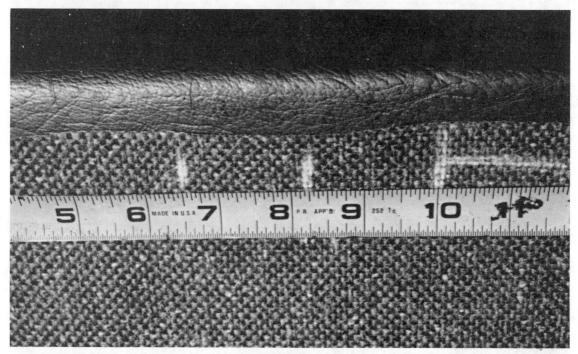

Fig. 11-4. Markings for "standard" 3 1/2-inch waterfall cushion: 8 1/4-inch mark is the centerline of waterfall cushion; 6 1/2-inch and 10-inch marks crown marks (or cushion thickness).

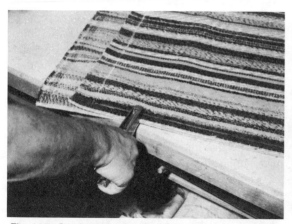

Fig. 11-5. Stapling marked waterfall cushion panel (folded along the centerline or 8 1/4-inch mark of Fig. 11-4) for trimming.

Fig. 11-6. Place staples inside the seam line to clear shear blade when trimming.

shown in Figs. 11-9 and 11-10. *Note:* The tucks should be approximately 1/4″ and terminate at the crown marks.

    6. Notch the centerline of both the cushion and boxing panels as indicated in Figs. 11-11 and 11-12. Round the front corners of both boxings as indicated in Fig. 11-12. Tailoring for the cushion is now complete.

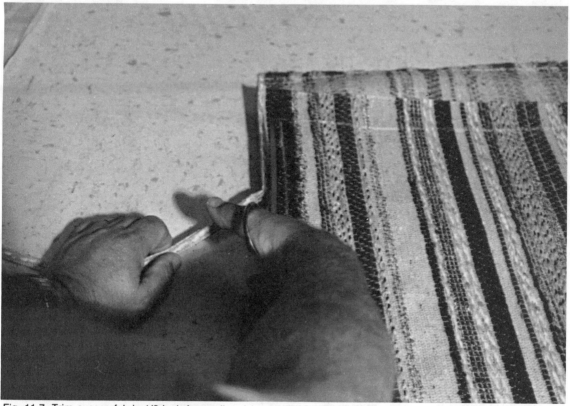

Fig. 11-7. Trim excess fabric 1/2 inch from tailored (seam) lines.

Fig. 11-8. Cushion panel trimmed to 1/2″ seam allowance.

CONSTRUCTION TECHNIQUES

Most cushions built for the furniture industry will make use of a zipper to facilitate stuffing and speed-up the closing process. In earlier times, many cushions were closed on the last or rear seam by hand sewing using the blind stitch. For those times a zipper would have been installed to make it easier to open and launder the cover. However, laundering no longer is much of a consideration; convenience and speed are the major reasons for including zippers in present practices.

Figure 11-13 shows a strip of #2 brass zipper stock and five glides—the preferred for most furniture upholstering. A dime has been included for size comparison along with one of the larger glides. (The larger glide would commonly be found on sleeping bags, tents, heavy jackets, etc.) Figure 11-14 shows a close-up view of the two opposite ends of a piece of zipper stock. The fabric has been trimmed as closely as possible from one side of each zipper in order to permit viewing the two in close proximity. "A" shows the cupped end while "B" reveals the opposite ball-end. This distinction is extremely important when it comes to installing the

Fig. 11-9. Fold tuck to each crown mark and staple for sewing (staple inside seam line).

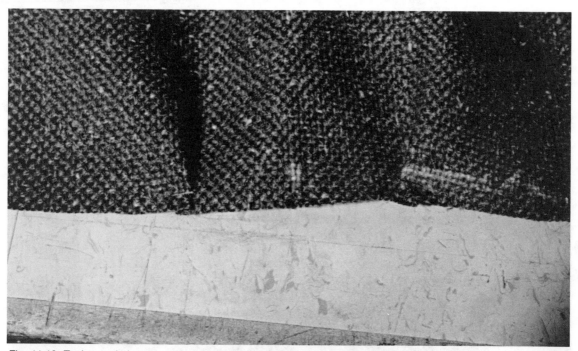

Fig. 11-10. Tucks stapled, ready to be sewn. (Note that tucks face toward centerline.)

Fig. 11-11. Notch at centerline of cushion panel for locating boxing center.

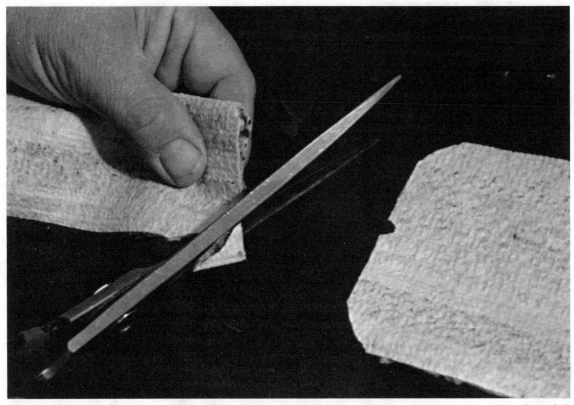

Fig. 11-12. Notching center and rounding corners of boxing front (left). Opened boxing showing center notch and rounded corners (right).

glide properly. The real problem here is that the glide can be put on either end, but will zip closed only when facing the right direction.

The ball-end of the zipper stock must point the same direction as the tapered end of the glide as shown in Fig. 11-15. To install the glide slip the square end down over the zipper stock (Fig. 11-16). While applying a light downward pressure on the glide with one finger (A), grasp the extreme top edges of the fabric and by rolling the hands away from each other at the top (B-B), attempt to separate the metal segments. This sometimes takes a little wiggling but is relatively simple to do. *Tip:* Raise the "pull" away from the glide body so the locking nib on the underside does not engage with the stock and prevent any movement. Notice in Fig. 11-16 that the pull is resting on the right thumb? That is to disengage the locking nib.

Once the glide has been installed onto the stock

slide it up and down to make sure it works smoothly. *Hint:* If it will open the zipper with ease but will not close with the same ease, chances are that the glide has been installed upside-down (from

Fig. 11-13. Zipper stock and Zipper glides. (Dime included for size comparison.)

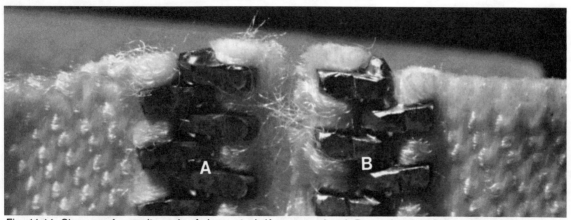

Fig. 11-14. Close-up of opposite ends of zipper stock (A = cupped end, B = pointed end).

the wrong end). Take it off, examine the ends carefully to assure the glide point facing the same direction as the ball-end of the stock and try again. How can it be taken off if it will not move? Just slide it all the way off the way it will move, opening the zipper completely! Ouch! Now the zipper is in two pieces, Fig. 11-17. Not to worry! That can be remedied with glowing ease! Start at the cupped end and roll the interlocking segments together as indicated in Fig. 11-18. By rolling from the bottom up, the segments can be felt making their interlocks. To speed up the process, once the bottom few segments are locked, place the zipper on a flat, smooth surface and with a pinching-rolling action, interlock the segments as illustrated in Fig. 11-19. Yet a faster way to completely close even the longest of zippers in a matter of seconds is to use a zipper glide that has been opened (It is no longer any good as a glide but a super closing tool!) and slide it along the top of the stock that is resting on a smooth, hard surface as shown in Fig. 11-20. *Note:* Not all zipper materials will work this way, but most upholstery stock will.

SEWING SEQUENCE (WATERFALL CUSHION)

The following sequence is suggested for sewing most styles of waterfall cushions. The one pictured in the sequence is a contemporary style, having no welt. However, as an aid for those who

would want to include a welt, the point at which the welt would be sewn on is also included.

1. Sew the first half of the zipper panel to the zipper stock (Fig. 11-21). *Note:* The 1/2" seam allowance has been folded under and the folded edge aligned with the center of the zipper stock. Proceed with the second half of the zipper panel so that the two folded edges meet over the center of the metal interlocks of the zipper (Fig. 11-22).

2. Sew the boxing (square end) onto the zip-

Fig. 11-15. Pointed end of zipper glide (Oriented the same as pointed end of zipper stock).

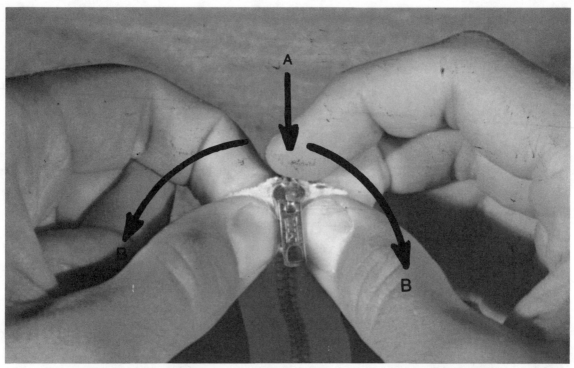

Fig. 11-16. Installing zipper glide onto zipper stock. (Arrows show direction of simultaneous pressures.)

Fig. 11-17. Zipper stock that has been separated. A problem? Not really!

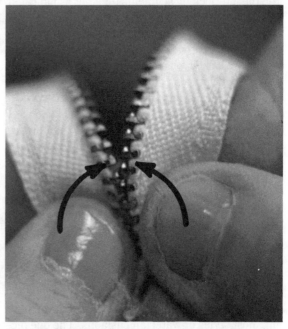

Fig. 11-18. Free-hand method of interlocking separated zipper stock. (Arrows indicate a rolling pressure to snap segments together.)

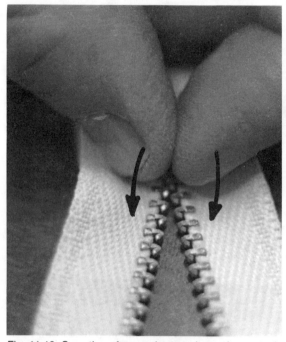

Fig. 11-19. Smooth-surface assist speeds up zipper stock interlocking. (Arrows indicate a rolling, pinching motion of the fingers.)

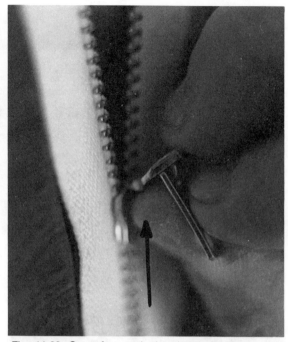

Fig. 11-20. Super-fast method to interlock zipper stock segments. (Straight-line run with opened zipper glide does the trick.)

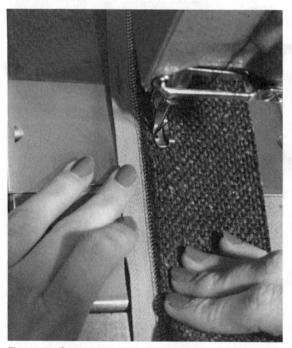

Fig. 11-21. Sewing folded first-half of zipper panel to zipper stock to create a concealed zipper.

Fig. 11-22. Sewing second-half of zipper panel to zipper stock.

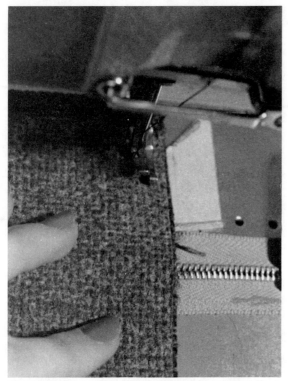

Fig. 11-23. Sewing boxing to completed zipper panel (face sides together).

per panel for trimming. (Some operators will make the zipper panel extra wide and trim it to the boxing width after sewing the boxings to the zipper.)

4. If welt is used: Sew welt to cushion panel so that the joining seam will be at the rear of the cushion. (On waterfall cushions, locate the single joining seam at the rear, bottom.) To join welt so the seam has the least bulk, follow this procedure.

a. Leave about 4″ of the welt free at both ends.

b. Unpick the ends of the welt strip, Fig. 11-27, so the fabric can be laid out flat where they will overlap (at least 3 inches from either end). This will be illustrated later.

c. Stretch the cushion panel and the overlapping welt panels taut to locate the center point (Fig. 11-28). Mark both welt strips at this point as shown.

d. Place opened welt strips face to face at center of chalk marks (Fig. 11-29). Push a skewer through the centers at the overlap point.

e. Place the skewered assembly on a flat surface and rotate the strips to be 90

per stock, Fig. 11-23. **Caution 1:** Be sure that the zipper glide has been installed before completing this step (refer to Fig. 11-37). **Caution 2:** Be sure that the fabric panels are face-side to face-side. (The excess zipper stock visible to the right of Fig. 11-23 will be trimmed off after the boxing has been attached.) *Tip:* Backstitching over the zipper stock (which is visible in Fig. 11-37) will reduce the tendency for the zipper to break through the thread.

3. Locate and mark the center of the zipper panel, Fig. 11-24, both sides. These marks are to be aligned with the center marks made (This is a hint!) in the cushion panel. Figure 11-25 shows a striped boxing sewn to the zipper panel. Notice that the stripes of the zipper panel will be aligned with the pattern on the cushion panels and that the boxing panel will have the pattern facing forward (the "down" direction). Figure 11-26 shows a seamstress marking the excess stock from the zip-

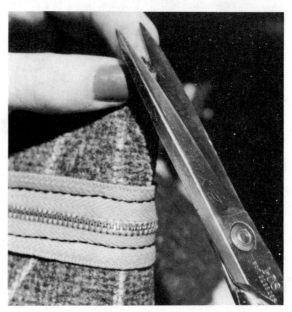

Fig. 11-24. Notching centers of zipper panel to align with rear, center of cushion panel.

Fig. 11-25. Trimmed boxing and zipper panel.

degrees to each other as illustrated in Fig. 11-30.

f. Hold the assembly in this position, remove the skewer and sew across diagonal corners such that when opened the strip will lay in-line and not overlapping itself (Fig. 11-31). *Hint:* To check this orientation, hold fingers at one of the diagonals and lay out the top strip. It will either lay on top of itself, or in-line; if on top of itself, sew the alternate diagonal.

g. Trim the excess to within 1/8″ to 1/4″ of the seam, Fig. 11-32, to reduce unnecessary bulk. Open the remaining flaps, shown at the left side of Fig. 11-33, to minimize remaining bulk.

h. Cut cording to make a butt joint at a spot not directly beneath the joint in the strip (Fig. 11-33).

i. Finish sewing the joined welt to the cushion panel (Fig. 11-34). The arrow points to the diagonal seam where the two ends of the welt are joined.

Fig. 11-26. Marking oversized (width) zipper panel for trimming prior to sewing to cushion panel.

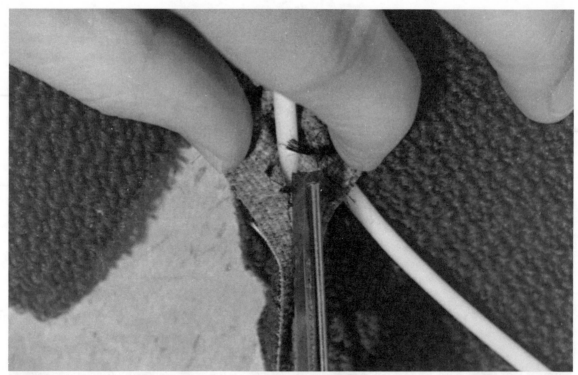

Fig. 11-27. Open both ends of welt at least 3 inches beyond overlap point.

Fig. 11-28. Marking welt at point of overlap.

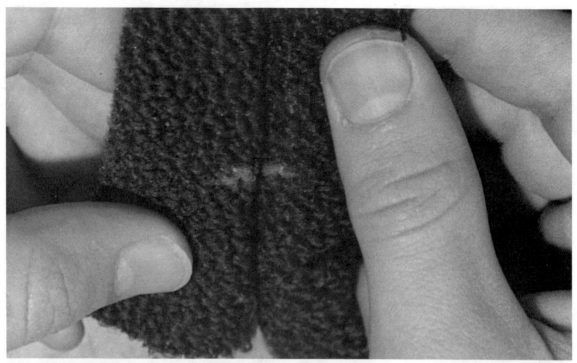

Fig. 11-29. Aligning centers of overlap marks (fabric is face to face).

Fig. 11-30. Pinned centers with top strip rotated 90 degrees to bottom strip.

Fig. 11-31. Sewing across diagonal.

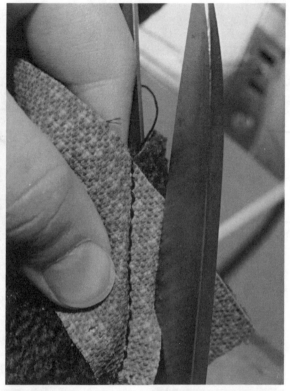

Fig. 11-32. Trim excess 1/8 inch to 1/4 inch from seam.

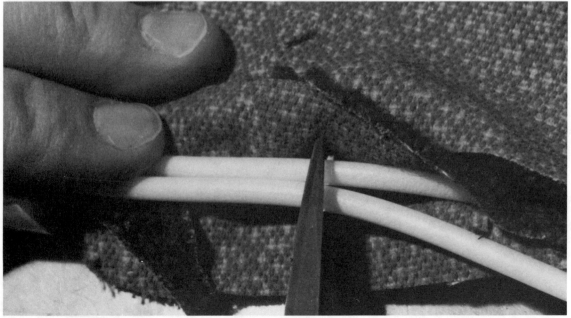

Fig. 11-33. Flattened seam with cording cut at point not beneath seam.

Fig. 11-34. Finish sewing joined welt to cushion panel. (Arrow points to diagonal joining seam.)

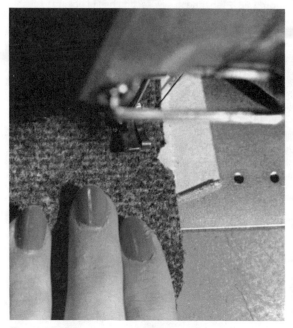

Fig. 11-35. Align boxing center with cushion center and sew around one side.

Fig. 11-36. Aligning zipper panel center with rear cushion panel center.

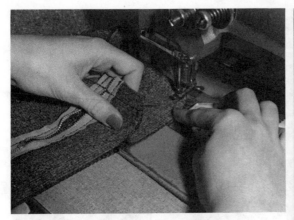

Fig. 11-37. Folding boxing to create zipper pocket.

5. Attach the center, front of the boxing to the center of the waterfall cushion panel as shown in Fig. 11-35. Sew the boxing to just around the rear corner of the cushion panel and then align the zipper panel center notch with the rear cushion panel center notch (Fig. 11-36). *Tip:* Leave the machine needle in the down position while making this adjustment to assure no movement from the previous stitch.

6. Now go back to the corner, fold over the excess boxing so the zipper panel will lay out straight, as shown in Fig. 11-37. **Caution:** Keep the center notches aligned, and sew straight over the top of the folded material. This creates the zipper pocket. Sew to just beyond the center notches and terminate sewing along this direction, cut the thread.

7. Go back to the front of the boxing and

Fig. 11-38. Preparing to sew second half of boxing to cushion panel.

prepare to sew up the opposite side in the same manner as indicated above. Figure 11-38 shows the seamstress aligning the panels for this final sewing step. When reaching a previously sewn area, always backstitch to prevent the stitches from opening later.

Chapter 12

Finishing Alternatives

In the past, "period" furniture designs could be identified by specific contours (Camel Back, Tuxedo, Barrel, Wing) and finishing techniques (Victorian, Colonial, Chippendale, Duncan Phyfe). However, much of the furniture in the American home involves a blending of the earlier "purist" features. Personal preferences have created a permissiveness of features, and almost anything is acceptable, except to the purist. Each style or blend has its place, and that place is determined in the mind of the proprietor.

This chapter will present a few of the alternatives to finishing an upholstered work, such as *bands, welt, blind stitching, panels, gimp, decorative tacks*. Each has its specialty use, and each can be incorporated successfully to create very interesting and pleasing effects.

BANDS

Bands are added to the tops and sides of arms and backs and to the bottoms of seats and outside panels to break up "plain" surfaces. Most bands are padded lightly which gives an added touch of elegance to the unit. A few upholsterers have installed panels with no padding at all. This is an exception rather than the rule, and is usually reserved for those units of the square, masculine appearance, and for the heavier weight fabrics.

For furniture styles having the band attached to the top of the arm rest, the (IA) panel is tacked to the top of the arm, a welt stapled in place, and then the band is blind tacked using tacking strip, either the flexible metal or cardboard. Figure 12-1 shows an arm band which has been laid in place at the stump with the operator holding the remainder of the band panel back to permit stapling. Normally, the full length of the band would be stapled in place with the entire panel in the full-open position. Desired padding would be added and the band folded over and stapled beneath the top arm rail along a line that will be covered by the outside arm panel.

Keeping a band even in width and parallel to the lines of the unit is extremely important. Using the combination square, set to a specified depth as illustrated in Fig. 12-2 is a convenient way to main-

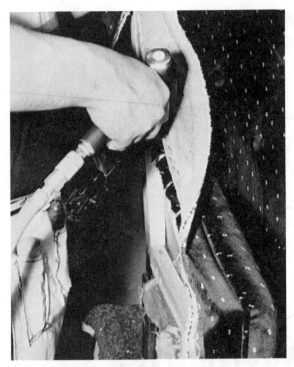

Fig. 12-1. Stapling tacking strip for arm band.

tain parallelism when the frame can be used. The welt is brought up tight to the tip of the blade. The installation pictured will be a back band that will extend from the top of the arm, up the back, across the top, and down to the opposite arm. The termination of the band will be concealed by the arm panels when they are installed. The finished chair(s) are pictured in Fig. 12-58.

WELT

Welt is used to finish off edges and junctions where two or more panels meet. Variations in the size of the welt cord create different impressions, from the delicate edging of a 1/16″ cord to the *bold* border of a 1/2″ fox edge. Double welt (refer to Figs. 12-50 through 12-52) is a variation occasionally used in place of the single welt as well as an "edge finish" in much the same situations as one would find decorative tacks or gimp used.

Another of the very popular uses of the single welt is to finish off the bottoms of arms, slip seats, and even the bottoms of chairs and couches. One

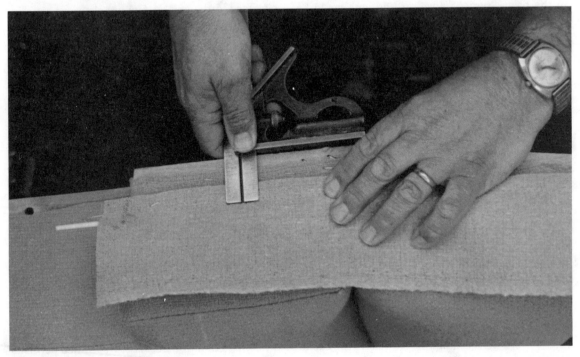

Fig. 12-2. Measuring to locate a back band.

Fig. 12-3. Welt marked for 90 degree cut-out to form square corner.

such application is shown in the beginning stage in Fig. 12-3. The welt has been attached along the front edge of the seat, will round the corner, and be joined at the spot immediately in line with and concealed by the arm post.

Welt is normally located so that the outside of it is either flush with or protruding beyond the edge slightly (1/32″ to 1/16″). In Fig. 12-3, the welt has been left unattached about 2″ back from the corner to permit cutting a 90 degree notch which will make a smooth, easy bend around the square corner. Notice that the point of the notch is at the spot where the outside of the welt will be and the point is rounded rather than sharp (Fig. 12-4). This makes a smooth yet square corner without a bunching of the fabric at the inside of the bend (Fig. 12-5).

The Finished Butt End

When welt is to butt against a post or other frame member and must "dead end" into it, a completely finished end can be created as follows:

1. Open the sewed welt for approximately three inches and cut the cord about 1/2″ short of the end of the fabric (Fig. 12-6). When the welt butts against a post, the cord is cut so it will end at the wood edge. The fabric will then be 1/2″ longer.

2. Cut straight into the fabric, toward the cord, but ending about 1/16″ short of the cord as

Fig. 12-4. Welt notched, ready to form around square corner.

Fig. 12-5. Welt making a square corner. (Raised edges, indicated by arrows, must be stapled down!)

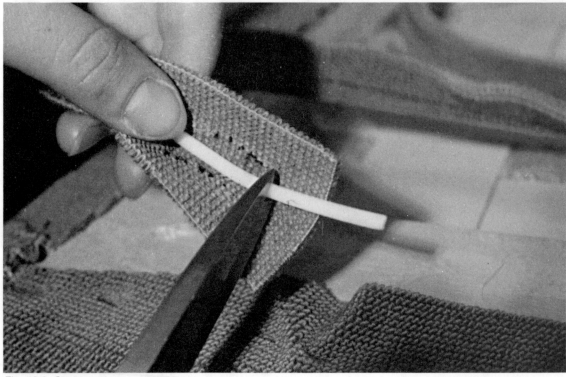

Fig. 12-6. Cutting welt cord for finished butt end.

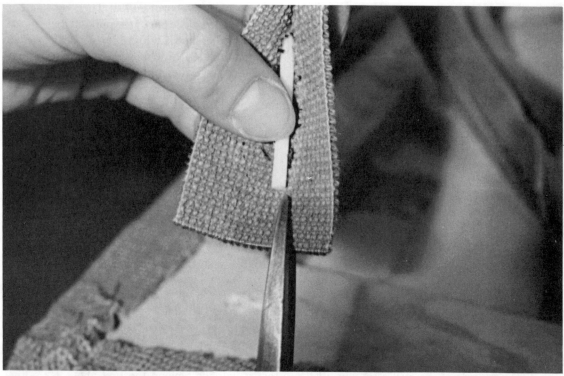

Fig. 12-7. Cut welt strip to within 1/16" of the cord, both sides.

Fig. 12-8. Cut wedges out of welt strip for "finished" butt end. One side is cut from the center to the edge, the other side is cut from the edge to the center as shown.

Fig. 12-9. Fold over center flap to cover end of cord.

illustrated in Fig. 12-7. Make two parallel cuts as illustrated in Fig. 12-8.

3. On one side of the welt strip, cut off the inside corner so the cut ends where the first cut (straight into the cord) ended. Then cut another wedge shaped piece out of the opposite but *outside* of the strip, as shown in Fig. 12-8 (notice the wedge laying on the seat?). This will leave three "ears" extending from the end of the strip.

4. Fold the center ear so it lays directly over the cord (Fig. 12-9).

5. Fold down the other two ears so the end is square, Fig. 12-10.

6. Now fold the welt as it was originally sewn. *Voila!* A finished end (Fig. 12-11).

The finished butt end is used successfully, with some fabrics, to create an almost unnoticeable union of the welt when it completely surrounds an area and meets itself, such as a slip seat. Figure 12-12 shows the beginning end being tacked to the bottom of a slip seat. Note the finished end and how the operator is using the finger as a measuring guide to assure a proper and even projection of the welt beyond the edge of the seat. Notice also that the welt is being stapled tight against the cord. If this is not done, the welt will seem loose and sloppy. To complete the perimeter, cut the ending welt so that it extends beyond the first about 1/2", Fig. 12-13. Open the welt, make the cuts, and fold the

Fig. 12-10. Fold over outer flaps to make a square end.

Fig. 12-11. "Finished" butt end.

Fig. 12-12. Stapling the first end of a "finished" butt joint weld to the frame. (Staple very tight to cord!)

Fig. 12-13. Cut welt 1/2″ long to form the second end of "finished" butt joint.

end as shown earlier in Figs. 12-6 through 12-11. Tack the second end tightly against the first as shown in Fig. 12-14. A butt union, properly done, displays very little deviation as is illustrated in Fig. 12-15 (the arrow is pointing to the spot where the two ends meet!).

Another form of the butt union is shown in Fig. 12-16. This union is formed by cutting the ends of the welt and cord flush and pressing the two together. This type of union works very well on only a few types of material, of which the short loop nylon frieze is one.

The Lap Joint

Another way to join welt is with the *lap joint*. The lap joint will work well on fabrics that do not tend to fray at the ends. It is especially suited for the vinyls. To make this joint:

1. Cut the cord and welt strip square and flush on the first end.

2. Determine where the joint is to be located (never on the front of a unit or cushion) and attach the welt around the perimeter, leaving 2″ of the beginning end unattached and about 4″ of the last end also unattached.

3. Cut the finishing end square and about 1/2″ long, Fig. 12-17.

4. Open the finishing end of the welt for about 2″ and cut the cord so it ends at the face of the beginning end as illustrated in Fig. 12-17.

5. Wrap the finishing end tightly around the beginning end as shown in Fig. 12-18.

6. Staple the union tightly to the frame and the result will appear as Fig. 12-19.

BLIND STITCHING

One of the oldest of the finishing methods, *blind stitching* is still used for numerous functions. Among these are (1) attaching new decking to an upholstered unit (Figs. 9-22 through 9-26), correcting an erroneous cut in a cover panel (which occurrence decreases as experience increases), closing pleats, folds or tucks, as illustrated later. The blind stitch is a square stitch that is sewn with a curved needle. The shorter the stitches are made, the more invisible will be the seam. Figure 12-20

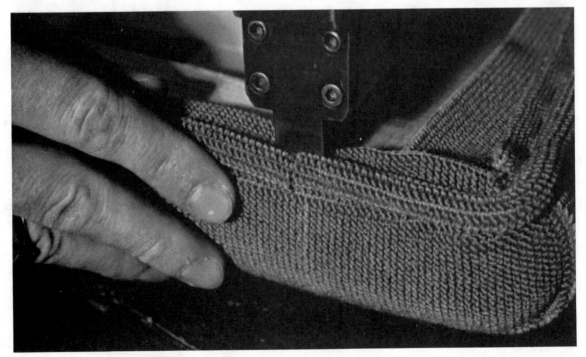

Fig. 12-14. Butting two "finished" ends together.

Fig. 12-15. Side view of a "finished" butt joint (junction above arrow).

Fig. 12-16. Making a plain butt joint.

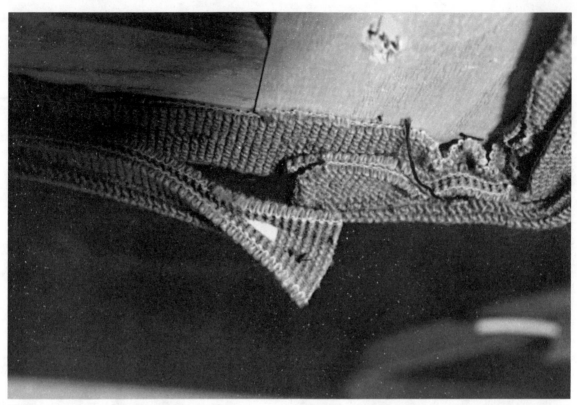

Fig. 12-17. First step to making a lapped joint.

shows a tucked corner of an attached cushion back in a crushed velvet. The tuck has been opened a bit to make it more visible. If the opening between the two layers of fabric is objectionable, close it with the blind stitch as follows:

1. Begin the stitch by inserting the curved needle into the fabric at a location where the knot in the end of the thread will be hidden with the closed seam. The preferred location is near the point where the overlap begins.

2. Exit the fabric a very short distance (1/16″ or less) to the side of the beginning of the fold. Figure 12-21 shows these first two steps.

3. Snug the thread and hold it at 90 degrees (square) to the lay of the fold, enter the fabric immediately beneath the thread and about 1/16″ away. Exit the fabric at the top edge of the fold 3/16″ to 1/4″ away. The point of the needle can be seen at the tip of the arrow, Fig. 12-22. Tighten this stitch.

Fig. 12-18. Tighten second strip around first end to form lap joint.

282

Fig. 12-19. Completed lap joint.

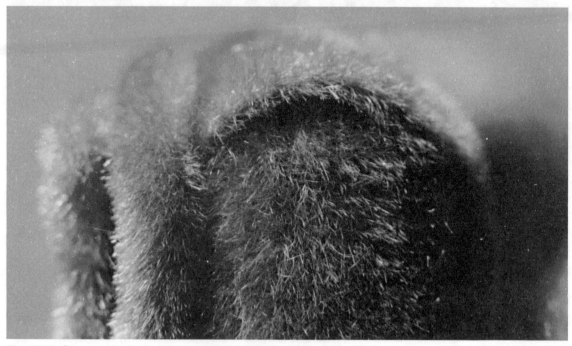

Fig. 12-20. Close-up of a tucked corner showing slight opening.

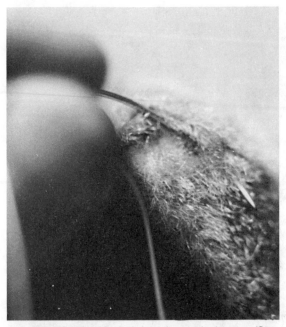

Fig. 12-21. Starting blind stitch to close tucked corner. (Start where knot will be concealed!)

4. Hold the thread square to the lay of the fold to locate the spot to enter and exit the opposite side as described above. Figure 12-23 shows the beginning of the next-to-the-last closing stitch.

5. Complete the closing with the last stitch being made in such a way that the final knot in the thread can be hidden from view. Figure 12-24 has the needle directed toward the small space that exists between the welt and the inside back cover. By pulling the welt open, as shown in Fig. 12-25, the needle can exit the fabric, the ending knot tied and concealed where it will not be seen. The finished sewing is shown in Fig. 12-26.

PANELS

The use of *panels* is one of the most popular, practical and fun finishing techniques used. Their primary function is to conceal the unfinished edges of fabric tacked to the frame in very conspicuous locations (arm stumps and back posts). Figure 12-27 shows an operator checking a panel pattern (a piece

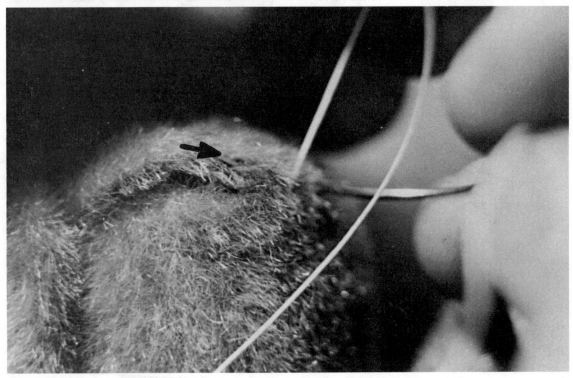

Fig. 12-22. Make first stitch with a short run.

284

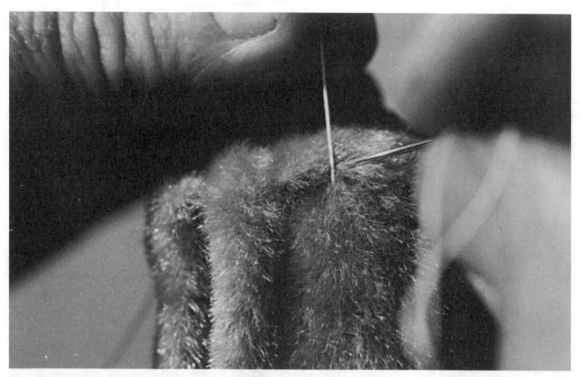

Fig. 12-23. Keep blind stitches square to seam being made.

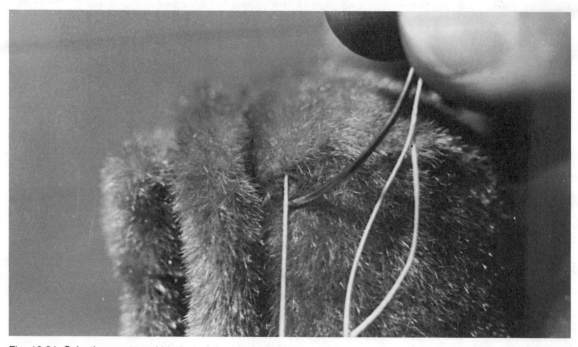

Fig. 12-24. Selecting a way to hide last of the blind stitches.

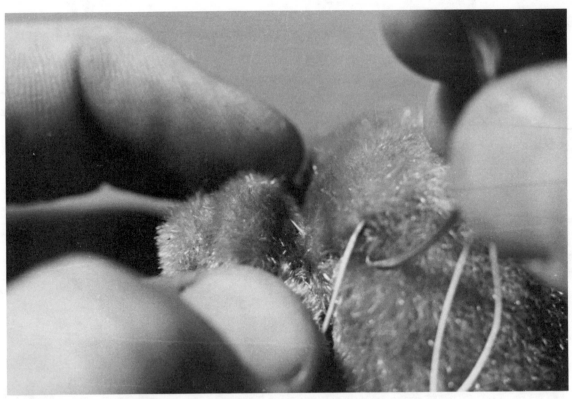

Fig. 12-25. Forcing welt open to hide the ending of the blind stitch knot (yet to be tied).

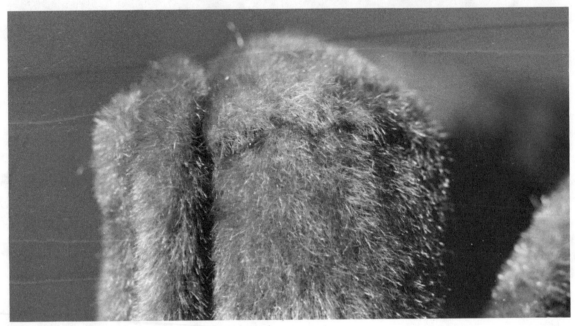

Fig. 12-26. Completed blind stitch closing a corner tuck.

Fig. 12-27. Checking panel pattern to a sofa back.

of 1/8″ hardboard) against the back post of a sofa. The panel itself will be made of 1/4″ plywood, 1/8″ or 1/4″ hardboard, or heavy cardboard especially made for that purpose. Figure 12-28 shows a pattern and two panels of 1/4″ plywood. The panel to the left is to be used on the front of the arm stump while the one on the right will, obviously, be used for the back post as illustrated by the pattern be-

ing checked in Fig. 12-27. To prepare panels, follow this procedure:

1. Bevel the outer edges of the panel so the outer edge is only about 1/8″ thick. Make the taper about twice as wide as it is deep. Figure 12-29 shows the bevel a bit more clearly than does Fig. 12-28.

2. Pad the face side of the panel. Either a full or half thickness of cotton can be used. Place the cotton on a flat clean surface. Lay the panel on top, with the tapered side against the padding. Press the panel firmly into the padding and tear the cotton so it extends 1/8″ to 1/4″ beyond the edges as shown in Fig. 12-30. A completed panel is shown to the right of the photo.

3. Place the padded panel on top of a piece of cover with the finish side down, as shown in Fig. 12-31. Fold the cover over snugly and staple to the back side. **Caution:** Use short staples, 3/16″ or 1/4″, for this purpose or they will protrude through the padding and cover on the face side.

4. When it comes to curved edges, place staples close (within 1/4″) to the edge and trim off

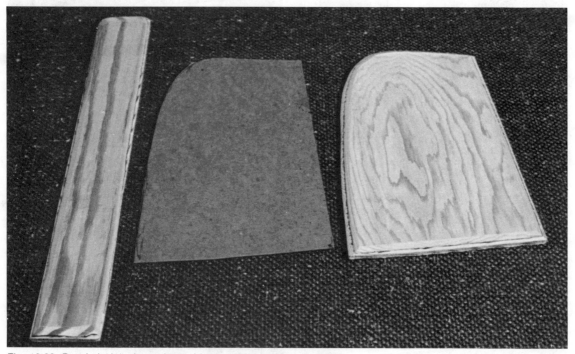

Fig. 12-28. Beveled 1/4″ plywood panel bases with back panel pattern.

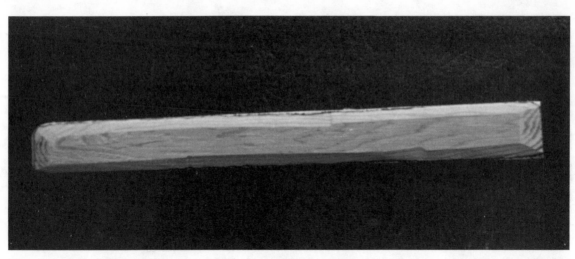

Fig. 12-29. View showing bevel of 1/4" plywood arm panel base.

the excess as progress is made. This reduces bulk and prevents ripples on the front side. Refer to Fig. 12-32.

5. Staple opposing sides before completing ends, Fig. 12-33. (The chalk mark was made to indicate the curved end of the wood.) Notice also the diagonal placement of the staple (arrow). It is located in that position to permit rounding of the corner. Cut the fabric along side of the staple to near the edge of the wood insert, as indicated by the dashed line.

6. Fold the cut tab under and pull the fabric into the corner as indicated in Fig. 12-34. Staple close to the edge (Fig. 12-35).

7. Work both sides around the corners and finish off by pulling the center of the rounded end straight into the panel, staple perpendicular to the edge and cut off the excess fabric (Fig. 12-36).

8. Finish off the square end last by stapling the two corners diagonally, cutting toward the corners, and folding the end over and stapling. Figure 12-37 shows one corner stapled and cut and a bit too much cotton remaining. Simply remove the excess cotton and staple the end flap in place and trim. *Note:* Occasionally the square end will be left unattached to the panel and be pulled under and tacked to the bottom of the front seat-rail. This creates a completely finished edge, preferred by some upholsterers.

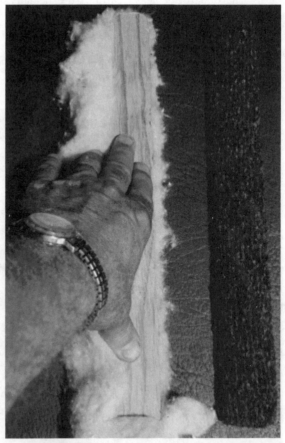

Fig. 12-30. Tearing cotton slightly oversize to pad arm panel. Finished panel shown on right.

288

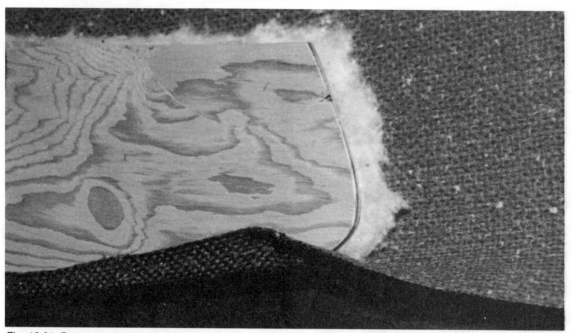

Fig. 12-31. Bottom and right side of cover stapled to panel base. (Keep pattern running true to the vertical center line of the panel.)

Fig. 12-32. Forming around curves of a panel. (Staple parallel and close (1/4 inch) to edge, trim excess, leave no ripples.)

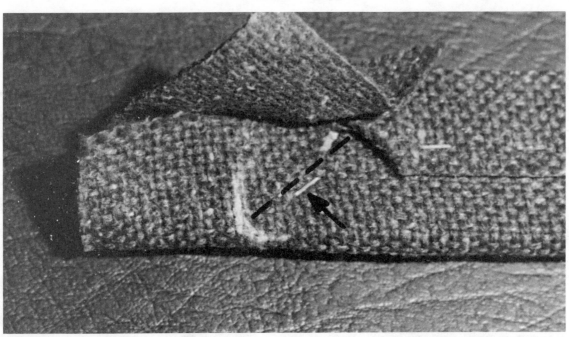

Fig. 12-33. Forming sharply rounded corners, staple at a diagonal (arrow), cut out excess (black dashed line).

Fig. 12-34. Tuck and form fabric tightly into corner.

Fig. 12-35. Staple close to edge and trim excess fabric.

Fig. 12-36. Trimming last of excess fabric on sharply rounded panel.

9. Attach the panel to the unit by driving four penny finish nails through the panel, fabric and all, from the front as illustrated in Fig. 12-38. Drive the nails until they snug against the wooden insert. A dimple will be noticed in the fabric, arrow (Fig. 12-38).

10. "Lift" the fabric over the head of the nail with the point of an ice pick as shown in Figs. 12-39 and 12-40. Figure 12-41 shows a chair with one arm finished with the panel, the other not yet installed.

GIMP

Gimp can be used anywhere fabric is to butt

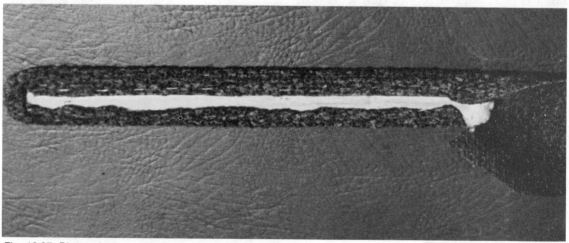

Fig. 12-37. Diagonal cut toward square corner of a panel.

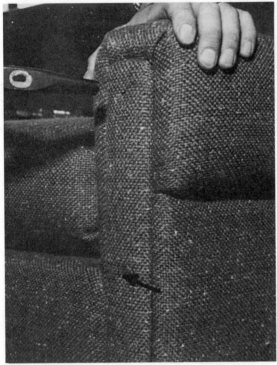

Fig. 12-38. Applying finished panel with small finish nails (4d or 1-inch brads). Set nails snug as indicated by dimple at arrow.

against show wood. Figures 12-42 through 12-49 show the procedure for installing gimp with adhesive. (The adhesive used should either be the white polyvinyl variety or a special fabric adhesive that looks very much like the polyvinyls.)

1. Staple the cover close and parallel to the show wood and trim the excess (Fig. 12-42).

2. Measure and cut the gimp to length. Allow about 1/4″ at each end to be tucked under to create a finished end, as indicated at the left side of Fig. 12-43.

3. Apply a ribbon of adhesive along the length to which the gimp is to be attached (Fig. 12-44). *Note:* Both of the adhesives mentioned above will dry transparent, making them virtually invisible when dry.

4. Gently press the back side of the gimp onto the glued area (Fig. 12-45).

5. Apply adhesive to the extreme ends of the gimp and tuck in place with the point of a stuffing regulator as shown in Figs. 12-46 and 12-47.

6. Use the regulator point to "regulate" the gimp to make a nice, straight edge against the show wood as illustrated in Fig. 12-48. Figure 12-49 shows the completed application.

Fig. 12-39. Insert regulator along side nail head to "Pop" fabric outward.

Fig. 12-40. Cover raised above head of finish nail.

Fig. 12-41. "Before" and "After" view of panel installation.

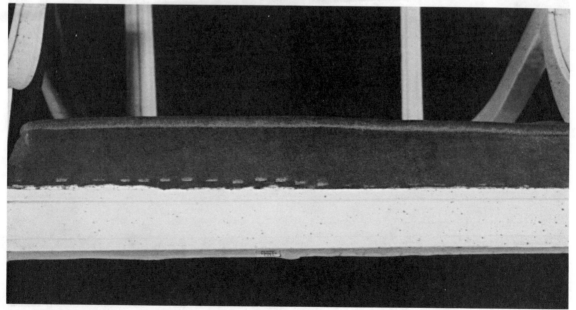

Fig. 12-42. Front of chair prepared for gimp.

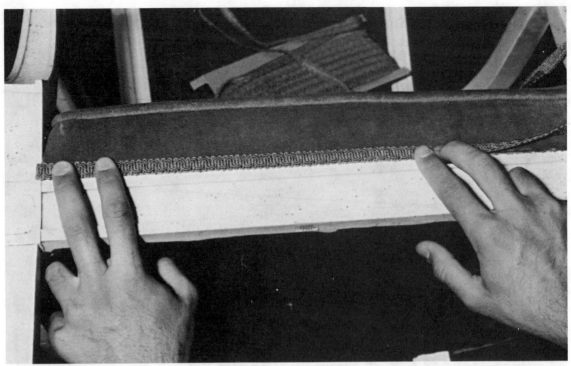

Fig. 12-43. Measuring gimp for length (leave about 1/4 inch extra at each end).

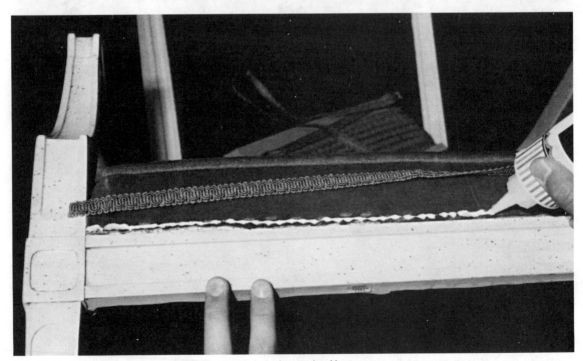

Fig. 12-44. Applying adhesive to bond gimp (chair is laying on back).

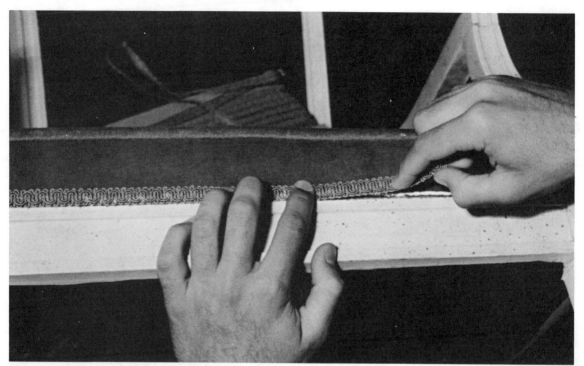
Fig. 12-45. Press gimp evenly into adhesive.

Fig. 12-46. Add extra adhesive to end of gimp to assure no fraying and secure bond.

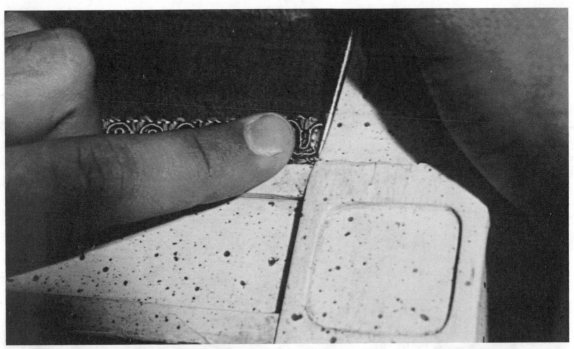

Fig. 12-47. Tuck gimp "Under" or "Into" at corners.

Fig. 12-48. Regulating gimp along edge of rail.

Fig. 12-49. Completed gimp finish.

DOUBLE WELT

The *double welt* was reserved to this point to discuss as it can be used in locations where single welt, decorative tacks, or gimp would have been used. Figure 12-50 shows the outside of a wing-back chair that displays show wood all around the perimeter. The cover has been stapled and trimmed very close to the wood in preparation for the application of the double welt. Figure 12-51 illustrates a double welt beneath a special foot that makes sewing a very consistent, tight double welt much easier. Application of the double welt is much the same as gimp, using either gimp staples or fabric adhesive. The installation around the carved leg shown in Fig. 12-52 gives an idea of what the double welt looks like as a finishing method. This is the leg of the chair pictured in Fig. 12-50.

IRREGULAR CURVES

A variety of techniques can be used to finish off edges which must fit against irregular curving contours. Figure 12-53 illustrates a modification of the Y-cut that is used to fit a seat cover around an arm post which is to butt into show wood. The tab

Fig. 12-50. Outside of a wing back ready for a double welt to finish the edges.

Fig. 12-51. Double welt shown under special walking foot.

Fig. 12-52. Double welt application around carved cabriole leg.

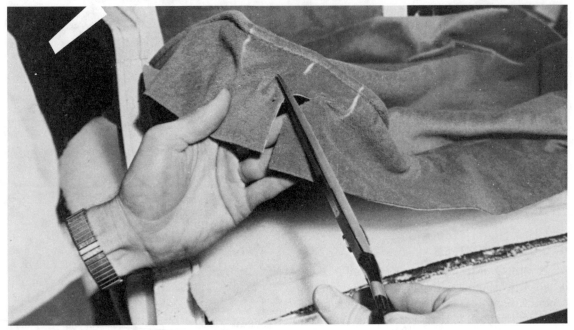

Fig. 12-53. Modified Y-cut for finishing around arm post.

will extend down the face of the post while the flaps will fold under and finish against the sides of the post as with other cases involving the Y-cut. Notice that the two angular cuts, Fig. 12-54, will not be as wide, proportionately, as with previous cases discussed.

Another finishing technique is the installation of a "*spanning panel*." This technique is used in situations where two finished edges of fabric must span show wood where there is no other convenient way to cover the framing wood behind it, as is illustrated in Fig. 12-55. The spanning panel is cut from a piece of cover to match the grain and pattern of the material that will span the show wood. The spanning piece is then folded so the rough edges will be against the frame, with a finished fold on the outer or visible edge.

RUNNING STITCHES

A couple of modern finishing techniques for ir-

regular surfaces are created by a slight change in sewing technique. Figure 12-56 shows a mid-back panel stay tacked in place which has no welt around the seam. This weltless seam gives the unit a smooth, rather streamlined air. A slight modification to the weltless seam is shown in Fig. 12-57. In this case, the straight-stitched seam is decorated by adding two running stitches alongside the seam. This approach maintains the streamlined influence and adds a flair of elegance. The two different styles of finishing, on the same chair base are shown in Fig. 12-58. It may be noticed that the cushions are styled differently. The chair on the left has a full box cushion while the one on the right is a waterfall cushion. Notice also the pleated corners on the seat panel.

DECORATIVE TACKS

Decorative tacks are used as a finishing technique in applications involving straight or irregular

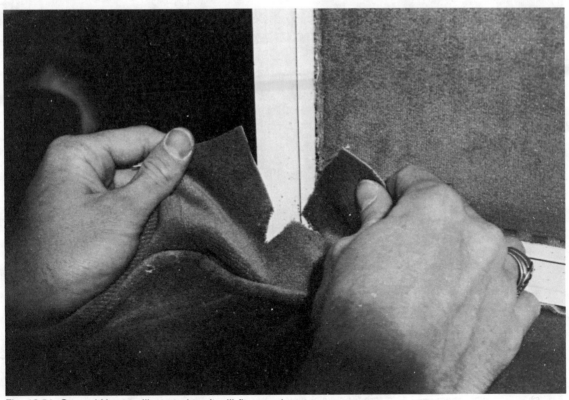

Fig. 12-54. Opened Y-cut to illustrate how it will fit around post.

Fig. 12-55. "Spanner strip" to cover frame wood at rear of show wood arm.

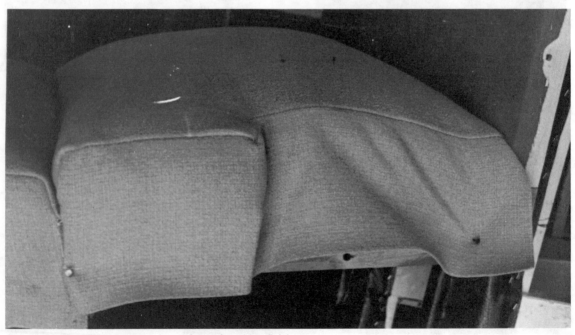

Fig. 12-56. The plain seam used as a form of cushion finish.

Fig. 12-57. The double top stitch as a finishing technique.

Fig. 12-58. "Twin" chairs, finished differently: left—box cushion, plain seams; right—waterfall cushion, double top stitching.

Fig. 12-59. Slitting cover to accommodate tucks around irregular curves.

curving lines. They could be used in much the same way as gimp, but where the "knobby" effect of the raised tack heads would be preferred to the feminine refinement provided by the gimp. Ir-regular surfaces around arm posts is an especially appropriate use for the decorative tack. Finishing off around carved legs can be a time-consuming ac-tivity when all voids and wrinkles are eliminated.

Fig. 12-60. Forming around irregular curves with regulator.

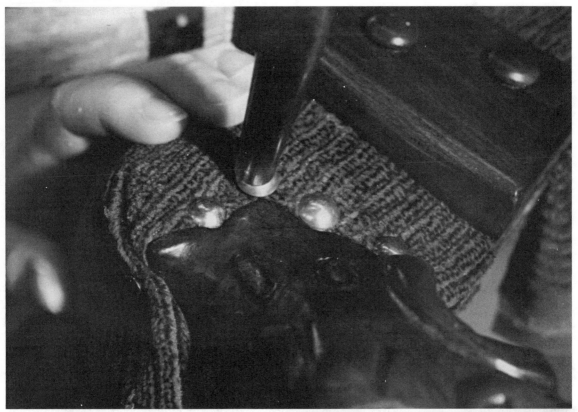

Fig. 12-61. Decorative tacks as a finishing touch.

The decorative tack process is illustrated in Figs. 12-59 through 12-62.

In Fig. 12-59, the seat panel has been pulled into place and tacked along the front and sides to within a few inches of the corners. The cover has been trimmed to overlap the show wood around the carved cabriole legs by about 1/4". A portion of the panel has been lifted up to show a short slit (just to the left of where the upholsterer's pin enters the fabric) cut into the cover to aid in tucking the material under to form a finished edge all around the irregular curves of the leg. Notice that a stay tack (Fig. 12-60, to the left of the finger) has been used to hold the panel in place while other cutting and fitting is being done. When all the fitting has been completed, a few decorative tacks strategically placed around the irregular perimeter, Fig. 12-61, will hold the cover permanently in place and give an "antique" air appropriate to the carved, cabriole leg, Fig. 12-62.

Fig. 12-62. Carved cabriole legs finished with decorative tacks.

Chapter 13

Vinyl Reupholstering

Vinyl reupholstering is just slightly different from working with woven "cloth" fabrics. The first difference is that when sewing vinyls, the stitch should be rather long, 4 to 6 millimeters (.158" to .236") to reduce the perforation effect. The second difference is that vinyls with no backing or a knit fabric backing are able to be stretched in virtually all directions to a greater extent than "cloth" fabrics. Another feature of this chapter is that all of the reupholstering work is done without the need of a sewing machine, of special appeal to the homeowner or do-it-yourselfer possessing only a light duty domestic machine.

STYLING

Inasmuch as kitchen or dinette furnishings are more subject to foodstuff and beverage spills than the average livingroom styles, easy clean-up is often an earnestly sought advantage, especially when small children are still visiting the facility frequently. For this reason, primarily, a furniture style having smooth contours, no welts (the habitual dust

and crumb catchers), and a minimum of tucks may be preferred. The primary style of reupholstering in this chapter will be known as the *Formed* style. Formed upholstery requires no sewing, eliminates the "crumb catcher," and displays a rounded contour having small or no tucks or gathers on the seat and only limited but unobtrusive tucks at the top corners of the back. As might be suspected, forming is best achieved with the more stretchable vinyl fabrics.

DISASSEMBLY

Kitchen chairs are built a bit differently than the furniture featured earlier in this book. Therefore a brief explanation of disassembly procedures may prove helpful. Generally, for convenience, speed and comfort, it is suggested that the backs be removed before the seats. There will be times when having the seat still attached makes it much easier to remove the back unit. This is explained in the back disassembly, style 4, below.

Backs

There are several basic systems for attaching backs. Several of these styles and methods for removal are included below:

1. Exposed steel frames with visible screws (from the back). Remove screws. Back will release easily. Ahem, usually!

2. Exposed steel uprights, back inserted between them, screws not visible—back may be attached with two screws at the top that slide down a groove on the inside portion of the tubular steel uprights, with the bottom locked in place with two steel dowels (or pins) that are inserted into drilled holes in the upright. To remove:

    a. Remove the caps (or plugs) from the top of the uprights. This will expose the sliding screws.

    b. Pry one side of the frame sideways from the back near the bottom. The pin will be seen. Continue wedging the two components apart until the pin releases from the hole in the frame. This takes some effort, so don't despair.

    c. Move the back toward the freed side to release the other pin. If this is not possible, wedge out the other side as before, to release the second pin.

    d. With both pins free, slide the back upward and out of the grooves.

3. Exposed wooden frames—screws are sometimes concealed by wooden plugs or buttons. *Carefully* pry the buttons from the frame by using a sharp instrument such as a knife blade, awl, or scribe. Voila, the screws! (Take care to not mar the buttons as you will want to reuse them.)

4. Press-fit back, no exposed frame (appears to be embedded within the back, which is actually the case)—back is removed by pulling it upward. This usually requires considerable effort. One of the best ways to get it off is shown in Fig. 13-1. Kneel on chair seat and pull up alternately, rocking it back and forth, on each side until back comes off. For obvious reasons, it helps to have the seat still attached to do this.

Tip 1: In some styles, the metal uprights have a cleat which digs into the wooden portion of the back to keep the back from slipping off when the chair is lifted by the back. The retaining power of the cleats, then, must be overcome to remove the back.

Tip 2: On other units, wooden dowels are pressed into the metal uprights, which in turn are pressed into the back unit. This style back is removed in the same manner as above. If pulling on the back as illustrated does not release it, rather than straining your own back, turn the chair upside down, and with the seat resting on a table or bench, knock the back loose by hitting it with a mallet alternately near each of the uprights.

Seats

Most seat assemblies for kitchen and dinette furniture are attached in basically the same manner, with screws through the frame from the underside of the unit. Thus, removal of the seat from the chair frame is usually accomplished by turning the chair upside down and extracting the exposed screws. Lift the frame from the seat unit. Occasionally, separation may require a little wedging

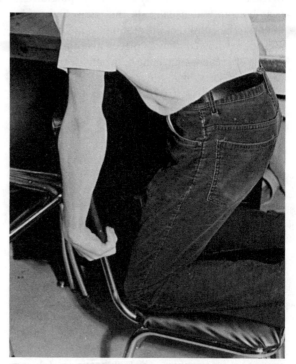

Fig. 13-1. One way to remove press-fit back.

Fig. 13-2. Rear view of press-fit back, OB attached with decorative tacks.

pressure to overcome fabric or seat base sticking to the frame. Raising the frame and tapping on the seat bottom will usually do the trick. Quite frequently, the bottom of the seat unit is covered with a cardboard piece. Those pieces are put there to reduce or prevent squeaking between the frame and the seat base, so save them if possible. If they are destroyed in the stripping process, just get some other lightweight cardboard or heavy paper and make new panels.

STRIPPING

The only real differences between stripping kitchen furniture and "overstuffed" are that (1) the kitchen units are much simpler and (2) the covered components are separate entities and are removed from the frame. Because the structure is slightly different, a short section on stripping is included.

Figure 13-2 shows a back (Style 4, above) that has been removed. In this case, the outside back panel was put on with decorative tacks, after a welt trim. This style is fast and easy. One disadvantage is discovered when this style chair is used against walls or other furniture—the tack heads scratch and mar other surfaces! Quick removal of the outside back and welt is accomplished by prying both out using a ripping tool as shown in Fig. 13-3. One style of back is shown in Fig. 13-4, wherein a cardboard

Fig. 13-3. One method to remove decorative tacks, OB, and welt with one operation.

Fig. 13-4. OB panel removed revealing cardboard and tacks holding IB panel to the frame.

Fig. 13-5. OB panel glued to reinforcing cardboard.

panel is applied directly to the frame *Before* the inside back panel is tacked on. Another style is shown in Fig. 13-5. With this style, the outside back panel is adhered to a cardboard panel and applied with decorative tacks *after* the inside back panel is installed. Figure 13-6 shows what happens when a back is driven off with a mallet or a hammer, and the pounding is done in the center of the back instead of near the frame members. Repairs are eminent. The procedure to repair the broken member is intended to be self-explanatory from the components pictured.

PADDING AND COVERING TECHNIQUES
Seat

Figure 13-7 shows a seat padding that was retained and merely covered with a new layer of cotton. The original padding consisted of a layer of foam rubber (V) and a couple layers of cotton felt (W).

1. The entire seat assembly is placed upside-down on top of an oversized piece of cotton and the excess trimmed to provide padding to the bottom edge (which is actually the top edge as pictured in Fig. 13-8) of the wood base. *Tip:* Note how worker is holding the cotton down while tearing around the perimeter of the base? *Reminder:* Never cut cotton, tear it.

2. Place completely padded seat assembly on top of seat panel. Tack the cover to the front center. Smooth and stretch vinyl fabric to the back and tack the center in place. Smooth, stretch and tack both side centers in place. *Caution:* Do not let the padding extend beyond the bottom edge of the wood as the cover is stretched into place. This is very important as a cover stapled with padding beneath it will result in an unintended and unattractive wavy surface, which is impossible to smooth except by completely redoing it. Notice the tendency for the outer padding to creep beyond the edge in Fig. 13-9? *Solution:* Slide the stretched fabric outward over the edge of the wood while applying a little pressure with the hand from the outside. Then, retaining that pressure, pull the fabric back over the edge and like magic the padding no longer

Fig. 13-6. Stripped press-fit back component: A = good bottom back rail, B = broken bottom rail, C = new, hardwood bottom rail, D = cardboard template used to make new rail.

Fig. 13-7. Stripped dinette seat showing padding in good condition.

Fig. 13-8. Tearing cotton oversize to pad the bottom of wooden base.

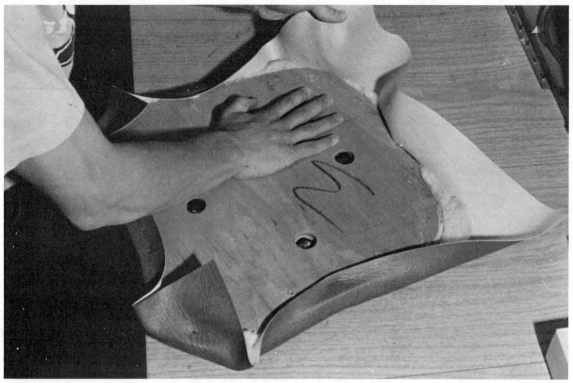

Fig. 13-9. Applying seat cover. (Tack centers first, then corners.)

extends beyond the edge but rather forms a nice roll just at the edge, with no lumps, bumps or ripples—if done properly.

    3. Stretch and fold corners at a 45 degree angle, staple at the center of each one. Note the third corner being stretched (Fig. 13-9). Note also that there is no padding coming around to the underside of the wood, at the tacking point.

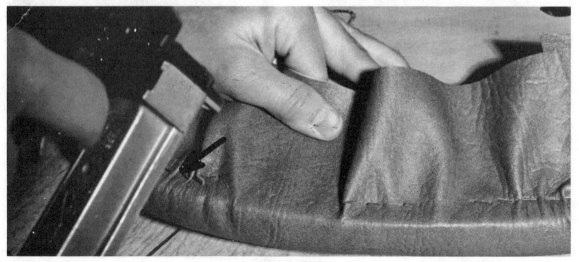

Fig. 13-10. Taking small tucks to remove excess fabric at corners.

4. Form Corners. Beginning near the center of the rounded corners, stretch cover at an angle toward the center staple to make a small tuck, on the bottom only. No wrinkle or fold should be seen at the seat edge. Staple across the tucks on a diagonal to hold them in place without slippage (Fig. 13-10).

5. Continue small tucks around corner to remove all excess fabric between the last corner staple and the adjacent center staple (Fig. 13-11). *Note:* Staples are very close together and the tucks are very small. This is what prevents wrinkles! Continue this procedure for all corners.

6. Prepare for bottom cardboard. Trim excess fabric 1/8" to 1/4" from the staples. Replace anti-squeak cover (Fig. 13-12). *Note:* Breather holes are provided in the base as well as in the cardboard—an absolute necessity to avoid entrapped air an and occasional embarrassing sound when one sits down.

7. Attach anti-squeak cover by stapling close to the edges of the cardboard as shown in Fig. 13-13. Secure the edges of any small tears that may have been created in the stripping process. *Helpful Hint:* Before attaching seat to the frame, rub some paraffin wax along the cardboard in line with where the chair frame will attach. This provides superior friction and squeak reduction. The "formed seat," ready to attach to the frame, is shown in Fig. 13-14.

Padding The Inside Back

Figure 13-15 shows the inside of a back component that is quite satisfactory for recovering. However, in this case, the customer wanted a bit more padding, so, another layer of cotton. *Helpful Hint:* Smaller pieces of cotton can be used successfully for padding if each one is "feathered" along the line where the two will join. Tear 1/2 the cotton thickness away to about 1 1/2" back from the edge, Fig. 13-16. Feather the joining piece in similar fashion and overlap the two feathered sides as shown in Fig. 13-17. If done with care this creates a union in which gaps and lumps are undetectable and the pieces joined do not slip apart.

Covering Inside Back

1. Attach Top-Center. Staple the top-center of the cover to the back at a point that will be beneath the fold line of the outside back panel. That

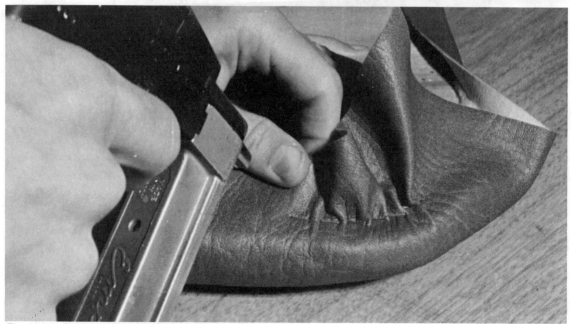

Fig. 13-11. Corner tucks completed, excess fabric removed, ready to tack toward center staples.

Fig. 13-12. Applying anti-squeek cover to bottom of trimmed, formed seat.

Fig. 13-13. Staple parallel to and close to edge of anti-squeek cover.

Fig. 13-14. Completed, formed seat.

Fig. 13-15. View of stripped back; padding is reusable.

313

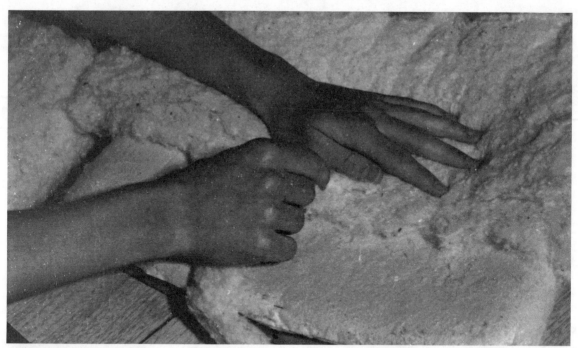

Fig. 13-16. Preparing to splice a new layer of cotton padding.

Fig. 13-17. Joining feathered cotton pieces for a smooth splice.

314

first staple is not quite visible at the extreme top of Fig. 13-18. Pull the fabric snugly over and around the top edge and down toward the bottom.

2. Tack Bottom-Center. Stretch fabric *very tightly* to bottom-center. If the center is not stretched very tightly, significant "bridging" will occur and the inside curvature of the back will be lost. Note that the cotton goes to the front edge (Fig. 13-18, arrow) but does not go onto the bottom surface. The cotton visible toward the outer edges of Fig. 13-18 will be tucked or rolled to meet at the edge but not beyond it. Ripples will be caused at the top (Fig. 13-19), as well as at the bottom but they will be removed as the "forming" process continues.

3. Form the Top and Bottom. Pull the top edge at a slight diagonal toward the corners (Fig. 13-20) and staple to within 4″ of the corner. Follow the same procedure to attach bottom.

4. Gently smooth (do not stretch tightly) cover to the side-centers and tack. Then form and tack sides to within 2″ of each corner, top and bottom.

5. Form Top Corners. As with the seat, take small tucks on the back side and staple. To create a smooth, rounded corner, take small tucks around the corner. (The small wrinkles beneath the joints of the thumb in Fig. 13-21 should be removed by taking out the last two staples and restretching.) Create the smooth rounding by pulling the fabric around the top of the corner in the direction indicated in Fig. 13-21. *Alternative:* Several tucks would also be acceptable; however, tucks must be facing downward and outward, and be located at the same spots on both sides and on all other units.

6. Major Tuck at Top Corners. Stretch the fabric to the side to take up the slack, and create the major tuck location that is attractive to *you*. *Tip:* Experiment a little at this point (refer to Fig. 13-22).

Fig. 13-18. Pulling bottom center to begin forming IB panel to frame.

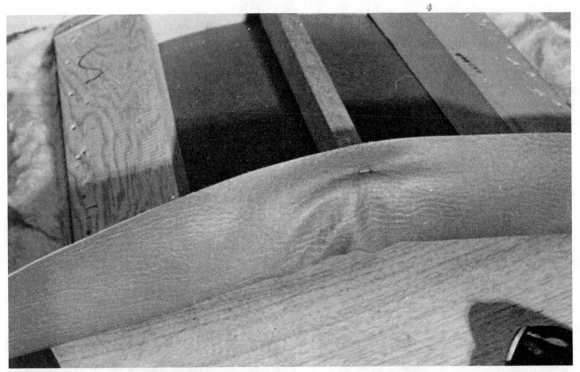

Fig. 13-19. View of top of IB prior to diagonal stretching.

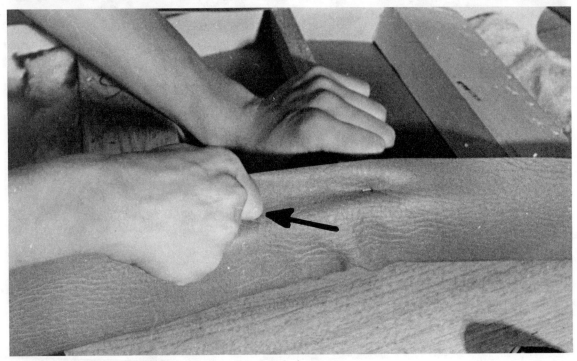

Fig. 13-20. Stretch top IB as indicated (by arrow) to form to frame.

316

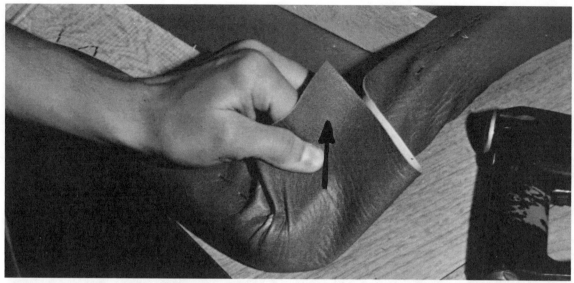

Fig. 13-21. Forming top corners of IB panel.

Relieve bulk from this tuck by cutting out the excess material. To do this, hold the fold tightly and open to expose the underside, and cut on a diagonal from just inside the last corner staple to within 1/4" of the fold, indicated by the tip of the shears, Fig. 13-23. Now cut along the fold, 1/4-3/8" away, to

angle into the ending point of the previous cut, Fig. 13-24. **Caution:** Do not let the fold shift when making this cut. This procedure removes the excess bulk from the corner and results in a smooth, flat tuck. The flatness of the finished tuck along with a slight variation is shown in Fig. 13-25 which

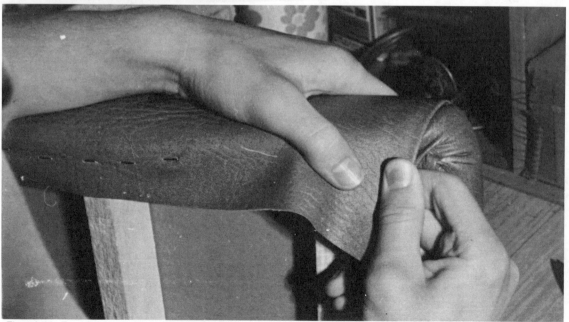

Fig. 13-22. Establishing major tuck at top corners.

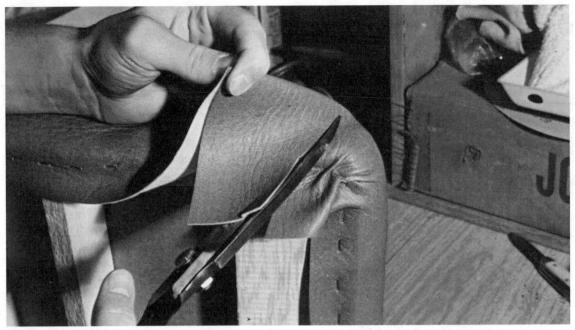

Fig. 13-23. Maintaining fold line and cutting to 1/2″ of fold.

includes a small, side tuck. *Note:* This side tuck has the fold facing downward.

Covering Outside Back

One of the most popular methods of attaching outside back panels is by *blind tacking*. The procedure is basically the same as with other upholstery styles, specifically:

1. Locate and tack top OB center. Mark the top and bottom centers of both the fabric (with a

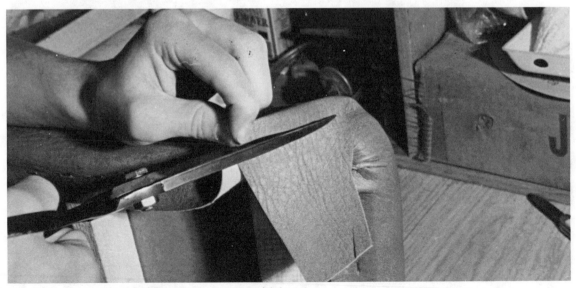

Fig. 13-24. Cut 1/2″ from fold line to remove excess fabric.

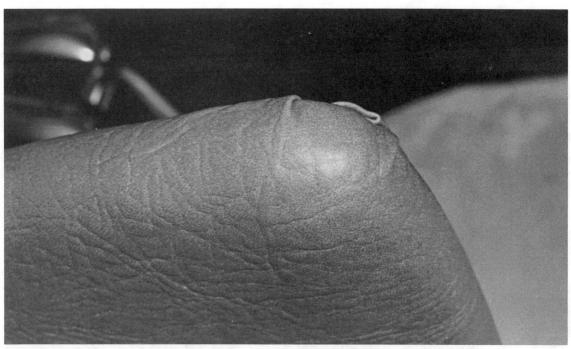

Fig. 13-25. Front view of completed corner of IB panel (OB is partially visible.)

"V" notch) and the frame (with a straight line) Fig. 13-26. *Note:* The OB cardboard is already in place.

2. Align and attach the center of the fabric with the back center and staple fabric toward the sides at approximately 3" intervals. Allow 1/2" to 3/4" for blind tacking, as shown in Fig. 13-27. This is merely to hold the fabric in place in preparation for the tacking strip.

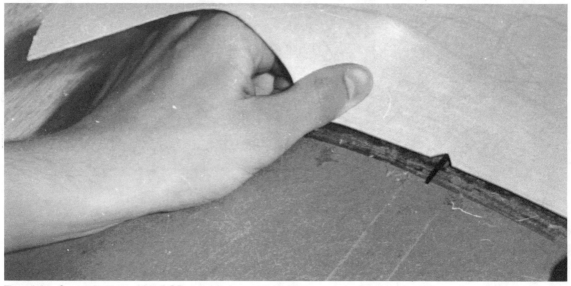

Fig. 13-26. Center reverse side of OB panel to top center of frame.

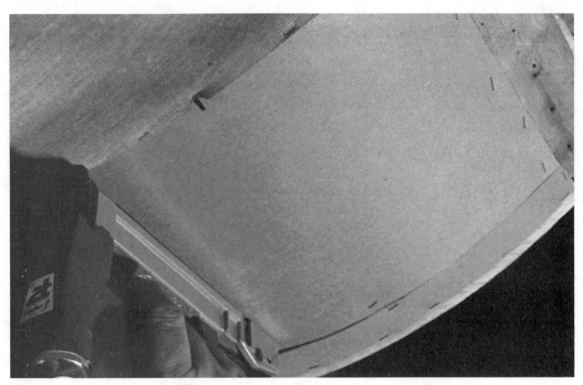

Fig. 13-27. Stretching and place tacking OB panel to install tacking strip.

Fig. 13-28. Installing tacking strip, working from center.

3. Center and attach the tacking strip so the top edge will be slightly beneath the top edge of the frame (Fig. 13-28). *Hint:* A good way to locate the center of tacking strip is to fold it in the center. *Tip:* Staples in the tacking strip should be quite close together and near the edge to be folded to assure a smooth, even edge. Cut tacking strip 3/4″ short of where the outside fold will be located, Fig. 13-29. This is to accommodate the tack strip that will be installed along the sides. *Note:* There will be times when staples should be placed at a diagonal rather than parallel to the outside edges of tacking strip. This is done when it is necessary to also hold the inner edge down, especially true when bulky fabrics are used.

4. Pad the Outside Back. Frequently it is desirable to lightly pad the OB. To do this, use 1/2 thickness of cotton or 1/4″ or 1/2″ polyfoam. Place padding to the top edge of the tacking strip, staple

1 1/2″ to 2″ apart, just to hold in place, then trim 1/2″ inside a line where the inside edge of the side tack strip will be located, Fig. 13-30.

5. Attach bottom of outside back by smoothing and lightly stretching OB panel down and around bottom. Fold cut edge under to make a finished edge and staple, progressing from center toward both sides (Figs. 13-31 and 13-32). Leave 2 or 3 inches from each edge unattached, as shown.

6. Apply side tack strips. Cut a length of tack strip for the sides. It should be 1/4″ to 1/2″ shorter than the distance from the top fold to the bottom edge of the back. Place the inner edge of the tack strip along the line where the side is to be folded over, Fig. 13-33. *Press Tacks Through Fabric.* Lightly pull (diagonally outward and toward bottom) OB panel over tack strip and press onto the tacks. Be careful! Those tacks are sharp! **Caution:** Press fabric onto tacks in two steps: (1) partially,

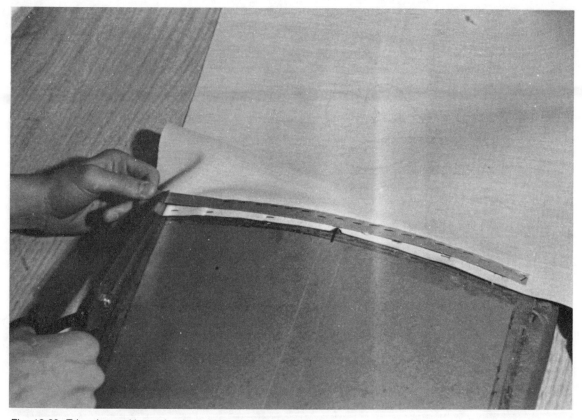

Fig. 13-29. Trimming tacking strip about 3/4″ short of side fold line.

Fig. 13-30. Tear cotton padding 3/4″ short of sides where tag strip is to be attached.

to orient the fabric (illustrated in Fig. 13-34), then (2) completely seated. *Do not* seat fabric completely until all tacks have been located and partially penetrating the fabric —or— sorrow will surely re-sult. Excess fabric should be trimmed 1/2″ to 3/4″ from the tack line. Once the fabric is completely seated, roll the tack strip and fabric under.

7. Seat tack strip by partially driving tacks.

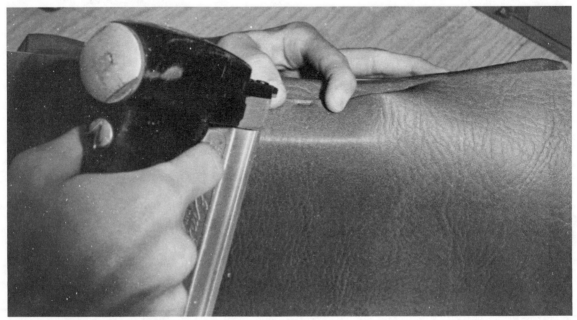

Fig. 13-31. Stapling finished edge of OB panel along bottom back rail.

Fig. 13-32. Center bottom of OB panel in place.

Stretching the fabric slightly to the side with one hand, begin at the top and tap the tacks *partially* into the frame, Fig. 13-35. *Caution:* Do not drive the tacks all the way in at first, that could cause the tack heads to puncture the fabric, distort the tack strip or both.

8. Drive tack strip flush. The second time over, set the tacks all the way in. Use a broad-faced

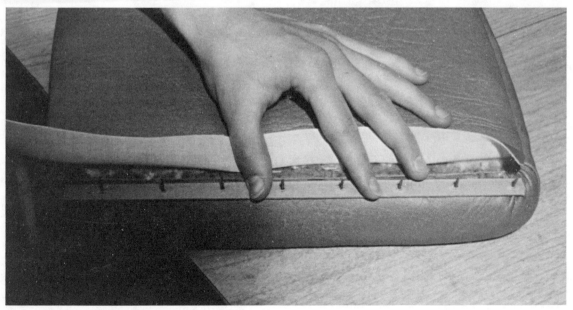

Fig. 13-33. Placing tack strip along sides of OB.

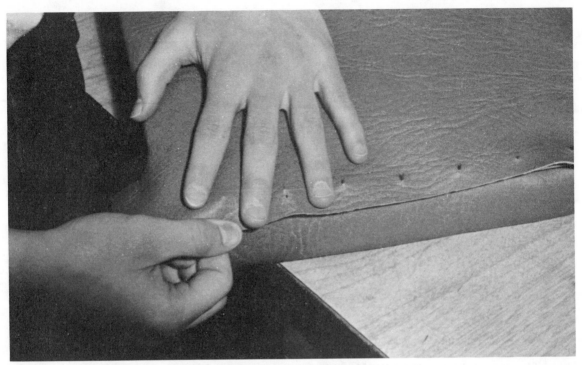

Fig. 13-34. Locating OB panel onto tack strip prior to turning under.

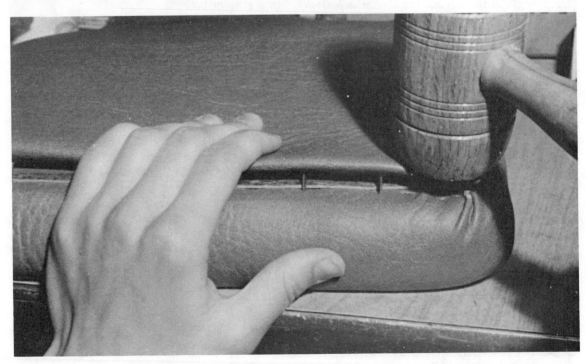

Fig. 13-35. Seating side tack strips.

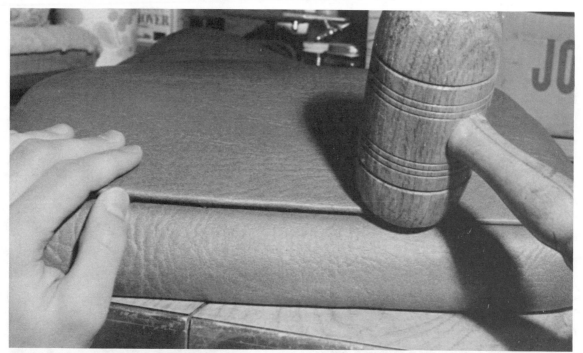

Fig. 13-36. Setting tack strips tight to back.

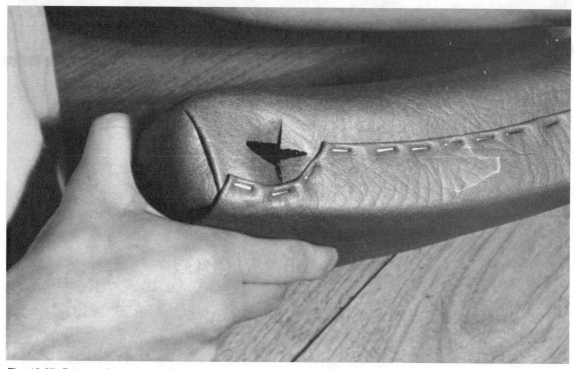

Fig. 13-37. Bottom of completed OB panel showing cross cut to tighten press-fit.

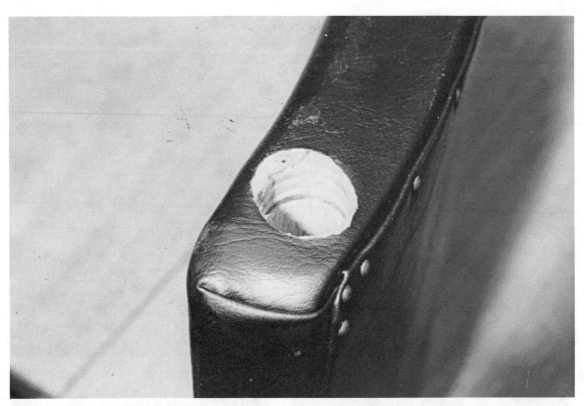

Fig. 13-38. Second style of back showing non-tightening cut-out and Ob panel that is glued to back cardboard and attached with button-head tacks.

hammer, a mallet (as pictured in Fig. 13-36), or the side of a tack hammer to set tack strip. *Tip 1:* Be sure to apply the major force directly above and straight onto the head of tacks rather than just anywhere along the tack strip. *Tip 2:* Placing a folded scrap of vinyl fabric over the OB panel when seating the tack strip reduces the potential to mar, scuff or cut the OB panel.

9. Finish off bottom as illustrated in Fig. 13-37. In this case, the fabric covering the holes for the frame uprights is slit from the center toward the edges. This procedure permits the fabric to fold inward when the uprights are inserted and serves to tighten the fit. In some cases the fit may be so tight that additional material would be unwanted. In those cases, cut a complete circle in the fabric as shown in Fig. 13-38. The back is now ready to slip back onto the frame.

Appendix

The checksheet recommended here is just that, a recommendation, not to be considered as an absolute necessity nor the last word in checksheet efficiency. It has been successfully used by numerous adult upholstery classes at Brigham Young University. It seems to work well. However, if this checksheet does not seem to fit your requirements feel free to make one that works better for you. But, it is strongly recommended, almost urgently recommended that some form of a checksheet be used, especially by inexperienced upholsterers, so the unit can be put back together with success and pride.

Instructions for this checksheet:

Comfort Test (performed prior to stripping): Sit in the unit and see how it feels to you. Is the seat too long? Too firm? Too soft? Too low? Too high? Is the back too short? Too firm? How about the arms? Are they too low for comfort? Need more padding? Should they be softer?

Style Changes: Where and what widths of bands do you want? Do you want to add or remove

panels? Do you wish to add or remove or restyle a skirt? Would it be better to change the methods of attaching certain components? Describe which ones and what the desired change is to be.

Cushions: Check what kind they were. Then in NOTES area, describe what you wish to do when recovering the unit.

Cover: List the pattern and color to be put back on the unit. Indicate the pattern repeat dimension.

Yardage: Chart: List what the chart calls for.

Actually Used: Indicate how much was really used.

EXACT ORDER OF FABRIC REMOVAL

This is the most important part of the checksheet. By recording, with extreme care and accuracy, which panels were removed first and how they were attached, a great deal of difficulty in determining what is to go back on first, second, etc. can be avoided. WARNING: When taking the various panels off, everything looks very simple and straight forward. But, by the time one gets to putting it all back together, it is surprising and a bit frightening how much has been forgotten and how strange it all looks. *Tip* 1: Don't take shortcuts until significant experience has been gained! *Tip* 2: Making sketches of areas and features which seem totally unfamiliar is also a great help, especially where several separate panels seem to or actually come together at the same point. Every help given at this point will be doubly paid back at the time of recovering.

STRIPPING CHECKSHEET

1. Comfort Test -- Changes that are desired

    Seat: Depth_____ Firmness_____

    Back: Depth_____ Firmness_____

    Arms: Height_____ Padding_____

2. Style Changes: Bands_____

                Panels_____

                Skirt_____

                Methods of Attaching_____

                _____

                _____

                _____

    Cushions: Removable__Box__Knife Edge___Waterfall___Attached___

        Notes:_____

            _____

            _____

Cover: Pattern - Style _____ Repeat_____

      Yardage: Chart_____ Actually Used_____

EXACT ORDER OF FABRIC REMOVAL

	Part	Tacked	Tacking Strip	Tack Strip	Sewn	Blind Stitched
Ex1	IB	Bot,T,R,L	--------------	----------	T,R,L (11 pcs)	T,corners
Ex2	OB	Bot	T, flex	R,L side	--------------	---------
1.						
2.						
3.						
4.						
5.						
6.						
7.						
8.						
9.						
10.						
11.						
12.						
13.						

HINT: Separate sketches of different areas are a great help!

COMMENTS:

Glossary

The definitions contained within this glossary have been written for descriptive and functional value rather than the traditional "dictionary approach." In some cases uses, techniques, and inclusion of other terms for reference have been added to enhance clarity and utility. Words appearing in italics will be found as separate entries within the glossary. With some entries, the same term is used for more than one meaning. In those cases the separate definitions are numbered as 1), 2), etc.

accordian pleat—See *pleat: accordion*.

attached cushion—See *cushion: attached*.

auger bit—A drill used for making holes in wood. It has a tapered *lead screw* at the cutting end, an auger section for removing the wood chips, a round shank and a tapered square end which fits into a grooved, two-jawed chuck of a *brace* (see Fig. 2-9A).

Baker clip—A trade name for a 3 or 5 prong steel clip used to fasten *edgewire* to spring wires. The clip is applied with a *spring clip plier* (also known by its trade name, *Baker clip plier*).

balloon arm—An arm on a chair or *couch* which is stuffed to the extent that it appears extra plump and full. Refer to Figs. 5-5, 5-7, and 5-36.

balloon cushion—A cushion of unusual thickness (greater than 5″).

band—A narrow, padded strip of *cover* material used to add "character" to certain furniture styles. May be located at lower portions of the seat, arm, and back; and at the upper and top sections of arms, *wings*, and back *rails* (see Figs. 12-1 and 12-3).

band clamp—A simple clamping device made from a long piece of nylon strap that is tensioned with a ratchet-locked, friction roller. Used to apply pressures around the full perimeter of articles to check fit and while glue is curing or drying (refer to Fig. 2-33).

bar clamp—A steel clamping device made from sections of pipe (1/2″ to 3/4″) or band iron of varying lengths according to need. One end of the "bar" is fitted with a screw-thread moveable jaw. The "stationary jaw" is adjustable along the length of the "bar" either by notches in the band iron or self-locking, spring-loaded jaws on pipe sections (refer to Fig. 2-14).

beading—See *welt cord*, *welt*, and *welting*.

bench cushion—An unusually wide seat cushion that gives a *unit* the appearance of a seat (see Fig. 5-1).

bench seat—A seat, wider than a chair, constructed as one continuous surface. It may have seams or welts, but not separate or separate-appearing cushions, thus giving the appearance of a bench. Refer to Fig. 5-1.

biscuit tufting—A style of *tufting* arranged in a square or rectangular pattern (refer to Figs. 5-10, 5-13, and 5-23). See also *diamond tufting* and *tufting*.

blind stitch—A hand sewn, square stitch which is started from the underside of the cover fabric and then alternates from one side of the seam to the other. When properly done, none of the sewing thread is visible, hence the name *blind* stitch.

blind tacking—A process of *tacking* a fabric to the frame from the back side in such a way that no tacks or *staples* are exposed to view. This is accomplished through the use of a *tack strip*, *flexible tack strip*, or *tacking strip*.

blind tufting clip—A metal clip used with the *blind tufting needle* to install *covered buttons* from the outside only. The clip, with *button tying twine* attached is forced through the *cover* and subsequent *stuffing*, but not through the back *cover*. The *blind tufting needle* is then withdrawn, leaving the clip and twine inside the *unit*. The looped button is then tied on from the outside (refer to Figs. 2-29 and 2-30).

blind tufting needle—A long (8 to 12 inches), straight needle which has a triangular point and a small "hook" a short distance from the point onto which a *blind tufting clip* is attached. Used to attach *covered buttons* to finished furniture where access to the inside for normal tying is restricted (refer to Figs. 2-29 and 2-30).

board foot—See *measurement systems: board foot*.

box cushion—See *cushion: box*.

box pleat—See *pleat: box*.

boxing—Side, front and occasionally back panels of a *box cushion*.

brace—1) A hand tool having a two-jawed *chuck* at one end, an offset handle near the center, and a swivel pad at the other end used to drive square-shanked tools such as *auger bits*. The combination is commonly called *brace and bit* (Fig. 2-9). 2) See also *brace block*.

brace and bit—See *brace* above.

brace block—Short, triangular wood pieces applied at the joints of *uprights*, *posts*, *stumps*, *rails*, and *slats*. The use of a brace block greatly increases the strength and rigidity of a frame.

bracket—A steel plate reinforcement used to provide added strength and rigidity to frame joints.

broad-faced seat panel—An unusually wide (more than 6″) *panel* of fabric which covers the entire front frame on a *unit* (refer to Figs. 5-7, 5-10, and 5-36).

burlap—1) A coarsely woven jute cloth used to cover springs and open frame areas to serve as a support for *stuffing* and *padding* materials. It is easy to work and resists stretching and tearing. 2) Also used to refer to any wear resistant, nonstretching fabric (other than jute composition) used to cover springs or open frame areas over which *padding* is to be placed.

button making machine—A hand tool designed for making covered buttons. There are a couple of different styles that are popular with upholsterers, two of which are illustrated in Figs. 2-25 and 2-26.

buttoned-pillow arm—An arm of a chair or *couch* which is finished off on the top surface with a *pillow cushion* that also has been buttoned to the *unit* (refer to Fig. 5-19).

buttoning—The process of applying covered buttons to a piece of furniture for decorative or contouring purposes. Similar to *tying*.

button tufting needle—A long (6 to 10 inches), straight needle having an eye 1 to 2 inches back from one end and a wooden knob at the other end, used for installing *covered buttons* that use an eye for attachment.

c-clamp—A steel clamp shaped like a "C", hence its name, having an adjusting screw through one side that creates the clamping action (see Fig. 2-8A).

cambric—A black, slightly stiff, sized and calendared cotton or synthetic fabric used to cover the bottoms of seats to prevent dust and stuffing particles from falling to the floor. It comes in light and heavy weights and 30 or 36-inch widths. A white cambric is used for cushion and pillow covers. The original "cambric" was made of flax linen at Cambrae, France, from whence the current name.

camel back—A *couch* or *loveseat* that has one or two compound curves contouring the upper lines of the back (refer to Fig. 5-25).

channel—A linear form of resilient *padding* around which the *cover* is usually sewn to a backing fabric making a pocket. A channel can be wide and relatively flat, fan shaped, curved and tapered, or narrow and rounded (*pipe*). Sometimes called *flute*. Refer to Figs. 5-7, 5-16, 5-24, and 5-26.

chuck—A component part of a tool which has two, three, or four opposing jaws for holding *auger bits*, *twist drills*, and other round, square, or hexagonal shanked tools.

claw tool—A tool with a notched, chisel-like blade and an offset handle used primarily to remove tacks in the *stripping* process. The notch is useful in gripping the tack, but can become a nuisance because (1) tacks may lodge in the slot, or (2) it does require rather close alignment. Sometimes called (though not preferred) "tack remover" (see Fig. 2-2A).

coil spring—See *spring: coil*.

comfort factor—Term used to identify the comfort of a *foam*. It is determined between the *ILD* reading of

25% and the *sag* reading at 65 percent deflection. Special foams, *HR*, can reach a *sag* factor as high as 2.4. No conventional foam can achieve that level of performance.

cording—See *welt*, *welt cord*, and *welting*.

cotton—A natural fiber or fabric made from the cotton plant. As a fabric it is not popular for a *cover*. See *cotton felt*.

cotton felt—A 1 inch thick (approximately) mat of loosely padded cotton fibers composed of varying percentages of gin flues, linters, staple and first cut fibers; also come in cotton-polyester combinations as well as flame retardant varieties. Used for *stuffing* and *padding* and is sold in rolls 27 inches wide and approximately 20 pounds per roll. Most commonly and simply referred to as *cotton*.

couch—A furniture piece designed to seat 3 or more people. Usually contains 3 or more cushions or *panels*, although some styles call for a two-cushion or panel unit. It is usually 72 inches or more in length and is frequently referred to as a *sofa*.

cover—The outer fabric of upholstered furniture.

covered button—A button covered with an upholstery fabric. The back of the button may have a nail, split prong or a loop by which it is attached to the *unit*.

cross tying—A method of tying coil springs for the purpose of providing a more firm, even spring support (see also, *eight-point tie* and *four-point tie*).

crown—That line defined by a 45 degree intersection of the horizontal top surface and the vertical side surface of an arm, back or seat. It is the line at which cuts must be made in *cover* fabric for proper *fitting*.

crowned back—A *couch* or *loveseat* having a back with a single, smooth upward curve which extends from one side to the other (see Figs. 5-7 and 5-26).

curve-ease—A brand name for *flexible tack strip*.

cushion: attached—Any cushion (back or seat) that is affixed to the main furniture piece by sewing, *buttoning* or *tying*.

cushion: box—A cushion having side panels and principally square corners. This gives the cushion a box-like appearance. May be made with or without *welts* (refer to Figs. 5-3, 5-5, 5-12, 5-17, 5-20, 5-35A, and 5-36).

cushion: clam-shell—A cushion (usually back) that has an extra-wide, extra-deep, single tuck sewn into it with the entire length pulled into the *stuffing* in such a way that multiple wrinkles radiate from the tuck, giving the appearance of a closed clam shell (see Figs. 5-33 and 5-34).

cushion: fixed—See *cushion: attached*.

cushion: knife-edge—Cushion with seams, and usually with large *welts*, located at the front and occasionally side centerlines of seat cushions, or the top and occasionally side centerlines of back cushions. The knife-edge gives the cushion sides a rounded appearance. *Welts* are usually made with 3/16 to 3/8-inch diameter cord, depending on size and style desired. See Figs. 5-1, 5-2, 5-6, 5-13, 5-14, 5-16, 5-19, 5-23, 5-26, 5-28, 5-29, 5-31, and 5-36C. See also *full knife-edge*.

cushion: L or J—A cushion which makes a short *right angle* bend in front of the arm *stump*. A cushion passing in front of the right *stump* is the "L" cushion, the one passing in front of the left *stump* is the "J" cushion. These cushions are usually found on *loveseats*, *couches* or *sectional units*.

cushion: loose—Any cushion (back or seat) that is not fastened to the main furniture piece.

cushion: ram horn—A cushion (usually back) that has the top *stuffing* tapered and the edges of the *cover* rolled under the ends in such a way that the side view resembles a ram's horn (see Fig. 5-32).

cushion retainer groove—A recessed linear region created 2 to 5 inches back (depending on the style) from the front edge of the *deck* which (1) acts as a retainer for a *loose cushion* reducing the tendency to *creep* out of the seat, and (2) permits the cushion to nestle-in by reducing the gap between the somewhat rounded cushion face and the *deck*.

cushion size—The outermost dimensions of a stuffed, completed cushion including the side bulging that occurs due to the oversized stuffing. This size is usually considered to be 1/2 inch greater per direction than the *finish size*.

cushion: squared-crescent—A *pillow cushion* having an inner contour in the shape of a crescent and the outer contour of virtually square corners (see Fig. 5-28).

cushion: T—A chair cushion that has a short section that goes in front of both arm *stumps*.

cushion: waterfall—A cushion on which the fabric continues in one piece from the back, around the front (waterfalling), and terminates at the rear of the opposing face. The *boxing* on this style is rounded at the front and is usually squared at the back. May be constructed with or without *welts* (see Figs. 5-4, 5-7, 5-9, 5-33, and 5-35B).

cut size—The size of a piece of fabric that includes all *tucks*, *pleats*, and *seam allowances* which are added to the *finish sizes*.

dacron—1) A curly, white polyester fiber mat used as

an outer layer or built-up layers of *padding* to provide extra softness in the final *feel*. It is also used to stuff pillows. Sold in rolls 27 inches wide weighing normally between 6 to 7 pounds. 2) A brand name for a thermoplastic polyester fiber or fabric.

davenport—See *couch* and *sofa*.

deck—The seat area upon which the cushion (*fixed* or *loose*) rests.

decorative tacks—Tacks or nails with large, domed heads which may have a hammered, antiqued, polished, brushed, geometrically contoured or a combination of these finishes. They may be made of brass, aluminum, steel, stainless steel; they may be plated, painted, or plastic coated. Used to add decoration, characterize period furniture, or strike a special motif.

decking—A durable fabric, cotton or synthetic, used to cover that part of the *deck* not normally visible when cushions are in place. It is often used to reduce cost as it is significantly less expensive than most *cover* materials.

density—The "weight" of a unit volume of *foam*, expressed in pounds per cubic foot. Many people erroneously use this term to indicate "hardness". See *ILD* for comparison. Most foams will have densities up to 2 pounds per cubit foot with seating foams being in the range of 1.4 to 2.0 PCF.

diagonal cut—A single, straight-line cut made in a piece of *cover*, *muslin*, or *burlap* that goes diagonally toward the inside corner of a *post*, *stump*, or *rail* where that fabric is to be *fitted* to two sides only of the frame member (Figs. 4-42, 4-43, 4-44, 9-3, 9-4 and 9-5).

diagonal cutters—A plier-like tool having a pair of cutting jaws that are placed at a slight angle to the handles (diagonal thereto) used for cutting wires and cords and for extracting staples and remnants (see Fig. 2-4B).

diagonal tying—See *eight-point tying*.

diamond tufting—A *tufting* operation wherein the *tufts* take on a diamond shape (see Figs. 5-14, 5-15, 5-21, and 5-22). See also *tufting*.

diamond tying—See *eight-point tying*.

dikes—The abbreviated yet popular name for *diagonal cutters*.

double-point needle—A straight needle pointed at both ends. The points may be either round (used for woven fabrics) or triangular (used for vinyls and leathers) having a single eye a short distance (between 1 and 2 inches) from one end. Used for (1) sewing *cushion retainer grooves*, or (2) installing *covered buttons* when a *button tufting needle* is not available (refer to Fig. 2-17).

dust cover—A fabric to prevent dust and stuffing materials from falling to the floor. See *cambric*.

edge roll—Generally a 1 1/4 inch diameter roll of twisted fiber-core material covered with 10 ounce burlap or polyester fabric and sewn snugly to form. Most edge rolls have some form of fastening lip, are fastened directly to the front seat or top back frame or to the *edge wire*, and most in use today are commercially produced. In years past, upholsterers formed, wrapped and sewed their own. See also *frame edging*.

edge wire—Heavy steel wire, 8 or 9 gauge, used to form a straight edge on *coil spring* construction or on *sinuous spring* systems incorporating the *V-arc* and *Z-arc* edge suspension. Edge wire is attached with metal clips called *Baker clips* or *spring clips*.

eight-point tie—A method of tying *coil springs* using 4 pieces of *typing twine* tied at 45-degree angles to each other, with two ties occurring per strand on each coil. Also referred to as *cross tie*. See also *four-point tie* for comparison.

fabric saw—A power driven (pneumatic or electric) saw used by production upholsterers, commercial textile fabricators, and tailors for cutting multiple layers of fabric to the same shapes and sizes. The saws will either have counter-reciprocating, very fine-toothed saw blades or a smooth, disc blade. Models of each are illustrated in Fig. 2-33.

fatigue—An expression of the loss in load bearing quality of a *foam*. The popular test for fatigue is derived from a static load being applied to an ILD of 25% for 17 hours at room temperature. The ILD loss is then expressed as a percentage of the original ILD value.

feathering—The act of tapering the edge of a *stuffing* or *padding* material to give a smooth tapered look to the *cover*, leaving no "end-of-padding" lines.

finish size—The size of a piece of fabric or cushion from seam stitch to seam stitch. *Seam allowances* are added to these dimensions to obtain the *cut size*. Refer also to *cushion size*.

fitting—The process of stretching, cutting, and *tacking* the *cover* into final location.

flap-panels—Thin, lightly *padded* cushions constructed on the order of a pillow that are attached to the arm or back (or both) of a *unit* by a flap sewn to the back of the cushion near the top. If these cushions were not further attached through the use of *covered buttons* they could be flapped upward by the flick of the hand, thus the name. Refer to Figs. 5-14—5-18.

flexible tack strip—A flexible, notched, metal strip that is formed to a *right angle* of approximately 1/2

333

inch each side. Used extensively for fastening *outside arm* and *outside back panels* having curved lines.

flop cushion—A cushion resembling a pillow, completely enclosed, usually having a zipped back, and is attached to a piece of furniture with an extra flap located near the rear, upper edge of the cushion permitting it to "flop". Refer to Figs. 5-29—5-31 and 5-36.

flute—See *channel*.

foam—The abbreviated term, most commonly used in upholstering practices to refer to *foam rubber*.

foam adhesive—An adhesive, usually in aerosol spray cans, formulated especially for attaching *foam rubber* materials to each other or to other fabrics. It is often used to fasten fabrics to other base materials such as wood or metal. This adhesive, when cured, remains flexible permitting resiliency while maintaining adhesion.

foam rubber—A porous, usually open-celled, urethane based, flexible material. Other materials have been used in the past, but with limited success. The industry uses urethane foams almost entirely. Most frequently it is referred to as just *foam*.

foam saw—A saw especially designed to cut slabbed *foam* to smaller or contoured shapes. It is usually an electric hand saw which has two counter-reciprocating, fine toothed blades and a tapered base (refer to Fig. 2-20).

foundation—The spring units, *webbing*, or solid (wood, plastic, or metal) base that provides the general support over which desired *stuffing* and *padding* is placed, and which gives the desired resiliency or rigidity for the furniture piece.

four-point stay—The application of tacks or *staples* at four points on an *inside arm panel* to hold it in place while final *fitting* is completed.

four-point tie—The two directional method of tying *coil springs* involving two pieces of *tying twine* with two ties occurring per strand on each coil. This is the minimum tie usually used and gives the softest suspension. The ties are made at 90 degrees to each other and square (insofar as possible) with the *frame*. Refer to *eight-point tie* for comparison.

fox edge—A rolled edging used to soften, round, and in some cases extend *rail*, *post*, and *stump* edges. Fox edging is a brand name and should not be mistaken for *edge roll*, but rather fits the *frame edging* classification.

frame edging—A roll of fiber or plastic material ranging from 3/8 to 1 inch in diameter, jute or polyester covered, with or without a fastening lip, designed to give sharp edges a rounded, softened effect. It is used

also to provide a recess for *panels* and reduce fabric wear at corners and edges. Refer to *edge roll* for comparison. Also called *fox edge*.

full knife-edge—A *knife-edge cushion* on which the center seam extends not only across the front (seat) or top (back), but around the sides as well (see Fig. 5-6).

gauge—The diameter of wire (*edge wire*, etc.) and the thickness of sheet metal used in plates, brackets and braces is expressed using this term. The higher the gauge number, the smaller the diameter of wire or the thinner the sheet metal.

gimp—A narrow band of decorative material used to conceal tacks, staples and *cover* edges that would otherwise be visible, and objectionable. It comes in ribbon form and is purchased by the yard, card or roll.

gimp gun—A pneumatic *staple gun* that uses narrowback staples especially suited for very low visibility in fastening *gimp* to upholstered *units*. It is also used for holding down other areas of *cover* where seeing the staple would be objectionable. Refer to Fig. 2-35.

gimp tack—A tack having a small diameter domed head used to attach *gimp* or to hold down corners, tabs, pleats or folds of *cover* material. The small head virtually disappears from view when used properly.

glide—Metallic or plastic (usually nylon) domes or caps placed on the bottoms of legs to reduce friction, marring and snagging of floor surfaces.

hand screw—A clamping device having two counter-threaded steel rods with handles and two wooden jaws which can be adjusted to apply pressure to parallel or slightly nonparallel surfaces. Used primarily to hold wooden pieces together while glue sets or dries (Refer to Fig. 2-13).

hard edge—A narrow strip of wood, often plywood, used as a retainer for the *seat* cover panel and as an elevator to raise the front seat *rail* to a height slightly above the crowned height of the springs.

helical spring—See *spring: helical*.

high resiliency foam—A urethane foam (classified "HR") possessing an exceptionally high degree of "life" or resiliency. Although more expensive than conventional foams, HR significantly increases the *comfort factor* and durability beyond that expected from the conventional urethane and latex foams.

hog ring—A steel wire formed in the shape of a "C" having pointed ends and measuring approximately 3/4 inch across its width. It is used extensively in auto upholstering and in areas where fabric is to be fastened to wire or rod anchoring systems. The rings are most successfully applied with *hog ring pliers* (refer to Fig. 2-20).

hog ring pliers—A plier having jaws with recessed grooves especially designed for holding *hog rings*. There are standard and spring-loaded models, the latter being much more convenient to use as they retain the ring within the plier without the need of any further pressure being applied by the operator. There are also straight and angled models.

HR—See *high resiliency*.

ILD—Indentation Load Deflection: a measure of load bearing (hardness of a *foam* material). A specimen 15″ × 15″ × 4″ is placed under a circular plate of 50-square-inch area, which is depressed 1″. This is 25% indentation. A reading is taken which shows the number of pounds required to make that deflection. If 20 pounds were required, the foam ILD would be 20 pounds at 25% deflection.

in-line—The abnormal, but occasionally necessary, practice of applying staples which are parallel, or nearly so, to a fold or tuck rather than perpendicular to it. This practice most often occurs when forming round-topped, padded arms at the *stump*.

interlacing—Crossing of one *webbing* strip alternately over and under other strips giving a uniform support base for *coil springs* or other *stuffing*.

innerspring—*Coil springs* contained within either individual fabric pockets or several coils linked together and enclosed as a group in a fabric (*Marshall unit*).

jute—A very durable, imported (from India), natural plant fiber that resists tearing and stretching. It is used extensively in *burlap*, *webbing*, and twines.

Klinch-it clip—Metal clips used to anchor *coil springs* to cloth *webbing*. The clips are applied with a *Klinch-it tool* which presses the clip prongs through the *webbing* and spreads them sideways, clinching the spring tightly to the *webbing* (see Figs. 2-28A and 2-28B).

Klinch-it tool—A dispensing-type tool having a long throat or tube into which *Klinch-it clips* are placed, and which is used for anchoring *coil springs* to *webbing* with the specially designed clips (*Klinch-it clips*). Refer to Figures 2-27 and 2-28.

knife edge—See *cushion: knife edge*.

lead screw—A short, tapered screw-like thread at the point of an *auger bit* which draws the cutting edges into the wood (until, of course, the lead screw extends out the back side of the piece being drilled).

legs—The two parallel sides of a staple that penetrate into the substrate.

loose cushion—See *cushion: loose*.

loveseat—A furniture piece designed to seat two people comfortably. It is wider than a chair and narrower than a *couch*, the normal length being from 54 to 66 inches. Can be made with a one-piece seat cushion or with two sections or cushions, the latter being the most popular.

low profile spring—See *spring: sinuous*.

mallet—A rubber, wooden, plastic or rawhide tool used to drive *ripping tools* or *claw tools*, set *tack strip* and smooth *stuffing* and *padding* after *cover* is in place. Rawhide or white rubber are preferred by most upholsterers (refer to Fig. 2-12).

Marshall unit—Coil springs sewn in individual *muslin* or *burlap* pockets and fastened together in strips or complete, ready-made units; used in seats, backs, cushions and mattresses. Also called *innerspring* units.

matching band—A *band* of the same proportional width as the remainder of the surface to which it is attached, usually along the front seat frame (see Fig. 5-5).

measurement systems—See below.

> **board foot**—A surface area of any material which is one foot on each side (one square foot) and one inch thick. It is calculated by multiplying the length of the material by the width (L × W) either in terms of inches or feet. If calculated in inches, conversion to board feet is made by (1) dividing the product by 144 (which is the number of square inches in one square foot) and (2) multiplying this product by the number of inches the material is thick. If calculated in feet, the area is already in terms of square feet, merely multiply the product by the number of inches the material is thick.

> **linear**—The term is derived from "line", meaning that this measurement pertains to one direction only, length. Examples of materials for which the linear measure is used are: ribbon, *gimp*, rope, twine, wire and wood moldings. Fabric, *cotton*, *dacron*, as well as some other materials are often sold by the linear measure. Also referred to as *running* measure.

> **metric**—Although much has been done preparing the United States for a conversion from the English measuring system to metrics, almost no binding activity has been noted in the area of upholstery and textiles as yet. Even the spelling of the standard for *linear* measure, the "meter" (as it is preferred by the U.S. Metric Board) is often spelled "metre", which is the preferred spelling of the ISO (International Standards Office).

running—A measurement referring to length only (see *linear* above).

measuring—The process of taking measurements with a cloth or metal tape from a finished piece of furniture to establish the proper *cushion* or *panel* size. Refer to *tailoring*, for comparison. Measuring for establishing cushion dimensions works well with straight-line seats. ("Tailoring" is recommended for units with any curvature in seat.)

metalene nails—Nails having extra large, flat heads that have been painted or vinyl coated to blend in with vinyl coverings. They are used to apply *gimp* and, in some instances, as *decorative nails*.

muslin—A lightweight, inexpensive cotton cloth used as a first *cover* over the completely padded furniture. Especially valuable for the learner as it provides experience in *tailoring* or *measuring*, cutting and *fitting* operations before the much more expensive *cover* material is worked.

nail head, set trim—A finishing style wherein the IB or IA *panels* are *tacked* to the front and tops of the frame respectively, then a *band panel* is attached with *decorative tacks* and stuffed to created a rounded *band*. Refer to Figs. 5-26 and 5-27.

narrow band—A *band* added to a piece of furniture that is proportionately more narrow than the remainder of the surface to which it is attached (see Fig. 5-4).

needlenose—A plier-like tool having long, tapered jaws, used to bend small radii in soft wires, grasp small objects in restricted areas, hold gimp tacks for starting, and other similar uses (see Fig. 2-4C).

no-sag spring crimper—Part of a hand tool unit, originally designed by the No-Sag Spring Company, used for reversing the bend in the cut *sinuous spring* (see Figs. 2-22 and 2-23).

no-sag cutter—Part of a hand tool unit, originally designed by the No-Sag Spring Company, having a single, hardened steel cutting blade that is pressed toward but stops at the face of a steel cylinder around which a section of *sinuous spring* is placed and subsequently cut (see Fig. 2-21).

no-sag spring—See *spring: sinuous*.

notches—Small cuts made in the *seam allowance* area of *cover panels* for the purpose of providing matching and aligning marks in the pieces which are to be sewn together. The cuts are usually made in a "V" shape, but may also be cut as double and triple V's; single, double or triple U's; as combinations of V's and U's; or simply as slits.

overstuffed—A piece of furniture on which virtually the entire surface is covered with a cloth or vinyl fabric, except for relatively small sections of *show wood*. Implied in this classification is generally the notion that the *unit* has one or more types of spring *foundation* and *padding*.

padding—The outer layer of resilient material just beneath the *cover* giving the desired feel (firmness) or appearance (plumpness) to the furniture *unit*. It may be used over the top of *stuffing* materials or alone, in which case it is both *stuffing* and padding, as in the case of *super soft foam* for a back cushion.

panel—1) A piece of heavy cardboard, light (1/8 to 1/4 inch) plywood, or other similar material cut to the matching contour of the front of an *arm stump*, the ends of a back, or the outside of a *wing*. The panel is added (usually), covered and nailed in place (usually with four penny finish nails) or wire brads, giving the *stump*, back or *wing* a pleasing, finished look. 2) Any of the major pieces of *cover* fabric which have been cut and readied for application, such as *seat* panel, arm panel, back panel, zipper panel.

pattern repeat—Refers to the distance from one point on a fabric to the nearest point at which the pattern repeats itself. Ranges go from 3″ to 27″ generally, with only a few being less or greater than this range.

pattern layout—A freehand sketch of all the *panels* of fabric that will be needed to cover or recover any given *unit* (refer to Figs. 6-13 and 6-14).

Phillips screwdriver—A screwdriver having a tapered, four-vaned blade that fits the recessed Phillips head screws.

pillow arms—An arm of a chair or *couch* that has as a final *padding* an attached *pillow cushion* (see Fig. 5-19).

pillow back—The back of a chair or *sofa* that has a *pillow cushion* as the final *padding* (Figs. 5-13 through 5-19, 5-22, 5-23 and 5-35C).

pillow cushion—A cushion that is constructed much on the order of a pillow, enclosed on all sides and having no *boxing* (see Figs. 5-13—5-19, 5-22, 5-23 and 5-35C).

pillow spring—See *spring: pillow*.

pipe—A *channel* produced by filling rather narrow tubes of *cover* material that are sewed to a fabric backing, giving a pronounced rounded appearance similar to the pipes of a pipe organ, whence cometh the name. Generally pipes are more slender than *channels*, although the terms are occasionally used interchangeably.

place tacking—See *stay tacking*.

platform—1) The wooden or metal structure upon which a piece of furniture rests, having solid footing on the floor while permitting the rest of the item to rock, swivel or both. 2) The flat, horizontal portion of a solid seat before installation of cushions, *stuffing* or *padding*.

pleat—Regular folds sewn into the *cover* fabric. Usually associated with *skirts*, *tufts*, *channels* or *pipes*. Also used at corners and other areas requiring a reduction of the perimeter of the fabric. Refer to *tuck* for comparison.

pleat: accordion—A *pleat* made with the folds all going the same direction, giving a stepped effect.

pleat: box—A *pleat* made by alternating the direction of the folds, giving an alternating planar effect.

pleat: kick—A small section of *cover* made in same manner as the rest of the *skirt* but separate from it, and which is attached to the frame at corners or at leg positions to provide complete coverage while giving the rest of the *skirt* mobility at these locations.

Pli-grip—A brand name for a notched, metal *flexible tack strip* capable of forming to compound curves with ease.

polyfoam—An abbreviated term referring to flexible urethane *foam rubber* of a "standard" firmness (*ILD*) and resiliency.

post—The front vertical member of an arm or back corners; normally narrower than 3 inches; arm may be covered, partially covered, or all *show wood*; does not involve use of a *panel* (compare with *stump*).

rail—The horizontal members of a frame that give the furniture the general form and structure.

recovery—The "bounce-back" of *foam* material. It is derived after the *sag factor* has been taken. The foam is again depressed to 25 percent *ILD*. This second reading is divided by the first 25 percent *ILD* reading to give a percentage of recovery. High recovery factors are essential for good cushioning applications.

regulator—See *stuffing regulator*.

right angle—An angle of 90 degrees; one which makes a "square" corner.

ripping tool—A chisel-like tool with a sharpened, square-ended, offset blade used primarily for removing tacks in the *stripping* process. Refer to *claw tool* for comparison (see Fig. 2-3A and C).

rubberized hair—Curled animal hair (generally hog) coated with a rubber film and processed in mat form approximately 1 inch thick. Used as a base *stuffing* in earlier upholstering techniques. Although still available, many upholsterers no longer use it as it gives a rather stiff, "crackeling" base and mats down rather readily.

running stitch—A straight stitch made close to and parallel with the seam, giving a very visible "stitched" appearance. It may be made on either or both sides of the seam. In some vinyl upholstery, a double running stitch is used to attach a fabric reinforcement strip to the back of the seam to relieve the stress on the vinyl seam and reduce the potential of tear-out. See also *top stitching* (Figs. 9-18 and 12-57).

sag factor—The cushioning quality or resistance of a *foam* to "bottoming out", derived from the ratio of 65% *ILD* to 25% *ILD*. A sag factor of 1.8 to 2.0 is considered in the normal range and is referred to as "standard."

sagless spring—See *spring: sinuous*.

scissor stapler—A manual, hand-held stapler having handles at one end, a pivot in the center, and the stapling end at the opposite end. It is used extensively in professional upholstery to temporarily hold folds and tucks in place for sewing. It also finds frequent use for fastening *dacron* edges together around cushion foam or spring units in preparation for stuffing into the cushion cover (see Fig. 2-7C).

screwdriver bit—A screwdriver tool having a point (*straight-slot*, *Phillips*, etc.) and shank, but no handle. The bit will either have the shank end round, square or with "ears" for inserting into a *Jacob's chuck* or *brace* respectively (refer to Fig. 2-15).

seam allowance—The amount of fabric extending beyond the seam itself which is not a visible part of the *cover panel*. For consistency and ease of reference, 1/2 inch has been designated for use within this text.

seat band—See *band*.

sectional—A set of two or more furniture pieces that can be used singly or in combination to form a variety of seating arrangements. These pieces are designed in such a way that they can be put next to each other and look almost as if they were one piece.

show wood—The finished wood surfaces that are supposed to be exposed (show) when the upholstery is completed.

silencer—A strip of fabric, oil impregnated craft paper, *webbing*, *foam rubber*, or other *stuffing* material used to reduce or eliminate noise of springs moving against the frame clips or support members.

sinuous spring—See *spring: sinuous*.

skewer—A slender pin usually 3 to 3 1/2 inches long, having a sharp, round tapered point at one end and a ring "handle" at the other. Also known as *upholsterer's pin* (not to be confused with shish kebob implement used at barbecues).

skirt—A horizontal segment of fabric, usually around the bottom of a piece of furniture that is fastened (*blind tacked* or sewn) at the upper edge only, leaving the bottom portion free to move. May be straight or *pleated*. Refer to *pleat: accordion*, *pleat: box*, and *pleat: kick*.

slat—A horizontal frame member, other than and between *rails* or arms that add strength and support and provide for tacking and stretching the *cover*. Refer also to *tack rails*.

slip-joint pliers—The proper term for the common household type plier. It is thus called because the pivot joint "slips" at the full-open position to accommodate size adjustments (see Fig. 2-4A).

slip seat—An upholstered frame seat constructed for easy removal and installation to a furniture frame. Usually attached by means of wood screws or bolts.

slip tacking—See *stay tacking*.

socks—Muslin casings for individual and rows of *coil springs* from which *marshall units* are made.

sofa—Another term for *couch*. There exists no universal distinction between sofa, *couch* or *davenport*. All three terms generally refer to a unit long enough to accommodate an adult reclining.

spring—The major suspension component for furniture provided by spring steel coils, bends, or curves.

spring bar unit—A group of two to five single-tapered *coil springs* fastened to a steel support bar which in turn is fastened to the frame of the furniture. Generally it is used for seat suspension.

spring clamp—A clamp which operates much like a pair of pliers except that a spring holds the handles apart and the jaws together (see Fig. 2-8B).

spring clip—The generic term for steel clips used to fasten two wire segments together. Refer also to *Baker clip*.

spring clip plier—A special plier having offset, pronged jaws designed for crimping the tabs of *spring clips* around *edgewire* and *spring* elements.

spring: coil—Coils of spring steel wire used as a major resilient base in furniture and mattresses. Coils can be wound with parallel sides or with single or double tapers. In double tapers, the smaller diameter is in the center of the spring rather than at the ends.

spring edge—See *edgewire*.

spring edging—An *edge roll* made in varying sizes for the purpose of closing the gap between the *deck* edge and the cushion. It also acts to help keep cushions in place while at the same time reducing the sharpness of the *spring edge*.

spring: helical—Small diameter (1/2 to 3/4 inches) coils of spring wire wound parallel, used (occasionally) as connector between *sinuous springs*, between *edge wires* and springs, and (frequently) between springs or *edge wires* and the frame. Light weight are used for backs and heavier weight for the seats. They come in open and closed form.

spring: low profile—See *spring: sinuous*.

spring: No-Sag—A brand name for a *sinuous spring* manufactured by No-Sag Spring Division of Lear Siegler, Inc. No-Sag has become the "catch-word" in the industry, probably because the company was the first on the market with the product, hence it carries the company name, much like "Formica", "Styrofoam", and "Masonite"—all being brand names for given products. Refer to *spring: sinuous* for gauge size and use area.

spring: pillow—A lightweight, basically parallel wound *coil spring* with both ends fastened with a clip to the last coil, preventing rips or punctures to a fabric. In spite of its name, this spring is not used in pillows!

spring: sagless—See *spring: sinuous*.

spring: sinuous—A steel spring wire bent in a serpentine form and wound on a roll. Also called *No-Sag*, *zig-zag*, and *sagless spring*. Heavy gauge wire (8 or 9) is used for seats while light gauge (11 or 12) is used for backs.

spring: zig-zag—See *spring: sinuous*.

staple—A wire fastener having a square "U" shape used for *tacking* upholstery materials to wooden or structural foam (plastic) frame members. Note: Should not be applied to fingers!

staple gun—A pneumatic, electric or manually operated tool that drives wire *staples* at the press of a trigger. It is estimated that the use of a staple gun reduces upholstery work time from 30 to 50 percent over the earlier use of tacks and *tack hammer*. Note: Should not be aimed at friends, relatives or other living things when firing (refer to Fig. 2-7).

staple remover—A tool used primarily for the removing of staples. There are two popular varieties: 1) A flat, two-pronged, patented model (commonly called the *Berry picker*, after the name of the inventor), and 2) a flat, wedge-shaped tool. Each has its advantage, but the *Berry picker* is preferred by most upholsterers and is discussed exclusively within this text except for the tools identification section where the wedge tool is illustrated (refer to Fig. 2-2).

stay tacking—The procedure of temporarily fastening a *cover panel* into basic position by driving a #8, or larger, *upholstery tack* part way in to hold the *panel* from shifting while final *fitting* is pursued. Stay tacks are easily removed when desired. Also called *place tacking* or *slip tacking, Staples* are very often used in modern practices instead of tacks.

stretcher—A strip of scrap material (*cover, burlap, decking*, etc.) that is sewn to the *cover* in areas where additional length is needed to stretch and *tack* and where the stretcher will not be seen as the *unit* is in normal use. The use of a stretcher can save on yardage of *cover* required, depending on size and cutting orientation.

stripping—The process of removing old fabric and damaged *padding, stuffing*, springs or other support materials.

stuffing—The under-layers of resilient materials used to provide the basic softness or firmness of the upholstered item. All upholstered furniture uses some form of stuffing. *Padding* and stuffing are often used interchangeably.

stuffing regulator—A sharply pointed, tapered, steel instrument used for inserting through *cover* or *muslin* cover to move (regulate) small amounts of *padding* without having to remove the *panels* (refer to Fig. 2-16).

stuffing tool—A tapered, wedge-shaped tool used to force *stuffing* or *padding* into corners, *channels, pipes* and areas which cannot be reached by hand.

stump—The front, vertical member of an arm. A stump is usually wider than the average arm *post*, being from 3 to 8 inches wide, may be contoured, most often is finished with a *panel*, and involves a covered arm.

super-soft foam—A very soft *foam rubber* used to make very soft cushions or *padding* (usually restricted to backs). It possesses just enough resiliency to return the fabric to its desired shape without giving a firm feel.

tab—1) The "V" shaped center portion of the *Y-cut* that is tucked under to create a *"finished edge"* when the *cover* is *fitted* against a *post* or *upright*. 2) A strip of *cover* fabric that is cut in a *panel* (like the rear portion of an inside arm *panel*) to permit stretching of the fabric on either side of a *rail* or around the *crown*.

tack—1) A metal fastening device characterized by a tapering shank (except in the case of *decorative tacks*) and a variety of head styles. 2) a term used to signify attaching a fabric to the frame of the furniture. The term originated from the earlier and exclusive use of tacks. Modern practices use *staples* for the same purpose, hence, tacking a fabric *panel* in place may well be done with *staples*.

tack hammer—A curved, slim, double-headed hammer having one head magnetized for the purpose of picking up and holding tacks making one hand installation possible. The flat sides of the hammer are often used to install fiber or metal tack strip, thus preventing cutting of the fabric. Also referred to as *upholsterer's hammer* (refer to Fig. 2-5).

tacking—The process of fastening fabric materials to the frame. Until the early 1950s, *upholstery tacks* were used exclusively for this task, hence the term. Even though *staples* are used by most shops today, "tacking" is the term still used.

tacking strip—A chipboard strip purchased in rolls or strips (or sometimes in sheets and then cut into strips) that is used for *blind tacking* the *cover* where straight sections can be reached from the underside of the fabric, like the tops of outside arm and back *panels*. Most common strip width is 1/2 inch. Also comes in a light weight, easy to bend metal strip (refer to *flexible tack strip*). See Figs. 10-4 through 10-6.

tackless—Note: Not to be confused with "tactless." 1) A term used by some upholsterers to refer to *tack strip* because, like its name-sake, it requires no addition of tacks. 2) The term is more correctly used to refer to the metal or wooden strips used for fastening carpeting to the substrates without the necessity of additional tacks.

tack rails—A horizontal frame member especially installed to provide a tacking surface in locations where the *rails* or *slats* do not meet upholstering needs.

tack remover—See *claw tool* and *ripping tool*.

tack strip—A rigid chipboard or metal strip into which tacks have been affixed by the manufacturer; used to accomplish straight *blind tacking* which must be installed and finished from the outside. Comes in strips 27 or 30 inches long with tack sizes of 8, 10, or 12 ounce (see Figs. 10-13—10-21, 10-27—10-32).

tailoring—The process of laying a cushion *panel* on a seat (or back) of a finished piece of furniture and then marking with chalk to the exact contour of the seat or back area, thus "tailoring" the *panel* to the precise size and shape. This process is more accurate and a little more time consuming than *measuring*.

tear-out—The occurrence of a fabric tearing away from a stapled or tacked area because of loose or insufficient fastening, excessive pressure, or the failure to *tack* an externally folded flap over the top of a partially attached *panel*.

top stitching—The process of sewing a normal seam again on one (single top stitch) or both (double top stitch) sides of the original seam creating a styling change as well as a stronger seam. The increased strength is accomplished by folding the seam flaps to one side and sewing through all layers from the top side of the fabric. The styling change is created by the thread of the top stitch(s) which are totally visible from the face side of the fabric. The thread may be in a contrasting or blending color. Additional reinforcement may be added by sewing a narrow strip of fabric to the back side of the seam. This is restricted to the double top-stitch, however. Sometimes called a *running stitch* (Fig. 12-57).

trestle—A saw horse-type stand with a padded, covered top used for elevating and supporting furniture during the upholstering process. The padded top, which is also recessed to retain furniture legs, protects furniture from being scratched or fabric from being snagged or torn (refer to Fig. 2-19).

tuck—A fold made in *cover* fabric for the purpose of reducing the perimeter.

tufting—The process of using *covered buttons, pleats, tucks* and *tying twine* in a patterned array to hold the *cover* and *padding* in place, giving styling and contouring to the furniture. Characterized by raised areas (tufts) that are generally diamond (*diamond tufting*) or rectangular (*biscuit tufting*) in shape.

twist drill—A drill having a smooth, round shank, usually two flutes, and smooth tapered point with no lead screw. The flutes look much like a flat piece of steel had been twisted. It is designed primarily for drilling metals and other materials of equal or lesser hardness (refer to Fig. 2-9B).

tying—The process of tying a strong twine to the seam flaps at intersections or through the *cover* fabric and padding for the purpose of creating depressions for design or contouring or for affixing cushions to the furniture.

tying twine—A tough, heavy twine, tightly twisted or braided of jute, nylon, polyester, flax or polypropylene. Used for tying springs, buttons and *edge wires*. Comes in 1, 2, and 10 pound spools.

unit—1) A complete piece of furniture such as a chair, ottoman, couch, recliner. 2) A set or subassembly of pieces which can be removed as an entity such as a spring unit, back or arm assembly, foot-rest, cushion.

upholstered—A furniture piece which has some form of *padding, stuffing,* springs, or a combination thereof, covered by either a cloth or vinyl fabric.

upholsterer's hammer—See *tack hammer.*

upholsterer's pin—See *skewer.*

upholsterer's shears—A heavy-duty pair of shears, improperly referred to by some as "scissors", used to cut the heavier upholstery fabrics, twines and threads (refer to Fig. 2-1).

upright—Vertical support members of a frame that do not serve as legs, *posts* or *stumps.*

V-arc—A *sinuous spring* construction wherein the end of the spring is formed to a "V" shape. This makes it possible for the end of the spring to also have a significant "spring" or return not normally found with the standard sinuous construction. If it is part of the sinuous spring, it also requires an additional *slat* for fastening the spring end as the end is now at a position shorter than that of the seat or top rail, where *sinuous spring* is normally attached. If it is a separate section, it fastens to the edge wire and rail. See also *Z-arc* and Fig. 4-36.

vents—Holes made in solid seat boards when a seat is covered with vinyl or any non-breathing *cover* fabric. If vents were not provided the seat would become an air pillow.

webbing—A strip of *jute,* cotton, plastic, rubber, or metal ranging from 1 to 4 inches in width and of various weights (thicknesses) used to provide a foundation for *coil springs* and other *stuffing* materials. Plastic webbing is often used as the only material on a piece of furniture other than the frame and necessary attaching hardware, as in the case of lawn furniture.

webbing pliers—A plier having corrugated, parallel jaws (usually 3 1/2 inches wide) used to grip and stretch *webbing,* leather or other fabrics (Fig. 2-10B).

webbing stretcher—A tool used to grasp *webbing* by pressure, puncturing or binding for the purpose of stretching it taught over the furniture frame. The tool may be designed with jaws, tapered steel pins or a slotted head (refer to Fig. 2-10).

webbing tack—A barbed tack used to fasten *webbing* to wooden or structural plastic frames. The barbs provide extra holding power which is helpful due to the heavy stresses placed on the tacks, holding *webbing.*

welt—A strip of *cover* fabric that has been sewn around a *welt cord* making a round, decorative edge that can be sewn onto other *cover panels* or tacked directly to the frame. This term is often used to refer to welting strips as well.

welt board—A straight length of board measuring 1 1/2" to 2 1/2" wide. The thickness and length are optional, usually 3/4" × 72", made of alder, poplar, birch, maple or other similar close-grained, hard woods (refer to Fig. 2-18).

welt cord—A round cord, purchased in rolls, of varying diameters used as a core around which upholstery fabric is formed to make *welts*. Made of a foamed polyethylene (preferred by most upholsterers today), twisted *jute,* or wrapped paper core.

welting—Strips of *cover* fabric before they have been made into the *welt*. Usually cut 1 1/2 inches wide and of the length necessary. Upholsterers often refer to these strips simply as "welt strips".

wrapped arm—An arm style wherein the inside arm *panel* wraps both over the top of the arm and completely around the front of the *post* or *stump* as well. This style is distinguished by pronounced, large, outward tapering tucks as the fabric rounds over from the front to the top of the arm. Refer to Fig. 5-5 through 5-7.

Y-cut—A straight cut made in the *cover, muslin,* or *burlap* that goes toward the center of a *post, stump,* or *rail* and which terminates by making two angular cuts, each toward the corners of the frame member. It is called the "Y-cut" because it looks like a "Y" has been cut into the fabric. This cut is used to provide a means for folding the fabric inward and *fitting* to three sides of a frame member, giving a *finished edge.* See also *diagonal cut* and Figs. 4-38, 4-39, 4-41, 9-32, 9-35 and 10-11.

Z-arc—A *sinuous spring* construction wherein the end has been formed to the shape of a "Z", or a commercially prepared spring unit of the same shape, that is used to give the spring edge a springiness that is similar to *coil spring* construction. The Z-arc provides a softer spring than does the *V-arc.* The end of a Z-arc is fastened directly to the front seat or top back *rail.* See *V-arc* for comparison.

zig-zag spring—See *spring: sinuous.*

zipper glide—Metal or plastic unit which "glides" along the *zipper stock,* opening and closing the zipper.

zipper panel—A *panel* of *cover* fabric into which the zipper is to be or already has been sewn, usually in cushions. For the hidden zipper, the panel is cut 1 inch wider (assuming a 1/2 inch *seam allowance*) than the cushion *boxing.* For a centered zipper, the panel is cut lengthwise in half.

zipper pocket—A pocket made at one or both ends of the *boxing* for the purpose of folding over and concealing the *zipper glide* when it is in the full-open or full-closed position. The pocket is made by making a "Z" or tri-fold in the boxing. Pocket depth varies with the normal being 1 to 1 1/2 inches. See Fig. 11-37.

zipper stock—A continuous strip of zipper material, purchased by the foot, yard, or spool from which any length zipper can be cut. It comes in several sizes. *Zipper glides* are purchased separately to match the stock size. See Figs. 11-13 through 11-22.

Index

Other Bestsellers of Related Interest

ATTIC, BASEMENT AND GARAGE CONVERSION: A Do-It-Yourselfer's Guide
—Paul Bianchina

Achieve the space, appearance, and functional practicality you want in your home using the space that already exists. This book combined with your own creative imagination will produce professional results. Information on tools and techniques is featured along with complete step-by-step instructions for converting underutilized basements, garages, and attics into spacious, attractive living spaces. 208 pages, illustrated, with 8-page color photo section. Book No. 3271, $16.95 paperback, $24.95 hardcover

DESIGNING AND BUILDING CHILDREN'S FURNITURE: With 61 Projects—2nd Edition
—Percy W. Blandford

Measure, mark, design, build, and finish child-size furniture. Projects include a baby's playpen, chest of drawers, safety gate, toy box, painting easel, rocking horse, and more. Percy W. Blandford is a recognized authority in woodworking and other practical crafts. His superb line drawings illustrate this step-by-step guide. 256 pages, 195 illustrations. Book No. 3064, $12.95 paperback only

KITCHEN REMODELING—
A Do-It-Yourselfer's Guide—Paul Bianchina

"*. . . offers all the know-how you need to remodel a kitchen economically and attractively.*"
—*Country Accents*

Create a kitchen that meets the demands of your lifestyle. With this guide you can attractively and economically remodel your kitchen yourself. All the know-how you need is supplied in this complete step-by-step reference, from planning and measuring to installation and finishing. 208 pages, 187 illustrations, Book No. 3011, $14.95 paperback only

KATHY LAMANCUSA'S GUIDE TO WREATH MAKING—Kathy Lamancusa, C.P.D.

Now, you can enjoy the inviting charm of handcrafted wreaths in your home all year long. Lamancusa clearly explains the most intricate aspects of wreath making. Beginning with the basics, you'll look at the materials used in wreath making with instructions for locating, cutting, and combining them. Then you'll move on to such projects as bows, kitchen wreaths, seasonal wreaths, wreaths for children, romantic wreaths, masculine wreaths, and special occasion wreaths. 128 pages, 133 illustrations. Book No. 3492, $10.95 paperback, $19.95 hardcover

WHOLE HOUSE REMODELING GUIDE
—S. Blackwell Duncan

Hundreds of remodeling, renovating, and redecorating options are described and illustrated step-by-step in this remodeling guide! Focusing on interior modeling, the possibilities that exist for floors, windows, doors, walls, and ceilings are comprehensively explored. Complete detailed, illustrated instructions for projects are easy to follow. 448 pages, illustrated. Book No. 3281, $19.95 paperback, $28.95 hardcover

FINISH CARPENTRY ILLUSTRATED
—Elizabeth and Robert Williams

This guide provides detailed instruction on completing all of the visible refinements that give your work that polished look. You'll learn step-by-step how to install doors, windows, shelves, shutters, bathroom and kitchen cabinets, moldings, and more. And you'll apply finishing touches without the frustration that often goes with delicate work. 192 pages, 74 illustrations. Book No. 3434, $12.95 paperback only

Look for These and Other TAB Books at Your Local Bookstore

To Order Call Toll Free 1-800-822-8158
(24-hour telephone service available.)

or write to TAB Books, Blue Ridge Summit, PA 17294-0840.

Title	Product No.	Quantity	Price

☐ Check or money order made payable to TAB Books

Charge my ☐ VISA ☐ MasterCard ☐ American Express

Acct. No. _____ Exp. _____

Signature: _____

Name: _____

Address: _____

City: _____

State: _____ Zip: _____

Subtotal $ _____

Postage and Handling
($3.00 in U.S., $5.00 outside U.S.) $ _____

Add applicable state and local
sales tax $ _____

TOTAL $ _____

TAB Books catalog free with purchase; otherwise send $1.00 in check or money order and receive $1.00 credit on your next purchase.

Orders outside U.S. must pay with international money order in U.S. dollars drawn on a U.S. bank.

TAB Guarantee: If for any reason you are not satisfied with the book(s) you order, simply return it (them) within 15 days and receive a full refund.   **BC**